Savannah Sideways

Jessica Leigh Lebos

ISBN-10: 0692950877
ISBN-13: 978-0692950876

DEDICATION

To all the people of Savannah—past, present and future.

CONTENTS

SAVANNAH SIDEWAYS: AN INTRODUCTION

I guess it's pretty obvious from the get-go that I'm not from around here.

Like the rest of the world, I had became fascinated with Savannah in the 1990s, after John Berendt pulled aside the moss curtain in his bestselling book, *Midnight in the Garden of Good and Evil.* Even then, I had only a fuzzy idea of an enchanted city full of fabulous antiques and eccentric alcoholics.

Around 1996, when I was working as a cub reporter and columnist at the long-running alternative newsweekly *Pacific Sun* in Mill Valley, CA, I met a cute surfer bum-sometimes-graduate student from Savannah. I found him extremely exotic as I had no idea the South even grew nice Jewish boys, and the Lowcountry boil he made for my birthday sealed the deal.

The first time I visited his hometown, I was struck by the regal architecture and slapped hard in the face by the humidity, which felt like a well-meaning old aunt trying to smother me with a crocheted blanket. I was charmed and confounded by how people walked and talked, and they seemed just as mystified by me: As soon as I opened my mouth, I'd see an eyebrow raise and that question would come: Where, exactly, are you from, honey?

Though it was always couched in polite Southern correctitude, the question always made me feel put on the spot, as if I would be either dismissed or embraced depending on my answer. Savannahians have always been a friendly lot, but I learned fast that your origin story is even more important that your cocktail order.

Born in New Jersey, raised in Arizona, and grasping at adulthood in the San Francisco Bay Area, I had only read about the South as a 10 year-old mooning over Scarlett and Rhett, then as a college student cynically dissecting Tennessee Williams and Flannery O'Connor. After Mark and I exchanged vows at Congregation Mickve Israel on Monterey Square in 1998, we continued to return to Savannah twice a year for long stays in midtown and on Tybee Island, letting the grandparents babysit while we explored downtown's new restaurants and old haunts with our friends in the know (usually, that meant working in the kitchen; this city's service class has the best taste of anywhere I know.) Our visits became more frequent after my mother-in-law was diagnosed with dementia, and we left the California redwoods in 2006 with our two small children to settle in for good.

Savannah's sense of place is so strong that people are defined by "from here" and "not from here," though that boundary has certainly loosened as the city has become a beacon for all kinds of folks from everywhere over the decades. (Similarly, it's much far more acceptable these days to order rosé without anyone pursing their lips.)

I got used to people taking in my batik skirts and feather earrings who'd then sniff "California," as if to say, "Oh yes, now you make sense." I jokingly began introducing myself as "southern by marriage" in an attempt to straddle the gap I felt.

In spite of my obvious otherness, I found myself in the unique position of everyone already knowing my last name, which got me through the front door: An outsider invited in, privy to histories and backstories, partly because I'm a savvy eavesdropper but mostly because Savannahians love to talk. But I wanted more than to be accepted, I wanted to *belong*. To be on the other side of that fence, to eat off the everyday plates instead of the good china only reserved for guests.

Wisdom dictates that a person must bloom where she's planted, and I've done my best to follow the lead of literary icon and Savannah native Flannery O'Connor, who promised that "all writers are local somewhere."

In 2011, I launched the Civil Society Column in *Connect Savannah*, the city's revered alt-weekly, and I bumbled my way through civic gatherings, art openings, charity events, ethical conundrums and Southern faux pas for almost seven years.

I aimed to see Savannah from a different perspective every week: From the top of a building under construction to the golden lines of the marsh to the underserved voices who deserve their say, filtered through the lens of my own skewed view. I've come to know a city where it's always possible to focus on the tour guide tropes (the food! The to-go cups! The pretty houses!) but far more satisfying to dig in to its most difficult challenges. It was always my hope to turn the clichés about what people may believe about the South upside down and sideways.

Savannah Sideways is a collection of essays about learning to live in one of the South's most storied, complex communities, each one chipping back another layer of paint to reveal more about a place that is never short on stories. Many are versions of Civil Society columns that have been updated, and others first appeared in other publications and online. While they serve as curtained windows into a particular point in time—2011-2018—in Savannah and our country, these stories have added up to my journey of searching out what it means to belong here, or at the very least learn my own way.

I'm not the first to write about Savannah, and I certainly won't be the last, but I've done my best to provide a peek into this glorious garden that goes beyond any guidebook.

So please, honey, go get yourself a drink, tuck in and let's have a look at Savannah turned upside down and sideways.

—Jessica Leigh Lebos, February 2018

1 LEARNING THE SOUTH

It takes more than a fake drawl and a hoop skirt to fit in around here, and navigating the social and cultural climate of Savannah is no cliché. I've followed real-deal Southern belles around to learn their ways, pretended to love SEC football and dug deep for non-existent Irish roots as part of Savannah's world-famous St. Patrick's Day celebration only to find more questions than answers. Sometimes I discovered answers in unexpected places, like a soulful Sunday service at a storefront church and a meaningful walk through a neighborhood most folks would never visit.

Confessions of a Hapless, But Not Hopeless, Southern Belle

When I first met the man who would become my husband in Northern California, I was fascinated by his Southernness.

The sexy drawl, the Lowcountry Boil he cooked up for my birthday, his refusal to wear a skirt like the other scruffily-bearded hippie boys...let's just say he stood out. He sugared me up with his "y'alls" and his "yes ma'ams," and introduced me to his mama, who patted my cheek and called me "dahlin'".

When we wed, I thought I might automatically become Southern, as if I could absorb by osmosis a dewy complexion, elegant gentility and the ability to make a tasty casserole out of nothing but some pencil shavings and a Vidalia onion.

I write thank you notes on heavy card stock. I wear lipstick to the grocery store. After much gagging, I have developed a palate for boiled peanuts. I once tried to make a dress out of the curtains, but it looked less Scarlett O'Hara than *Project Runway* Reject.

Instead of rising pretty and fluffy as your grandma's knitting, my breakfast biscuits resemble something knocked out of a granite quarry. My Derby hat is a fedora. My children, no matter how many pointed looks of death are shot their way, cannot seem to remember to address their elders with "Yes, sir" instead of "Whatevs." Try as I might to be a true Southerner, it is clearly hopeless that I will ever get it right, bless my heart.

So it was with some trepidation that I approached The Southern C Summit, a resplendent gathering of Southern tastemakers, bloggers and brandmakers held at Jekyll Island. Surely I would out myself as an imposter by lapsing into Valley Girl-speak or not knowing the difference between bourbon and whiskey.

It did not help that instead of booking a hotel room on the island like normal people, Mark and I stayed up the road in Brunswick at the Hostel in the Forest, a rustic respite where cells phones tend to freeze and the only streetlights are fireflies. This hippie girl will take any excuse to escape into nature, even if it means the paradox of blow-drying my hair in a treehouse.

Hosted by the Southern Coterie, a vibrant online social network to "connect, congregate and converse" about all things below the Mason-Dixon line, the Southern C Summit was far from a bunch of ladies chirping about china patterns. Creators Whitney Long and Cheri Leavy brought a tremendous line-up to the glassed-in halls of the stunning Jekyll Island Convention Center, where Southern media's biggest brains shared strategies for entrepreneurs on how to capture the essence of the front porch aesthetic.

"The South is hot right now," advised Erin Shaw Street, the travel and web editor for *Southern Living*, that publishing icon successfully forging the identity of the New South while preserving the unique heritage of the Old. While china patterns remain a charming mainstay in *SL*'s content, the classic magazine keeps a manicured finger on the pulse of new trends in culture and cuisine. It rolled out a sleek digital edition last year and commands Pinterest like a sweet-tempered colonel.

The South's role as major player in the new economy was also a summit theme: Confounding the stereotypes was Charlestonian Stanfield Gray, the executive producer of the interactive techfest DigSouth, who entreated that though we might have once been dismissed, Southern culture is now coveted in the mainstream conversation about innovation and the digital era. "We are mentally, physically and spiritually mobile," said Gray. "We no longer have to move to succeed here."

Success in the contemporary South comes down to one simple adage: "Be authentic," counseled Street.

I learned early on that you can't fake Southern. No matter how much I try to blend, within three minutes of being anywhere some well-meaning person will look me curiously up-and-down and ask, "Now honey, where're you *from*?" The true belles have a gimlet eye for wannabes and liars, though they'll be as sweet as tea to your face while you wax on about your pimiento cheese dip recipe that you obviously purloined from *Southern Living*.

So I decided to stop trying. You don't have to be Southern to live and love the South, and I've found that if you mind your manners and handle your drink properly, the South will probably welcome you in like family anyway.

I pulled the stray twigs out of my hair and settled in with a cadre of fabulous Savannah folk who know me well enough to forgive my endless repertoire of *faux pas*. The Hostess City was well-represented in this well-coiffed coterie: Ruel Joyner of Broughton Street furniture shop 24E set up a cozily chic living room in the lobby. Hunter Cattle Company sent their marketing mama Kristen Fretwell to the Southern C for tips on how to handle sudden massive success. It was a wonder to watch artist Katherine Sandoz dashing off delightful renderings of summitgoers that then flashed across the live Twitter feed wall as I shared a bourbon cocktail with public relations powerhouse Jennifer Abshire and marketing whiz Cari Clark Phelps, who has recently turned her talents inward with her line of luxury bath products Salacia Salts (really, only a genius could tie together Roman mythology and Tybee Island lore.)

Photographer Jade McCully, stylist Liz Demos and event planner Andrea Gray Harper patted the chair next to them, just like in *Steel Magnolias* when Clairee tells Truvy, "If you can't say anything nice about anybody, come sit by me." No matter what they said about me later, they didn't bat a single eyelash when I told them I showered *al fresco* that morning.

The lines began to blur between the hippie hostel and the convention center, the fireflies and Twitter, between who I really am and who I still hope to become. By the time bowtie designer and quintessential Southern gentleman K. Cooper Ray took the stage as keynote speaker, I felt right at home among so many genuine Southern belles and beaus. Even if I did forget my lipgloss in the woods.

A revelation came when Ray, an Alabama-born international stylemaker who strikes the perfect balance between the traditional and the eccentric, described his new Social Primer tuxedo line—a black tie collection without any black—thusly:

"Colorful and eclectic, just like we want our Southern women to be."

Maybe there's hope for me aftah all, dahlin'.

May 8, 2013

Tale of an SEC Widow: How I Learned to Stop Fuming and Love Football

Most weekends from fall to spring, my sweet-tempered husband disappears. In his stead, a hollering barbarian arises, a beer-swilling beast that pounds his chest and screaming at the TV like it just stole its dinner. Sometimes, Sasquatch escapes the confines of the living room, loping madly to the nearest sports bar to find others in his species.

Whether this unrecognizable fiend stays home or heads out in the wild, football season invariably means I'll be sitting by myself. It used to upset me, this abandonment of weekend husbandly duties. *How could ESPN take precedence over our Home Depot shopping list?* I would fret as I loaded the car with mulch.

It would be one thing if he only vanished for games involving his beloved Georgia Bulldogs, but his obsession extends to the entire Southeastern Conference. From Tennessee to Auburn to Alabama, every SEC college team deserves equal attention, every single game affecting everyone else's overall rankings. All else is irrelevant when he is discussing these statistics with others in his herd, many of who count SEC colleges as their alma maters.

I have observed how these alliances can turn a friendly barbecue into a small riot, where grown men cry over linebacker's pulled hamstrings and throw deviled eggs across the room over a poor offense strategy.

That's when I realized it wasn't such a terrible thing to keep my distance. Still, it would be helpful if he extended the impressive level of focus he gives to four quarters (plus OT!) to other areas of our life.

How can he know the height and weight of UGA's freshman quarterback yet cannot remember the name of our child's teacher? Does he not look at the pristine green field on the screen and wonder at its contrast to the leaf-covered, overgrown lawn right outside our front door?

You'd think dressing up in a cheerleader outfit and dancing around the room would get his attention, but I bruised myself on the piano trying to do a cartwheel before he asked me to keep it down because he couldn't hear the referee.

The best luck I've had in shaking him out of spectator stupor is to yell, *Hey! I just saw the Gator mascot run down the block with his tail on fire!* But that only worked once.

Fortunately, I have other SEC widows with whom to commune. A few weeks ago, we arrived for the Georgia-Alabama game at one of our friends' homes, bags of gluten-free pretzels in tow (no more salsas or dips; they're too hard to clean off the ceiling.)

As the husbands and a few wives hunkered down in front of the gargantuan screen, the deserted partners set up the snacks, got a tour of the house and compared quinoa recipes. Which took all of about ten minutes.

"So, what do we do now?" I asked.

"Roll Tide," said our hostess as she rolled her eyes and poured the wine.

While it is unlikely the allure will never diminish for my spouse, I have learned over the course of 18 seasons that there are advantages to temporarily losing one's spouse to football.

First, you have a set schedule of unfettered time to indulge in your own pursuits. One year during the championships, I planted 200 daffodil bulbs, choreographed a Zumba routine and watched *Magic Mike*—twice.

It's also a good time for important conversations that I'd like to go my way, as he's not listening and will usually agree to anything, especially on a fourth down. This is how I acquired a gorgeous pair of Frye boots and got him to agree to accompany me to the entire season of my favorite community theater.

Most importantly, I've realized that I can entice my man to return if I can sit down, crack a beer and watch the game. Of course, this only works for a few minutes before someone misses a field goal and the beast surges back again, howling and flinging popcorn.

But it's fine, really. I just take a sip, smile and remember we've got front row tickets to *Godspell.*

A version of this essay appeared in Good Grit, *October 2016.*

I Sing A Song of the South, But I Ain't Whistlin' Dixie

When I was 10 or 11, summer in Arizona was horrendously boring and hot as hell. To keep me from burning holes in the pool furniture with a magnifying glass and O.D.ing on *Days of Our Lives*, my mother handed me the biggest book she could find.

The paperback edition of *Gone with the Wind* looked like a brick and weighed about as much, and I dubiously hefted it onto my lap.

It took me all of a week to devour all 1,087 pages, love-hating spoiled Scarlett as I pined for Rhett and sobbed for Melanie. The burning of Atlanta seared my heart, and for years I fantasized about making a dress out of the Venetian blinds.

Between *GWTW* and repeated viewings of the adorable Myrtle Beach chick flick *Shag* at the local dollar theater, I formed some rath-*uh* romantic notions about the South in my youth.

By the time I met the surfer from Savannah who would become my husband, however, I had also acquired also a comprehensive liberal arts education that put me eye-to-eye with the true bloody history of the Civil

War and the hard-earned legacy of the Civil Rights Movement. These fermented a passion for social justice and filled in the gaps of my imaginary petticoats. I married into the South with my eyes wide open, ready to embrace its complicated charms and difficult paradoxes.

Any wise person will tell you, marriage ain't all about the romance, dahlin'.

As an outsider, I know I'll never be considered a real Southerner no matter how deliciously I fry my okra. (It's all about the coconut oil, y'all.)

Such tacit acceptance has always been fine by me. As a Jewish hippie chick, I figured I was absolved from the past's persistent evils and the loser apologists of the Lost Cause, as though I could line dance and swill bourbon with the South's fun-loving side and tiptoe away when it gets all blackout drunk and waves its guns around. I could be up to my earlobes *in* it, but not *of* it, so to speak.

I think that changed forever last week. We were at a wedding in upstate New York when the horrific shooting at Charleston's Emanuel African Methodist Episcopal Church hit the news, ripping off the gauze on a wound that still seems to fester as deeply as it did 150 years ago. It can be argued that the South's racial issues aren't any more or less intense than the rest of the country's—the most violent cases of racial unrest in modern history have taken place in the Midwest and Southern California—but slavery's painful legacy remains embedded in its soil, in its history, in the heritage some of its citizens champion so fiercely.

I felt the backlash as we introduced ourselves to the other wedding guests and told them where we were from. There was an exception when one person asked excitedly, "Georgia? Did you see the zebras running through the streets?" I had to explain gently that last month's flooding incident involving the escaped zoo animals actually took place in the *country* of Georgia, "like, near Russia." She seemed very disappointed.

Mostly though, I watched eyes frost over warily, as if I was going to break out a Confederate flag bikini and an AK-47 and start spitting tobacco juice all over the furniture.

It was real strange to be judged as Southern. I mean, I did not put a boiled peanut in my mouth until I was well into my 30s. I birthed my babies in California with a doula and a bottle of Rescue Remedy. *I was born in freaking New Jersey*, for criminy's sake.

Wait, y'all have got me all wrong! I wanted to shout. *I am not responsible for this hot mess!*

Instead, a surprise entered my heart: I found myself defending the South. Maybe I was just rebelling against the Yankee snarkiness that assumes everyone below the Mason-Dixon line has a fried Twinkie in their purse and a Glock in the glovebox. But I could not let my chosen home be reduced to the actions and attitudes of a few violent, inbred cockroaches.

Hackles raised, I spoke passionately about the joyful diversity of my kids' public schools. I described the miles of forest and marsh, the kindness of strangers, the humble goodness of a paper plate of boiled shrimp caught in one's own castnet.

Granted, I live in a lovely city with a racially balanced city government, an organic farmers market and a thriving arts scene, a little bastion of progressive thinkers and educated transplants. It also helps that we've got *The New York Times* fawning all over Savannah like we're the most covetable girl at the cotillion. (Three articles in two weeks? Any more of this courtin', honey, and you're gonna have to put a ring on it.)

Absolutely, Savannah is a precocious exception to the South that regularly sells out its natural resources to the highest bidder and still refuses to expand Medicaid benefits to millions.

But this is the only South I know: One where for every Confederate flag on an F-350, there's a "Coexist" sticker on a Prius. Where the most heated argument I've ever witnessed between a white man and a black man was over who made the best barbecue. Where there are more people authentically concerned and engaged with economic equality and social justice than any place I've ever lived.

The South I laud is the birthplace of Martin Luther King, Jr. and a seat of the national food justice movement. It is where, in the wake of horror and death, we stand up, link arms and march together, black, white, brown, young, old, straight, gay, trans, and everyone in between.

To this adopted daughter, being Southern is to own the good, the bad and the ugly—and then work for better. It is a bittersweet row to hoe, which is probably why we put so much goddamn sugar in our tea.

The Confederacy's been dead and gone a long time, and even the most delusional debutante must know deep in her bones *that* South ain't rising again, no matter how much starch it put in its white hoodie.

But as God as my witness, I do believe that *this* South, *our* South, can and will rise above the ignorance and the corruption, heal the wounds and show the rest of America what forgiveness, perseverance and gentility really mean.

And what will we do with all those retired flags?

Frankly, my dear, I don't give a damn.

July 1, 2015

Let The Flannery Freak Flags Fly

If you weren't born in the South, or you were but you've got dark secrets, or maybe you're just a general run-of-the-mill weirdo, there is temptation, I think, to believe that you don't belong.

The key to happiness, then, is to be OK with that. In fact, when a bunch of us non-belongers get together and beat a drum—or many drums—it's something to celebrate.

The freak flags were flyin' high at the Flannery O'Connor Homemade Parade and Block Party last Sunday, transforming normally bucolic Lafayette Square into a haven for Savannah's most delightful misfits and fruitcakes. I say that out of utmost respect, and humbly offer that it takes one to know one.

Honoring what would have been the 89th birthday of our own native literary icon and her legacy of gothic, spiritual, disturbing, quintessentially Southern stories, this was an inside joke for the literate outliers: Here was the requisite guy in the gorilla suit, and another in seersucker carrying a prosthetic leg over his shoulder. Chicken costumes and peacock flourishes abounded.

Organizer Christine Sajecki donned vintage tweed and a tambourine for her ringleader role, and tech guru Kathleen Fritz came in full Church Lady garb complete with white gloves. Artist Katherine Sandoz appeared as Flannery herself, handing out handmade azalea crowns, hair tucked back just so.

Obviously, no gathering of local eccentrics would be complete without Tom Kohler and his amazing beard. Same goes for beautifully bizarre grande dames Carmela Aliffi and Jane Fishman, the latter resplendent in a vintage fuschia jumpsuit she's schlepped around since the '70s.

"Check this out," crowed Jane, flashing a wad of cash she'd raised for the Flannery O'Connor Childhood Home from the Chickenshit Bingo booth. "Turns out, chickenshit has another use besides fertilizing the garden."

Freakdom is a family-friendly affair, and the next generation of odd ducks got plenty of play: Artists Scott "Panhandle Slim" and Tracy Stanton watched their boys hula-hoop for hours, and Deep Center's executive director Dare Dukes did his best to divert his littlest from poking fingers into the bingo chicken's cage. Vendors Vinson and Jillian Knight-Miner sold massive shark teeth and hand-crafted leather journals while chasing daughter Kegan through the dappled sunlight. Much to the squee of all ages, teacher Rich Copeland brought bunnies to pet. (Good thing this wasn't a Steinbeck convention.)

Perhaps it is O'Connor's bemused narrative tone or her gimlet eye for hypocrisy, but her dark, often macabre stories have come to represent a sense of seditious "otherness," offering salvation to anyone who's ever questioned the status quo. Tales like *A Temple of the Holy Ghost* and its unorthodox meditations on saints and sexuality remind us that the sacred and profane exist together at all times, a bittersweet balm against the small-mindedness and violence.

"She was an insider and an outsider at the same time," considered azalea-wreathed Allison Hersh, writer and longtime board member of the Flannery O'Connor Childhood Home. "And she brought that together in a distinctively southern way."

For sure, the square seemed presided over by a prism of cheerful absurdity, like a giant, rainbow-shaped, wryly-arched eyebrow. But like O'Connor's discomforting stories, there was a sense of depth in the revelry, as if identifying as a weirdo precludes the knowledge that life can be as difficult and stupendously unfair as it is mysteriously glorious.

Thus even the most heretical among us bowed their heads as Rev. Michael Chaney invoked the novel *Wise Blood* in his opening proceedings, bemoaning "where's all my sweetness gone?"

The funereal giddiness was only amplified by author Zach Powers' solemn saxophone, followed by musical badass Anna Chandler crooning Nina Simone's "Sunday in Savannah" with such soulful abandon it's a wonder the live oaks themselves didn't start singing along.

There was clapping all around as the unapologetic procession began, led by snare drum maestro Andrew Hartzell and the Sweet Thunder Strolling Band that included mandolin wunderkind Jameson Murphy, Jon Waits, Philip Seymour Price, Joel Varland, Andy Young and some others whose names I didn't catch because I was holding my crown on tight and running to keep up.

I held my sweetie's hand as we meandered past The Cathedral of St. John the Baptist, singing terrible but heartfelt harmonies on "I'll Fly Away" and grateful for the camaraderie.

Our kids conceded to donning peacock feathers for the occasion but hid behind a tree when it was time for the parade itself. No matter; they're not fooling anybodye—they wear their weirdness like a birthmark, and maybe one day they'll be proud.

I don't presume to know how Flannery O'Connor would feel if she knew she'd become the patron saint of Savannah's freaks and weirdos. As we scraped the birthday cake sheet clean, I'd like to think she would have approved of any effort to make something beautiful out of the confusion and ugliness of the world and love it anyway.

And now that I've been thinking on it, maybe she'd also agree to this, merry misfits: You belong because you say you do.

April 2, 2014

How to Go Bragh

Welcome to the week of green, when Savannah rivals Oz for the title of Emerald City.

With St. Patrick's Day preparations and pre-partying in full effect, the enthusiasm is as contagious as the bubonic plague, without the fleas. The line around here goes that everyone's a wee bit Irish on St. Patrick's Day in Savannah, whether you possess leprechaun DNA or not.

But how does a person go about feeling authentically Irish in order to join the fun? I'm positive it takes more than a vat of Jameson and a shamrock-shaped loincloth, though the soused gentleman I observed dancing a jig on Congress Street Saturday night may disagree.

History is always an excellent place to begin. The city's storied Irish heritage hearkens back to the city's Revolutionary War days, when Sergeant William Jasper laid down his life during the Siege of Savannah. In the decades before the Civil War, Irish immigrants were imported for the work deemed too body-wrecking for slaves, including laying tracks for the Central of Georgia Railroad and digging out the Ogeechee Canal by hand.

The descendants of those maligned laborers found their way into all strata of civic life, preserving their traditions while assimilating as true-blooded Americans. One of those recognizable traditions is Irish dancing, performed throughout the year at various events but especially at the Irish Festival and Tara Feis.

In my quest to deepen my genetically-nonexistent Irish roots, I asked for tutorial from my daughter, who spent a year as the only Jewish girl in the Irish Dancers of Savannah.

My little lady of the dance patiently demonstrated the fast footwork and stock-still upper body of the tradition, her chin high and elbows pointed, skipping around the room like a bonnie lass. I proved to be an impossible student, as I am incapable of dancing without waving my arms like the cast of *Hair* performing "Age of Aquarius."

So I moved on to the greening of the Forsyth Park Fountain, hoping to absorb a dose of Celtic pedigree by osmosis. Turns out swimming in the fountain is not allowed, but I was edified in other ways. Little girls in smocked dresses and boys in seersucker suits held their grandparents' hands as members of the exclusive St. Patrick's Day Parade Committee—a member must die in order for a new one to be inducted—filed by in their natty green jackets and embroidered sashes, lending a sense of solemnity to the proceedings at first.

Soon, however, cheers and squeals erupted as the children poured bucket after bucket of dye into the shallow pool. As we oohed over the spectacle of the fountain's regal swans and muscled mermen suddenly gushing green, I began to feel a little more part of the family.

City of Savannah Park and Tree employee Baby Boy Pinckney is a 20-year greening veteran and assured me that the product he was surreptitiously adding at the fountain's pump to speed things along was not Soylent Green but a food-grade dye manufactured by Pylam Products. He added that it takes about a day to flush the fountain clear again with chlorine bleach after the festivities. All perfectly non-toxic, but swimming is still not recommended as it comes with a $1,000 fine.

It occurred to me that perhaps one can convert to Irishness. To find out, I headed over to Ground Zero for Savannah's Irish community, the Parade Committee Headquarters on Liberty Street. There I found General Chairman Brendan Sheehan dodging a PR bullet for the parade's rejection of a group of New York firefighters. He and local fireman Mike Dodd were busy explaining to a TV crew that while this particular group's record of past bad behavior earned them *personae non gratae* status this year, there will be plenty of Savannah's, New York's and other cities' finest marching in the parade.

Sheehan seemed relieved that all I wanted to know is how to become more involved in the Irish community. But his brow furrowed as he gently explained that no matter how good my organizational skills, I would not be able to wear one of the Parade Committee's snazzy green jackets anytime soon. Or ever.

For that honor, you have to be nominated by another committee member basically at birth, and then someone has to pass on to the verdant fields of eternity. Sheehan himself says he waited almost 26 years for his name to come up before he could join the ranks of this most respected Savannah organization, a group that works all year long to engineer the country's second largest St. Patrick's Day parade.

Also, you have to be a man.

Ahem. Now, it is true that it is a *tremendous* amount of work to host a half million people and make sure the streets run smoothly, but 800 dudes to plan a parade? If the women were in charge, there would only need to be 50 of them and a big ol' pot of coffee. Just sayin'.

If I couldn't join the parade committee, maybe one of the other Irish organizations would have me. I called my good buddy Chuck Loncon, a member of the Hibernian Society, the country's oldest Irish cultural association. Established in 1812 on St. Patrick's Day, the Hibernian Society has always been traditional but wholly devoid of religious strife. In fact, Chuck told me one of the society's founding members, Isaac Minis, was actually Jewish. So there ya go, I crowed, I'm a legacy!

Chuck cleared his throat and clarified that while the Hibernian Society is indeed inclusive, apolitical and without religious preference, it is also composed only of men.

Ohhhh, *fine*, I get it. To get officially Irish around here, you have to swing a shillelagh.

I gave it one more go last Sunday, when I found myself at the Celtic Cross Ceremony at the Cathedral of St. John the Baptist, its spires still breathtaking under its scaffolding cloak. Everyone—even a Jewish girl who can't cook a decent corned beef to save her life—is welcome at this glorious mass that ends with a procession to Emmett Park.

Many say this is the true St. Patrick's Day Parade. A far cry from the downtown drunken ruckus, the ceremony is a sobering testament to how far the Irish community has come in Savannah and what a triumphant heritage it has to bequeath to future generations.

That's when I realized the true meaning of being Irish in Savannah is to honor faith and family, no matter where you worship or from where your ancestors hail. Hold both close, and you're as green as it gets.

Of course, there's still an epic party to get started. But please, keep your shirt on (and your pants, for Pete's sake) and be grateful you were born with the luck of the Irish.

March 12, 2013

Walking the Fifth Ward

"What, exactly, are you doing here?" the young man in the hooded sweatshirt wanted to know.

I couldn't blame him for being suspicious. What business could a middle-aged lady carrying a pen possibly have in his neighborhood after dark?

I live only a few blocks away, but until today I had no business at all in the Fifth Ward. This two-block tinderbox off Waters Ave. where gunfire and sirens are an almost constant soundtrack is identified by SCMPD Chief Jack Lumpkin as the headquarters of one of the city's most active criminal groups—some would call it a gang—also called the Fifth Ward. Tiny clapboard houses founder behind brown lawns, most of them rental properties belonging to a handful of slumlords who haven't bothered to fix a fence or a screen door in decades. It's not the kind of place you walk the dog.

But to Ylana Abbott and Eugene "Trae" Priester, organizers of the grassroots non-violence group Solidarity in Savannah, the Fifth Ward isn't some gang hideout—it's home to several protégés who have responded to offers of a path out of crime and violence. Since last summer, their team of volunteers has arranged job interviews, provided information on the GED and acted as mentors and stand-in parents for anyone who asks.

I have tremendous respect for SIS' efforts to bring compassion and counsel to some of Savannah's sparkiest neighborhoods, though I mostly tend to express that from behind a desk. But after the recent flurry of press about the city's crime stats and the initial successes of the city's End Gun Violence initiative, I had to agree with Ylana that a certain perspective was missing.

"You know, there have been articles on crime from everyone except those who are in the midst of it," she mused in a text earlier in the week. "What if there was something from the young men's point of view?"

So I bundled up for a late evening stroll and tagged along as Ylana and Trae walked the blocks of the Fifth Ward, checking in with the neighbors and handing out SIS newsletters to clusters of men leaning against cars. There were people standing around everywhere despite the frigid air, some possibly working illicit business and others simply relaxing.

"All right?" called Trae to a rail-thin gent standing in an open garage.

"Jus' chillin' with my Icehouse and my Newports," the man cackled back, lifting a paper bag in a toast.

We came up on a group listening to a car stereo, and two younger men peeled away to join us. One was a 22-year-old with whom SIS has been working closely—we'll call him "Mr. H"—who I had met earlier in the day with Ylana, who often comes by the Fifth Ward during her lunch hour from her job at Savannah Law School.

We picked up Mr. H in front of his house and drove around while he told me his story: He dropped out of Windsor Forest High School at 16 to take care of his grandmother. At 18, he served two years for assault after a bar fight and was recently turned down for a minimum wage job at a fast food joint because of his record.

He admits he's sold drugs in the past to get by and has also worked warehouse gigs near the port, though finding reliable transportation is always a challenge, since most of those job sites aren't on the bus route.

"No one wants to give me a ride home once they find out where I stay," he said, the lines around his eyes making seem older. "Everyone's scared to come around here except the police and the Jehovah's Witnesses."

Lately he's found a little work cutting grass and trimming trees with his father, an ex-felon who's never been able to find a steady job after he got out of prison over two decades ago.

"You're forty-something years old, you haven't been in trouble for 20 years and you're still being judged for your criminal background," said Mr. H, shaking his head at the system that also strips felons of their right to vote.

He doesn't need a fancy infographic to show him how the revolving door of poverty, lack of education, lack of knowledge about and access to services leads to violence, desperation and prison. It's pretty damn obvious. And it's a cycle that's nearly impossible to break without help.

"Yes, someone is shooting every night. The thing is, they're not doing it for no reason. They're trying to survive," he told me as we sat with Ylana's car heater running.

"You got these young kids out here—their parents aren't what you expect parents to be. They're fucked up. On drugs, drinking. So these kids got to go out and help the family, and they do it their own way because no one ever taught them the right way. And once they mess up and get in trouble, they're in the system and they're stuck. There's no point in trying to better themselves because they're already looked at as hopeless."

He wants more than anything to figure out how to provide stability for his two small daughters, ages 1 and 3 months, maybe use his natural gift for fixing appliances and radios after Ylana helps him get his GED.

His real dream, though, is to open a dog kennel, he confides when we meet again on the street that night. One of his dogs, a mellow, caramel-colored pit bull named Coco follows obediently as he and Ylana walk ahead to discuss the details of his upcoming GED test.

The other kid, the one in the sweatshirt, waits expectedly for me explain my presence.

"I'm here to talk to you, if that's cool," I say. His face breaks into a smile.

"Mr. J" grew up a few blocks over and now lives with Mr. H and his family, helping out with the rent. They call themselves brothers, though the kinship is more spiritual than genetic. They grew up together on these same streets, kicking empty cans and doing their best to avoid trouble.

Though he calls the Fifth Ward home, Mr. J says he doesn't feel limited by the drama. As we walk, he tells me he's just finished his kitchen shift at Ole Times Country Buffet and proudly shares his plans to go to Savannah Tech to earn his welding certificate.

"I think it's because my parents were around more when I was coming up," he says thoughtfully when I ask where his self-direction comes from. "But other people, they don't have that. When no one shows you the way, you don't even know it exists."

That's what Solidarity in Savannah aims to do: shine a light on the possibilities without judgment, following up with a text, a ride to the DMV to get a driver's license, a safe place to study. Volunteers are also trained to gently disrupt conflict, and more recruits are always needed.

An East Savannah native now in his 40s, Trae embraced Islam while in federal prison, serving a 10-year sentence on non-violent gun charges. We pass the Fifth Ward house where he was arrested, caught up in a raid instigated by someone who rolled over on his friends for a lesser plea.

With his calm demeanor and gray coming into his beard, Trae is a respected elder on this street, his credibility compounded by his time on the inside. He counseled others on keeping to the peaceful path in jail, and came home committed to help others from getting caught up.

"The feds are big on peer-based programming, but the state and the city haven't caught on yet," he sighs as we discuss SIS' need for funding in order to grow its outreach team.

There was expectation that the End Gun Violence budget would include money for such community work, but thus far the initiative has focused on the necessity of corralling the city's most dangerous criminals.

Part of the strategy of the End Gun Violence smackdown hinges on not only pursuing perps but their friends, and Ylana worries how this "guilty by association" will further erode already broken communities like the Fifth Ward. Being at the wrong place at the wrong time can destroy a young man's life and those around him, further perpetuating the cycle.

Though only 30, Ylana seems comfortably maternal with these boys, and indeed expresses a mother's unconditional empathy for the deep pain that can lead to their downfall.

"It's absolutely imperative that violent offenders are taken off the streets," she says. "But it's important to understand the gaps that are left when these men—fathers, brothers, providers—are gone."

The next stop on our walk is at a house strewn with trash in the yard, its cement stairs crumbling. We're here to check on 19-year-old "Mr. S," who went back to finish his senior year at Savannah High after finding a SIS flyer and texting that he wanted to change his life.

A boy cracks open the door, and there's concern that Mr. S isn't here. But a few moments later a compactly-built kid in a pressed school uniform rides up on a bike, offering apologies.

"We call her the 'Hood's Hope," grins Mr. S as Ylana checks his progress report.

We're deep in a discussion about the uselessness of advanced algebra when two dark figures walk up suddenly, their faces covered with bandanas. Their eyes dart over me, my pen. For the first time, I feel fear, understanding viscerally how vulnerable these young men are every day.

The laughter stops, and we all exchange wary greetings. The two men move on quickly. I don't ask who they were.

"Things are fucked up," offers Mr. J in explanation. Everyone nods solemnly.

We stand under the stars for a more few minutes, and a car full of pretty girls rolls up, asking Mr. S. if he wants to get food.

"Gotta go!" he says as he sprints off, but not before catching me up in a quick hug.

Mr. J. and Mr. H. also hug me too as we part ways, and I feel my own maternal instincts blossom for these bright young souls, who can hardly be called innocent. Yet their sweetness prevails, in spite of knowing how the world sees young black men from bad neighborhoods.

We have demanded solutions to the city's crime, and the sweeping arrests and harder sentences ought to yield progress in removing violent offenders from the streets. Those measures are welcome and necessary for a safer Savannah for all, and I hope we'll see significant decreases in shootings and homicides and more gun busts and arrests as time passes.

Yet, always, behind the stats are the stories and struggle of individuals who would do it differently if they only knew how. Can we as a community support those willing to walk beside them and point the way?

January 27, 2016

Take Me to Church

They had me at "hallelujah." The two singers on the small wooden stage had started off softly, but when the keyboard began to hum and the drums kicked in, their voices really began to soar, and I was up out of my padded chair, arms in the air.

Now, I'm not much of a churchgoer these days. I can barely make it to synagogue on the regular, let alone branch out into other religions. A girl needs at least one day a weekend to have late brunch and do yard work, am I right?

Over the years, however, I have had the honor of visiting a few Christian houses of worship. My parents instilled in me great respect for all religions and encouraged my burgeoning spiritual curiosity when I was 8, driving me all over town to the Sikh ice cream shop and a Buddhist meditation class and a babysitter's Catholic confirmation. ("Get back here right now!" hissed my mother when I started down the aisle for a communion "cookie.")

As much as I've meandered the spiritual path, it's always led me straight back to myself, where my heritage suffuses with meaningful traditions, a deep awe for the natural world and an unshakeable belief that we're all in this together.

I may be a flower-worshipping daughter of Israel, but I sure do adore the Christmas story, what with all the kindness and frankincense. And I've always had a major girl crush on Our Lady of Guadalupe, which is what's bound to happen when you grow up the only Jewish feminist on the block in Tempe, Arizona.

I've lit candles in Italian basilicas, walked the Stations of the Cross in Jerusalem and attended glorious weddings in some of Savannah's most impressive churches. In my practice of radical religious egalitarianism I have always strove to be a respectful observer, a humble heretic seeking unity in a world that drives us apart at every turn.

But detached reflection isn't an option at Resurrected Faith Ministries, where the gospel is a highly participatory activity. My family and I attended a service recently to support Britannia Jones, who cared devotedly for my mother-in-law through her long decline. Our kids grew up together in those eight years, and the Jones family never left us in the days following her death a few weeks ago on Thanksgiving. It is one of the great privileges of my life to have shared with Britannia the task of bathing Marcia's body for the last time.

Just a week after we buried my mother-in-law, Britannia's father, Mr. Jake Cox, passed away, as well. So much loss in such a short a time tightened our circle in a ribbon of grief. And so we went from sitting *shivah*—the Jewish ritual of mourning—to singing hosannas in the tradition of Resurrected Faith.

The congregation of about 25 meets in a tiny storefront off Highway 80 in Bloomingdale, a long way from the tall steeples of downtown and the stained glass sanctuary of our own Congregation Mickve Israel. At first, our motley Jew crew—me, Mark, the kids, my father-in-law and brother-in-law—felt conspicuous as we took our seats.

"Do they do the cookies here?" my daughter whispered loudly.

"Shhh, no, different church," I murmured, as the grandmotherly woman next to her gave us a wink.

Then the music started and the uneasiness lifted as Britannia's husband, Willie, held down the baritone. While we didn't know the words to sing along, we're prenty used to religious services bringing us to our feet. (Synagogue = Stand up. Sit down. Stand up. Sit down. Repeat for an hour and a half, three on major holidays.)

Britannia went first to pay homage to her father, followed by her aunt and other relatives. Tears flowed freely and shouts of worship filled the small room, a welcome release for all the emotions we'd tamped down over the last few weeks.

It was especially touching to witness my normally reserved father-in-law give testimony for Mr. Cox, who was an accomplished craftsman and carpenter and had helped my father-in-law with several projects around his home.

"He was very strong, a real man," he sniffed to calls of "Amen!"

After the words of remembrance, it was all over but the preaching. A tall woman in gold shoes approached the pulpit, and with a bow of heads, Pastor Veronica Skipper began to speak.

"We are here to celebrate a life. And yet, we *all* have an appointment with death," she intoned in a voice that rumbled to my toes.

"What are you doing to prepare yourself for your appointment?"

I know she meant Judgment Day with a capital "J," which doesn't get much play in the Torah. But the question piqued even the agnostics among our group, reminding that we are accountable for our actions on earth, starting with the ones we love.

Pastor Skipper made it clear her job isn't to judge anyone, only to spread the Good Word of repentance and forgiveness.

"I know y'all have different words for it," she said, nodding to our family. "But we are all praying to the same God. All the paths lead to the same place."

This struck me as Truth with a capital "T", and I heard myself holler "Hallelujah!" right back. Soon enough, all of us were up clapping, no longer visitors to a different religion but welcome members of the family. Surely one of the great peaks of my spiritual path was watching my husband in his new Goorin Bros. fedora dancing and high-fiving with Willie's mother.

The songs filled our souls, andt all that joyful noise makes a body hungry. Afterwards, we gathered in the back room for a meal prepared by the restaurant that Pastor Skipper runs during the week, Sarah Jane's Southern Kitchen in the Savannah Mall food court. Our bellies rumbled as we piled up plates with fried chicken, mac 'n' cheese and yellow rice.

"The green beans are cooked with pork," warned a new friend apologetically.

"That's OK," I said, confessing that our family doesn't mind repenting for bacon now and again.

Some might consider it blasphemous not to care whether we pray perfectly, or all alike, or even at all. But the more I embrace and am embraced by beliefs other than my own, the more I suppose that the keys to heaven—which may for some be a metaphor for happiness on earth—have less to do with the dogma than the faith.

I'm no theologian, but maybe the diamond-cut common denominator of all religions isn't agreeing on a deity or a scripture, but sending off our own and each other's loved ones with grace.

And perhaps the greatest faith means believing in our own inherent value and purpose, and that the most holy acts are the kindness and inclusion we show others.

It's what I'll be meditating on this Christmas, in between watching the new *Star Wars* and enjoying the sacred Jewish tradition of Chinese food.

Too soon to get an "amen?"

December 23, 2015

2 HALLOWED GROUNDS

More than 11 million tourists visit Savannah every year, dutifully taking in the historic sites and ogling the antebellum architecture to soak up some of our storied beauty and charm. But it takes more than a trolley ride to take in more than three hundred years of history, and I've made a little minor history of my own chasing a fox through Bonaventure Cemetery, searching for ghosts afterhours in the Olde Pink House and wearing a gorilla suit at the Flannery O'Connor Childhood Home. The guidebooks might give background on those oft-treaded places, but no other tour guide will dish like this about the Davenport House, the Ships of the Sea Museum and Congregation Mickve Israel.

Get Sick at the Davenport House

Feel that lovely breeze? Notice the absence of demonic insects gnawing at your ankles? Welcome to fall, good people. We made it.

This is the best weather these parts have to offer, and even the couch potatoes ought to take it outside for the next few weeks. For reals, move your couch outside. Better yet, push it on over to Picnic in the Park, traditionally held the first Sunday in October.

This is also the time to get sugared up, grossed out and scared 'til you pee your pants.

Mine is a family that prepares for Halloween like other people wait for the Apocalypse. We start discussing costumes after Fourth of July and buy fake blood by the bucket. The kids hassle me like hyper hyenas until I bring down the Big Box of Decorations on the first day of October. (Any earlier is Halloween sacrilege. You hear that, neighbor with the skeleton lawn ornaments up since Labor Day?)

As soon as the androgynous life-size doll we call Bobby is hanging from a noose on the front porch, the children then begin their lobby for our yearly tour of haunted houses, ghoulish groves and creepy corn mazes anywhere in a 50-mile radius. Sometimes when we run out of thrills to satisfy them, we just drop them off in a grody alley in a dark part of town and let them explore.

This year, I suggested we kick off our macabre junket at the Isaiah Davenport House Museum, where director Jaime Credle and a cast of volunteers have revived their living history production, *Dreadful Pestilence: The Yellow Fever Epidemic of 1820*. Set in various parts of the refined American Federal-style domicile on Columbia Square, the hour-long show chronicles the horrific illness that killed one out of five Savannah citizens and provides a fascinating and germane context of social norms, race relations, media propaganda and medical inefficacy.

According to my children, Halloween shouldn't be educational.

"Ugh, history?" complained my son. "We want ghosts."

"And goblins," added his sister. "And scary clowns on tiny motorcycles."

I don't mention that when clowns show up anywhere, including the circus, both of them keep their faces in my armpits the entire time.

"Plus, it sounds unsanitary. Didn't yellow fever make people puke black vomit?" sniffed my first born, ever the germophobe.

"It can't possibly be as disgusting as the festering herpes sores on the zombies at that place we went to last year," I pointed out.

"But that wasn't real," he countered.

"Proving my point. Get in the minivan," I commanded.

Dreadful Pestilence begins inside the former Kennedy Pharmacy on the east end of Broughton Street where the cast sets the tone of 19th-century Savannah: The port is thriving, the construction trade is up and folks are flocking here to start new businesses, explains show co-creator Raleigh Marshall as he greets guests at the door in a sateen striped waistcoat. Savannah Arts Academy theater major Catie Morris delivers a cute commercial for a snake oil that's supposed to cure yellow fever, and young songstress Kate Bosen tries to keep the mood high as the death toll mounts.

It's morbidly entertaining as well as historically correct: Much of the script is lifted word-for-word from Savannah's two competing newspapers at the time. Jeff Freeman and Iain Woodside play the dueling editors, one warning the public about the coming epidemic, the other completely denying any danger whatsoever and encouraging folks to mingle in the markets.

"This isn't scary," whispered my daughter. Speak for yourself, kid.

But she clutched my arm tightly after the intro, when guests are separated into small groups and escorted into the grand main house, the only time of year the museum is open at night. We climbed the candlelit staircase to the unfinished attic, which is honestly the scariest place I've ever been in my life, not counting my children's bathroom.

Here the production's other co-creator, Jamal Touré, plays a free African named Mingo Bwa who has been tapped to help bury the many uncounted slaves dying of the fever. Touré, who researches local African history for his tour company Day Clean Journeys, explained that whites would not inter blacks nor count them in the death numbers. Thus the historical record can only guess at how many African slaves died during the epidemic.

"It is a pandemonium of darkness," he cried, gesturing to unseen bodies.

Next we found Shakespeare-spouting Lauren Purcell awaiting treatment, which was frighteningly primitive compared to modern medicine, no matter how you feel about the Affordable Care Act. Back in the day, a prescription might have included having your arms cut and bled, drinking cayenne pepper tea or a tying a pigeon to one's arse.

My daughter snorted with laughter at that last one, but her brother got busy digging in my purse for the Purell.

Even if they'd had gobs of anti-bacterial goo back them, it wouldn't have helped. Though yellow fever was blamed on dirty air, the Irish and/or inauspicious astrological alignments, the true cause of yellow fever wasn't discovered until the 1890s, when Army doctor Walter Reed confirmed that the disease is carried by the most sinister monster of all: The swamp mosquito.

Finally, we came to the salon, somber as mourner Jan Vach hovered over the coffin her young daughter. Surrounded again by Bosen's lilting voice, we chose our fates from a basket: Three of us barely survived the dreadful pestilence, one did not.

With everyone satisfyingly freaked out, I felt a little sorry for the tourists clopping around outside hearing made-up ghost stories. Though Marshall assured me that the Davenport House is "not haunted in the least," it is definitely one spooky place.

Just goes to show that real history is creepier than fiction. And according to my personal Halloween police, every bit as cool as vampire zombie clowns with chainsaws.

However, my son still wants to remind you not to forget the hand sanitizer.

Oct 3, 2013

Notes from the Graveyard

While a piece of chocolate cake can do wonders for a lagging spirit, it's best not to overindulge your sweet tooth. Similarly, meditations on mortality can light up one's motivation, but we mustn't give too much time to our thoughts about death.

Unless you're Don Teuton, in which case, you think about the latter like it's your job, since it is.

The Savannah native spends almost every day in Bonaventure Cemetery amongst the city's most prominent dead people, giving tours for the living, for a living. But unlike some of us, the nature of his obsession is more pragmatic than philosophical.

"I've always been fascinated by this place, how people are memorialized after they're gone," muses the middle-aged dad who goes by his guide name, Bonaventure Don. "These monuments and headstones tell the city's history."

True enough. Around every marble corner is a Tattnall, a Telfair, a Jones or another famous local figure—some who were exhumed from elsewhere and brought here posthumously in the 1840s at the behest of then-Evergreen Cemetery entrepreneur Peter Wiltberger to drum up business.

The macabre marketing ploy worked, and the former rice plantation is now the final resting place of notable local characters from all over the centuries, from settlers and soldiers to songbird Johnny Mercer to revered local fashion designer and Chanel licensee Sophie Meldrim Shonnard, who constructed the pink bouclé suit Jacqueline Kennedy Onassis was wearing the day of her husband's assassination.

This is the garden of cadavers and crypts that put Savannah on the tourism map, but Don, who is also on the board of the Bonaventure Historical Society, is adamant that it offers only a partial history.

"These are the names we read about, but there are many important Savannah people who aren't buried here," he admonishes, adding that the city's African American narrative, told through the hand-carved headstones of nameless slaves and the monument to civil rights activist W.W. Law, can be found on the west end of town in Laurel Grove South, segregated by I-16 from its northern counterpart.

Though an avowed lover of local lore, I'm embarrassed to admit that I've only visited Bonaventure once, for an actual funeral, and did not tarry to enjoy the moss-draped ambience. I've never been a big fan of cemeteries, all that fussy formality and somber granite. And frankly, my neurotic notions don't need any encouragement.

I haven't given much thought at all about what's to be done with my meat puppet once I've vacated it for the next dimension. Maybe I'd like to be cremated, my ashes sprinkled via hot air balloon over a snowy mountaintop, like toppings on a sundae. Or wrap me in a cotton sheet, bury me in the backyard and plant a cherry tree on top. In any case, I'm going out how I lived, with dessert on my mind.

The only reason I'd called up Bonaventure Don at all is because I'd heard reports of a fox scampering around the headstones during his tours. In addition to sweets, I'm a huge sucker for friendly wild things.

I pulled along my colleague, Arts & Entertainment editor Anna Chandler, for a fox finding field trip, since we'd had so much fun stalking the owls of Skidaway Island earlier this year.

"Don't worry, I won't dig up any bones this time," she whispered as we traipsed along the grounds.

Don led us down Mullryne Way towards the bluff where the fox had been seen the day before, pointing out the intricate Gothic flourishes and serene marble angels that watch over the dead. We passed the graves of Little Gracie Watkins, whose eerie, life-like statue inspires visitors to leave candy and toys on the steps, and poor Eleanor Whitaker, a proper young woman who had to live with the sobriquet Hard-Hearted Hannah, the Vamp of Savannah, given by a spurned suitor.

Spurred by low blood sugar, I mostly pondered the thousands of forgotten names that time's relentless maw swallowed long ago, their only legacies a set of dates and a pithy epitaph. My favorite is Martha Kirksey's, who died in1889: "She did what she could." Sounds like poor Martha could have used more chocolate.

Some graves had piled rocks on top of the headstones, a worldwide Jewish practice that has been curiously adopted by Bonaventure visitors for many of its permanent residents, regardless of religion. Perhaps it's a testament that we all meet each other in the end anyway.

Listening to the wind whistle through the 250-year old-oaks, I began to appreciate hanging out with the dead, how contemplating eternity in this lovely place might help time slow down enough for a person to catch her breath in this insane world.

We had just strolled past former poet laureate Conrad Aiken's final resting place when I saw a flash of copper fur out of the corner of my eye. I turned just in time to see a black-tipped tail disappear past a stone cherub.

"There's the fox!" I gasped. Anna and I hopped around the headstones, trying to catch a glimpse of our vulpine crush without treading on anyone's sacred ground.

We searched for over an hour, but the fox stayed shy. Our wildlife quest did, however, yield soaring ospreys, graceful egrets and several butterflies as big as my hand. A red-tailed hawk alighted on a marble slab a few feet away, then took off again with a blue-tailed skink in its talons.

All this life finally distracted me from the grim heft of the last week's news: The horrific murders of two journalists at the hand of yet another sociopath with a gun. The fatal shooting of yet another young person, a college student. Too many beautiful friends fighting for their lives against the demon cancer and other diseases. My dear, infirm mother-in-law still resisting the end with every shallow breath.

The existential angst of it all is bad enough, and sometimes the visceral loss can be too much to bear. The fact that the only death that we don't have to fear living with is our own provides little solace. It was comforting to find that chilling with the dead is a decent way to cope. Maybe even more effective than a cream-stuffed éclair.

I've visited Bonaventure several more times since, telling myself I was going back to look for the elusive Mr. (or Ms.) Fox. But I keep lingering, walking further among the paths, greeting the now-familiar etched names like old friends.

I still haven't seen the fox, only a set of tiny footprints that could just as well have been made by someone's Chihuahua.

But I have wandered across a grassy open space in the Jewish section, where the dates are more recent. My mother-in-law will lie here sooner than later, and apparently there are a couple of spots in the plot for both Mark and I, thanks to the foresight of family. (Despite its fame, Bonaventure still has plenty of room for you and yours, too: Only about half of the 60,000 individual sites are occupied.)

I guess it's a bit weird that hanging out in a graveyard has been an antidote for ruminating too much on my own mortality. Yet sitting on the damp ground, the Wilmington River rushing by and the sparrows chirping in the marsh, I felt a little less averse to the idea of a headstone with my name on it.

Not that I expect it to be a stop on Don's or anybody else's tour. But should you happen upon it some day in the far, far future, feel free to leave a few rocks. And maybe a piece of cherry pie.

September 2, 2015

Cool refuge in the North Garden

Maybe you can't actually fry an egg on the hood of your car right now, but surely, it's possible to poach one's brain in this unabating heat. Going outside in the middle of the day right now seems like a terrible idea.

I've stopped taking calls during daylight hours because I'm concerned I'll conduct my own inadvertent science experiment about how much time it takes for an iPhone to melt into the side of a human face. (Siri, has anyone ever drowned in their own sweat?)

I'm of the mind that August is for Southerners to hibernate, a time to cozy up under the air-conditioning vent and subsist on cold sandwiches and Popsicles. To those among us who remember what summer was like in Savannah before the advent of AC and before tank tops were socially appropriate, I bow to you for simply surviving.

So, no, I think I'll stay right here with my sweet tea, thanks. But as I make another trip to my refrigerator ice machine, I think guiltily of Savannah's first settlers, who must have been furious with General Oglethorpe for plunking them down in Mephistopheles' boiler room. If generations of women in white gloves and petticoats can withstand the heat, the reasonable part of me *tsktsks*, surely I can handle wearing a cotton sundress to the midday dedication of the Ships of the Sea Museum's new North Garden.

When I arrive at the museum's secret garden entrance off MLK Blvd., I thank heaven I'm not a man for the umpteenth time in my life. *They* have to wear suits to these types of functions with a freakin' TIE. I don't care how "breathable" seersucker is; it's still a jacket over a shirt and that sounds positively asphyxiating.

Thankfully, refreshment awaits under the stunning beamed pavilion called the Assembly Room, an outdoor ballroom built to host music concerts and workshops that now serves as one of the breeziest, best venues on the Savannah Stopover Festival circuit.

Folks gather strategically near industrial fans to hear about the latest in the legacy of Mills Bee Lane IV, the benefactor who continued his father's passion for restoration and maritime history by moving this unique and charming museum of expertly-built ship models to the Scarbrough House in 1997.

The stately Greek Revival manor was built in 1819 by Owens-Thomas House architect William Jay for shipping magnate William Scarbrough, and for 70 years it was the West Broad School, one of the first African-American educational institutions in the city. Now it houses its impressive collection of large-scale model ships (I admit I thought model ships were kind of nerdy until I actually wandered through the displays; they're amazing) and offers the city's largest private garden that's open to the public.

"If the garden gate's open, come on in," invites linen-clad Executive Director Tony Pizzo, who worked closely with Lane until his death in 2001. Along with the SOS board, Pizzo remains committed to Lane's vision of shared resources. "Mills was the kind of person who wanted to make life better for everyone in the community."

Following the axis of the older brick courtyard, visitors encounter a stunning assemblage of five carefully planted green zones designed by renowned local landscape architect John McEllen, who created the museum's original formal garden in 1997. Though McEllen added more color to Lane's earlier green-on-green garden scheme, he kept to the magnate's primary intention of lush wildness.

"Mills basically wanted an environment that seemed like if you sat there too long, it might swallow you up," says Pizzo.

For sure, the pockets of new flora give off an impression of outstretched arms, even in their nascent stages: The "naturalistic" area of native sweetgrasses and fragrant magnolias along the Assembly Room's back wall wave in the welcome breeze, and the vines of wisteria, red honeysuckle and Muscadine grapes seem to sneak up the 100-foot Pergola right before my eyes. Deep green podocarpus trees stretch up along both sides of the walkway, awaiting the time when their height will allow McEllen to pleach them into a natural arch.

The Sisters Garden echoes the original plantings of those hot, weather-hardy species put in the ground by the original 1734 Trustees, including mulberry trees, heirloom roses, and verdure favored by Scarbrough's three daughters, who managed to suffer their pre-spaghetti strap wardrobes in the heat just fine. In fact, middle sister Charlotte Scarbrough Taylor grew up to become one of the world's first and finest female entomologists. To which I say, of course she did! What better occupation could there be for a curious young woman in 19th century Savannah than studying the area's prolific bug population?

Also on the museum compound—which now spans an entire city block—is the exotic Citrus Garden, abundant with enough kumquat and Key Limes and blood orange trees to bowl over the senses with scent as they bloom.

Savannah will feel the true payoff in the years to come, as the museum's North Garden entwines upon itself and anchors the revitalization coming to pass on MLK Blvd. From the second-story vantage point of the Belvedere balcony, one can take in a unique view of the Talmadge Bridge as well as the geometric perfection of the Trident maple grove, where Pizzo hopes to see locals and tourists alike lounging under the lush, deciduous trees.

"The leaves will change in the fall," foretells Pizzo, commenting that SOS' greenspace is a distinct location from other parks, offering a place "more for reflection than recreation."

Free wi-fi throughout the grounds means I could maybe get some work done this afternoon. But it's already 95 degrees and 90 percent humidity, and my laptop keyboard might burn off the pads of my fingers.

Literally drenched in my own sudor, I instead sneak away and lay down quietly panting under the maples on the soft grass, where it becomes obvious how our ancestors dealt with the heat: They planted trees, then waited patiently and took refuge in their shade.

July 31, 2012

What Would Mother Mathilda Do?

When I find myself in times of trouble, I'm always hoping some nice lady will come to me and whisper words of wisdom, just like in the song.

The thing is, I'm never quite sure who I'm supposed to be looking for. My idol-adverse people don't have a go-to spiritual maternal figure, and our last visitation I'm aware of involved a burning bush.

I guess I envision the Holy Mother as a divine superheroine, an enigmatic combination of Wonder Woman and Mother Theresa, infinitely loving but not here for our self-created separations and sufferings.

Lately the picture I've been holding in my mind looks a lot like Mother Mathilda Beasley, Georgia's first African-American nun and one of Savannah history's most mysterious characters. Maybe it's an unlikely girl crush for a Jewish mother, but ever since I read the historical marker near the Sacred Heart Catholic Church on Bull Street a few years ago, Mother Mathilda has fused into a corner of my cluttered spiritual consciousness, an esoteric place that resembles a cross between Solomon's Temple and the Aughra's den from *The Dark Crystal.*

The more I learn about this sacred sister, the more otherworldly her legend becomes. The records show that "Matilde Taylor" was born a slave in New Orleans in 1832 and arrived in Savannah as a free young woman who signed her own name as "Mathilda." She worked as a seamstress, operated a secret school for slave children ten years before the Civil War and married wealthy black restauranteur and landholder Abraham Beasley in 1869.

After her husband died in 1877 and left her a portfolio of money and property, the widow Beasley traveled to England to take the vows of the Poor Clares, a branch of the Franciscan Sisters, and returned to Savannah to found the state's first African-American order. The newly-minted Mother Superior oversaw a school and orphanage at Sacred Heart then at St. Benedict the Moor, the city's first black Catholic Church.

After her husband's estate was spent, she reportedly took in sewing gigs to pay for books and clothes for her students, an early precursor to today's educational martyrs. (Not to be confused with Susie King Taylor, another local renegade who sacrificed much to teach African American children both in secret and in the open.)

It's humbling and inspirational to learn that Mother Mathilda devoted her fortune and the rest of her life in service to her students. But it's the description of her death that puts my reverential imagination over the edge: On Dec. 20, 1903, parishioners entered her cottage to find her body in repose in front of her private altar, hands clasped and arms outstretched in prayer.

Her funereal instructions and burial garments were folded neatly beside her, giving the scene an eerie yet holy prescience. Even now it gives me goosebumps.

Mother Mathilda's whole tale seems to transcend history into legend, and so many questions remain about this mythical mystic: How did she escape slavery? Where did she learn to read and write? Why did this "commanding figure" of "extreme height" risk fines and public lashing to share knowledge—and therefore power—in one of the South's most stubbornly segregated strongholds? What were her thoughts in those last moments before her spirit rose from the earthly plane?

Her enduring enigma is fed by two photos that supposedly depict Mother Mathilda Beasley: One is a portrait of an ethnically ambiguous face with striking cheekbones and hypnotic eyes; the other features an elegantly dressed, young African-American woman posed with a parasol.

Though they have been used interchangeably in stories about Mother Mathilda, they are clearly not the same person. (Artist Michael Porten solved this conundrum by presenting her likeness in bas relief profile as part of SCAD's Women of Vision installation in Arnold Hall.)

I consulted Georgia Historical Society archivist Katherine Rapkin to find the angel in the details: The first photograph is undated, part of the vast Walter Charlton Hartridge Collection documenting two centuries of Savannah history. The latter is from the Georgia Historical Society Collection of Photographs, and Katherine notes that specific details of the dress place it taken in 1890, when Mother Mathilda would have been almost 60. It seems pretty unlikely that she would have looked that fantastic at that age, unless the nuns made a secret beauty product out of saintly relics that we don't know about.

More reasonable is that this lovely lady is Josephine Beasley, wife of the younger Abraham Beasley and Mother Mathilda's step-daughter-in-law. (Abraham Sr. had a son from a previous marriage, and while she was a maternal figure to many, Mother Mathilda never bore any kids of her own.)

Added confirmation comes from a corresponding portrait of Abraham Beasley, Jr. in the same collection.

"It's possible that Josephine has been mistaken for Mathilda because Abraham shared the same name as his father and people presumed the couple to be the elder Beasleys," explains the archivist of the confusion, adding that "confirming identity of people in photographs from the 19th century presents challenges because in many instances there may be no other representative depiction for comparison."

I'm going with the first one because the features seem to align more with her obituary, which notes her lineage as French-Creole and Native American. Plus the expression on her face is righteously beatific while conveying the weariness recognized by every mother who is pretty dang tired of trying to take care of all y'all.

Both images appear in a fascinating installation at Mother Mathilda Park on East Broad Street, where her tiny cottage was lovingly restored and relocated in 2014 and currently maintained by Chatham County Parks & Recreation. The agency recently hosted a birthday celebration outside the cottage, the start of a campaign to raise Mother Mathilda's profile. CCPR Director Steve Proper has reached out to tour guides to include the site and hopes to increase the hours at the cottage in 2018. (It's currently open Wednesdays from 11am to 1pm and Saturdays from 10am to 3pm.)

"We want to re-introduce Mother Beasley to the Savannah community and its visitors," said Proper as kindergarteners from nearby East Broad School listened intently to her story. "She was a very special person and important figure in the city's history."

I can't think of a more appropriate icon to ascend to a higher place in the metanarrative, a reminder that we can affect change while comporting ourselves with dignity and grace.

I admit that I was hoping for some kind of divine visitation as I stood in her modest rooms, imagining her laying prostrate on the wooden floor, caught between heaven and earth. Instead I could only think about the challenges of the world and all the broken-hearted people in it, doing their best to keep the faith in the face of violence, sickness, fire and war. I realized that there's no wisdom in waiting around for the answers, which have always come from real human beings who use their time here to figure out how to help.

Yet a few days later as I was worrying over my personal problems and walking the dogs around her gorgeous park, I do believe Mother Mathilda came to me.

Nah, not an angelic vision or a tall, austere woman with piercing eyes. Just a breeze rustling the oaks and a trace of a thought:

Do the work set before us as best we can, and let the rest be.

Dec. 17, 2017

The Bucket List and the Bell Tower

It used to be enough for humans just to grow up, spawn a kid or two and leave behind a good-looking corpse.

But no, now we've got to have Bucket Lists to keep things interesting. We decide we need to do certain things before we die, even if those things could possibly contribute to the dying.

A decent bucket list should always include a few points that overreach the boundaries of common sense, such as dressing up like a man and running with the bulls in Pamplona or performing an interpretive Afro-Judeo dance with Lady Gaga wearing my very own pair of prosthetic horns.

Then you mix those up with achievable activities, like finishing a novel and cooking a soufflé to feed the illusion that we're actually in control of our own lives.

It's always fabulous to cross things off the Bucket List, even if they're the easy kind like finishing a mosaic art piece made from the shards of the many dishes and teapots accidentally broken over the years. (And by "accidentally," I might mean thrown across the room because someone got backtalky after failing the recognize the advanced symptoms of PMS.)

Once in a while, you're presented with the opportunity to slash a Sharpie through a biggie. From the moment I set foot in Congregation Mickve Israel many years ago, before Mark and I were engaged and my mother-in-law still had her wits, I have been obsessed with the idea of climbing to the top of the bell tower.

The yearn to climb old buildings began when I traveled around Europe with my friend Amy after college. I tipped my head back to the glorious arches and columns of Notre Dame Cathedral in Paris and thought it would be super tough to sneak in and explore Quasimodo's tragic path. Amy, the smart friend, pointed out that tourists are actually *allowed* into the bell tower, and what's the fun in that? She also talked me out of taking the speed train over to Pamplona with the pair of steel-toed boots I'd schlepped around six countries in my backpack, which probably saved my life.

Years later, standing in awe in the nave of my future husband's childhood synagogue, the zest to take in the view from the highest point in a holy place was renewed. It was my first trip to Savannah, and my mother-in-law, who created the docent program at the synagogue, proudly led me through the churchy Gothic sanctuary, explaining that it was the oldest one of its kind still in use.

As my future mother-in-law recounted the history of the third-oldest Jewish congregation in America, founded by descendants of Portuguese refugees and a handful of German Jews just a few months after General Oglethorpe claimed this piece of the New World, I peeked around the pipe organ balcony for an entry point to the bell tower but discovered nothing but a metal folding chair and some old sheet music. I vowed that should it work out with this Savannah guy, I would one day find the way up to the tower, standing from the dozens of pointed church steeples spiking in the Savannah skyline with its rounded, oxidized bronze *yarmulke.*

Decades have gone by, earning me an honest history with Mickve Israel: Our fall wedding, our move to Savannah from California, my very own classroom where I made popsicle stick sukkahs as a Shalom School teacher. All the while, the thought of climbing the tower fluttered like a moth around my dimly-lit brain. I would clamber up to the organ loft any chance I got. During Friday night services, when I would turn around to wish the pew behind me "Good Shabbos," my eyes would wander up, wondering how, *how* to get in.

Well, I figured it out a few weeks ago. I'm not going to reveal any specifics because I don't want to get kicked out of the Purim schpiel. Let's just say that what was hidden in the shadows became clear.

I've been biding my time, waiting for the combination of opportunity (i.e., not during Yom Kippur services) and wearing the correct outfit for stealth (this is not an undertaking for high-heeled boots).

Last Sunday, when I was wearing sneakers and yoga pants and supposed to be helping make challah dough for the Shalom Y'all Food Festival, I seized the day.

The first ladder was no big deal, except that it was kind of dark and I had to move a trapdoor with one hand. The next three were a different story. I climbed hand over hand to the second level of tower, light spilling in from the windows on unfinished concrete. I was surprised that it wasn't painted, though I guess it was never meant to be for the tourists like at Notre Dame.

Then I looked up and saw a series of the rustiest, scariest wrought iron ladders that appeared to have been excavated from Dostoevsky's Russian prison.

I almost chickened out, big time. But that *meshuggeh* 22 year-old who really wanted to run with the bulls kept whispering "C'mon, you can do this. You'll feel like a douche for getting this far and not going to the top."

I'm not one to succumb to peer pressure, even from the voices in my head, but this felt truly important. Not just to have something to check off my Bucket List but to prove that I love this temple and its history. This was a way to have an intimate connection with its story, a visceral experience that combines body, soul and spirit.

Of course, baking challah with the rest of the Sisterhood is a wonderful visceral experience, too, but maybe I do need a little bit of badass factor.

It's also true that's there's a new rabbi and a new chief administrator in the synagogue's near future, and should someone do a security sweep, I might never get another opportunity to climb the bell tower.

I put hand over hand on the rusty rungs.

Someone had nailed a couple of 2'x4's across one section, but I scaled them pretty easily. At the first landing, I made the mistake of looking down. I pictured my broken body on the wooden scaffolding and realized if I fell, no one knew where I was. My mangled corpse might not be found until some other moron had the same demented idea. But then I decided I was not going to die in ugly old yoga pants and kept on.

The second landing was bolted to the concrete wall under the pointed windows just like the other ladders, but for some reason, it WOBBLED. My intestines in my throat, I shook it a few times. Would it pull out from the wall under my weight? Surely it had been built to withstand someone bigger than me, generous tush and all. Then I started wondering why ladders had been built in the bell tower at all—because, it occurred to me suddenly, I had never heard any chimes from my synagogue. I had come all this way only to finally put together the truth: There. Was. No. Bell.

But I'd gotten this far. Above me, just one more orange-flaked ladder up, was another trapdoor. By now my arms were weak as egg noodles, my legs tensed from fear. I stood on the shaky landing for what seemed like a long time, talking to myself, talking to God, wondering what the right action would be.

Did I climb all this way to fail? Was the attempt enough to be a part of the larger story of Savannah's Jewish history? What the hell kind of mother and decent citizen does this anyway? What is wrong with me?

I put my hands on the rungs of this last ladder and took one step. Thirty seconds later, I took another. I made it to the top this way, slowly, and wrapped one arm around the iron to steady myself while I pushed up on the trapdoor with the other. Nothing. I couldn't budge it an inch. It was too heavy for me to move with my adrenaline-depleted arms. I stood suspended in the air, breathing heavily with the top of my head touching the thick wooden slab. I'd made it to the finish line and couldn't cross—perhaps a lesson to the insane person who lives inside me who should not be allowed to handle any decisions (or come to think of it, dishes.)

Suddenly, I pushed my head up. With the strength of my shoulders and the hardness of my skull, I lifted the door up three inches, feeling the breeze immediately on my cheeks. From my raccoon mask-sized gap, I saw a view few have seen of the city. I could hear children laughing in Monterey Square six stories below. I saw the Talmadge Bridge and the church steeples and the rooftops and the trees and the blue, blue sky.

If you had been a bird cruising the city's highest points or flying by in one of the Army's ubiquitous fighter jets, you might have caught a glimpse of the wide eyes of a terrified but exhilarated 40 year-old woman who'd just pushed past her many demons to achieve a dream—a weird, inappropriate, probably illegal one, but a dream nonetheless.

I whispered a prayer of thanks to Whomever Is Responsible, and another for getting me back down safely, pretty please.

I made it all the way back down in under ten minutes. I was just starting to creep down to the sanctuary when I heard my son's voice. His Shalom School teacher had chosen this exact moment to bring the class in and quiz them on Shabbat prayers.

I flopped down to my belly like a Mossad agent—how would I explain THIS? My face pressed against the intricately carved wood, I examined the six-winged angels along the columns from a whole new perspective and *kvelled* quietly as I heard my dear boy get all his answers right. I sent up another deep-hearted prayer of thanks that my children won't have to do anything to belong to the story of this historic synagogue: They already do.

The fifth-graders finally marched out and I meandered back to the challah-braiding workshop. All in all, I had been gone less than an hour, and no one seemed to notice my absence. I jumped right in line with the other Jewish mothers and grandmothers and proceeded to make a total mess trying to braid six lines at once. But privately I felt I'd accomplished something far more important than baking a perfect challah, though that's on the Bucket List, too.

To anyone offended, I apologize and promise never, ever to climb the bell tower again, and not just because my legs are still so sore. But I won't guarantee I won't get myself another pair of steel-toed boots and head to Pamplona before I turn 50.

Oct. 14, 2011

Haints' Night In at the Olde Pink House

It's close to midnight, and something evil's lurking in the dark. Under the moonlight, you see a sight that almost stops your heart. You try to scream…

Yes, these may seem to be the lyrics to Michael Jackson's "Thriller," but it's pretty dang close to how it all went down.

See, when I pulled up to the Olde Pink House late last Monday night to meet Ryan Dunn and Guieneverre Cutlip of the local paranormal investigative team 3-D Ghosthunters, I wasn't scared at all.

Mostly, I was annoyed that this expedition had to take place at an hour when I'd have been horizontal for at least two hours, earplugs snugly in place. Stupid specters. Why can't ghosts socialize at five in the afternoon like normal people? So inconsiderate, the undead.

Turns out it's the live folk that are the problem.

"It needs to be as quiet as possible for us to collect data," explained Dunn as we sat on worn leather couches waiting for the downstairs Tavern bar to clear out. "During the day, there are all kinds of noises that cover up any unusual activity."

Dunn founded 3-D Ghosthunters two years ago with his wife, Kim, after spending an unusual date night in Colonial Cemetery that yielded a bizarre recording of mysterious voices. They began investigating purported local haunted hotspots like the Savannah Theatre and The Foley

House and have collected a library of enigmatic EVFs ("electronic voice phenomenon") that reveal whispers and phrases when analyzed with audio software. In this Most Haunted City in America, their hobby is flourishing into a big business.

Joined by marketing director Cutlip and photographer/resident skeptic Ryan Reese, the small team does an exhaustive historical timeline of each location and is careful not to promise proof of otherworldly entities. Unfortunately on this night, the babysitter cancelled, so Kim was home with the couple's two little girls, presumably reading them Edgar Allen Poe.

As the barflies toasted another round, Dunn educated me on the two types of ghosts: "Residual" phantoms are imprints that repeat the same action over and over, and "intelligent" spirits interact with the living, sometimes dropping things on heads or speaking through television static. (Any one remember Carol Anne…Carol Anne?)

Often when either kind passes through a room, he said, a density in the air can be detected and the temperature drops.

I felt sudden chill and shrieked.

"We try to offer rational explanations of why something is happening," Dunn laughed, pointing to a vent over my head. "Really, paranormal is our last conclusion."

Finally, the last of the port-soused patrons stumbled into the night and the ghost hunters got to work. Digital recorders received fresh batteries and cameras were set up in the dining rooms of the Olde Pink House, which you may have gleaned is old and pink and incredibly creepy in the wee hours of the morning.

Built in 1789 for Revolutionary patriot James Habersham, Jr., this mansion-turned-restaurant has for decades spawned reports of mysteriously locked bathrooms, disembodied faces in mirrors, and on several occasions, old Mrs. Habersham drifting past to play with patrons' hair. Dunn chose to begin the investigation in the tavern hallway, where a smoky apparition was captured on a security camera last year (it's on YouTube.)

Pink House manager Meghan Littlefield, who spotted the ghost on camera while working in the back storeroom (and can be seen running down the hall at 33 seconds into the video), didn't seem to mind being charged with staying late with the team. "I get all the ghost stuff now," she grinned.

Restaurant people are always up late anyway, and sommelier Jason Restivo also stuck around to tell tales of eerie shadows and a stack of bowls that broke themselves. When I asked maitre d' Sean Dempsey if he'd ever experienced anything supernatural at work, he reluctantly answered, "No. Well, yeaaah…" and shared stories of candles that relit themselves and brought out a framed photo taken by a customer of a strange cloudy figure standing in front of the bar.

At this point, Dunn announced we should split up and beckoned me to follow him to the very dark third floor. He placed playing cards on tables along the way—"trigger objects" that can attract movement from the Other Side.

The hair on my neck did a little dance as we passed by a portrait of Mr. Habersham giving us the stinkeye from over the hostess station—I swear his eyes followed me as we wound our way up the spiral staircase. I crept along with my back to the wall in case anything tried to pet my hair. We had just tiptoed into the low-ceilinged Brown Room when Dunn asked loudly, "Are you here? Can you make a noise to let us know?"

Oh hell no, I thought, he's talking to the ghosts? I was told we were *observing.*

I stepped away from my guide, trying to make myself as small as possible. "Does it bother you that we're in your house?" he boomed, recorder held high. I scrunched into a fetal position in the corner. Suddenly I felt a buzz in my back pocket. OH MY GOD. The ghost is here and it's touching my butt! I almost screamed, then realized it was just a text from my insomniac son.

After a few more questions, Dunn sighed. "I don't feel much up here, let's go back down to the tavern."

There we sat quietly again in the hallway with Cutlip, Reese and the rest of the gang, watching the EMF sensors light oscillate, a possible indication that ghosts were disrupting the magnetic field. I had just decided that 3 a.m. was late enough for a school night when Dunn asked the empty space in front of us, "Are you lonely?"

And there it was, a distinct *skreeeeeeky* rustle that seemed to come from the chair right next to me. We all jumped and turned wide-eyed to each other.

"Everyone heard that, right?" chirped Dunn, busily rewinding the recorder.

That was enough paranormal activity for this girl. I don't care whether you believe in ghosts or not: When the air speaks, it's time to go home.

The 3-D Ghosthunters stayed until dawn and are still analyzing the recordings from the Pink House to share on their Facebook page, but Dunn sent me the cleaned-up clip of the rustle the very next day.

I've listened to the whispered "Help, help" about a hundred times now, and all I can say is I hope the poor soul trapped near one of the finest wine cellars in town with no way to partake finds some solace soon.

As for the happy ghosts, some say Halloween is when they really come out to play. Bring your cards, if you dare.

Oct. 23,2012

Don't Feed the Animal

I was a few minutes late for the bi-monthly board meeting of the Flannery O'Connor Childhood Home, but I still took a moment to compose myself on the stairs.

There's something about entering this modest, Greek Revival townhouse-cum-museum that requires correctitude, as if the author and her family still lived here. You don't just rush in with your sunglasses falling out of your purse and lipstick on your teeth.

Offering an apologetic whisper, I squeezed in at a corner of the dining table, where my fellow board members were munching on cookies and discussing the details of the upcoming Flannery O'Connor Parade and Street Fair.

The Sweet Thunder Strolling Band had been booked, the local authors procured for the Book Lady's vending tables. Only one small matter remained.

"So, who wants to be the gorilla?"

A few of my fellow board members politely stared at the antique china cabinet that houses first editions of the author's books. Others engrossed themselves in the budget spreadsheets expertly prepared by treasurer Christian Kruse. President Bishop Kevin Boland cleared his throat. Secretary Allison Hersh held her pen poised above her legal pad, ready to record the minutes.

Since I joined this board of brilliant and competent people last fall, I have found myself qualified to contribute very little, other than helping Mary Lawrence Kennickell arrange the snack table at September's Ursey Memorial Lecture with Roxane Gay and volunteering to drive the best-selling author to the airport.

Even then, distracted by my own fangirl chatter and the seemingly sudden sprouting of the new Tanger outlets on I-95, I managed to miss the damn exit. Poor Roxane Gay probably thought I was trying to kidnap her and dump the body in some remote South Carolina outpost in the vein of the Misfit in "A Good Man Is Hard to Find."

Now, finally, here was an opportunity to redeem myself from that terrible, awkward failure of duty.

I slowly raised my hand. Joseph Schwartzburt raised his eyebrows. Ann Moffett smiled at me encouragingly.

"I'll do it," I said, lifting my arm higher and waving like a prom queen. "I will be the gorilla."

The more I thought about it, the more I liked the idea. The lively parade that takes place every year in Lafayette Square outside "the Childhood Home" (as it's referred to in order to differentiate it from the author's adult home, Andalusia Farm in Milledgeville) is one of the reasons

I joined up in the first place, with its unique combination of literary homage and reverential silliness.

Plus, I've totally got the skills for once. Not to brag, but I served as the mascot of the high school football team my sophomore year, spending every Friday night trying to keep up with the pom-pom squad on the sidelines and out of the way of the marching band. Since my school had won the Arizona state championship two years before, it was afforded two mascots, a boy *and* a girl horse. My friend Cathy and I rotated between the full body suit of the boy horse and the far more preferable girl costume, a heavily-eyelashed equine head and an old cheerleading uniform. No matter what, we looked like teenage disasters at the after-game dances in the gym, where we mostly spent drinking stolen wine coolers in the locker room.

So I figured I have the fortitude to pull off a few hours as an ape with no choreography. But I felt I needed more background to fulfill the role justly, sniffing out meaning and context through the nostril slits of the fur mask. Call it gorilla journalism, if you will. (Heheheh, you probably already did.)

Though I remembered it making appearances in her work, I wanted to know what a gorilla is doing at the Flannery O'Connor parade. But first I had to understand why a literary icon universally described as "reserved" and "private" has such a wacky parade in the first place.

The answers lay with artist and former FOCCH board member Christine Sajecki, who discovered an edict from the 1970s proclaiming March 25, Flannery O'Connor's birthday, a city holiday. She already knew that percussive ringleader Andrew Hartzell—now on the current board—used to throw spontaneous (i.e. unpermitted and unsanctioned) parades back in Portland, Oregon, and together they invited their favorite literary-minded rebels to reclaim the celebration.

The first seditious procession took place in the late afternoon of MLK Day 2012 around Lafayette Square, a ragtag bunch of 20 weirdos carrying signs bearing Dr. King quotes and the Flannery battle cry, "Beauty is our money crop."

The following year, the parade was officially adopted by the FOCCH and acquired legitimate paperwork, but it still retains the atmosphere of family-friendly anarchy, with its azalea crowns and chicken poop bingo. Over the years the event has become a beacon for anyone with an askew view of the world, taking a cue from the writer's famous quote about recognizing freaks.

All the weirdos must converge, or something like that.

Still, it's hard to picture the honoree joining the fray. Instead, I imagine her observing wryly from her former bedroom window, thinking up ways to describe yet another ludicrous band of Southern idiots.

"I don't know that she herself would enjoy it," agrees Christine, who moved to Baltimore a couple of years ago and was back in Savannah last week for a short spell with her husband and adorable baby son, August. (Perhaps you bid on one of her beautiful encaustic paintings at a recent Southern Discomfort art show at Non Fiction Gallery to benefit the Childhood Home?)

"Her writing was radical, but she was a fairly proper person. I doubt she would appreciate having such a spectacle made of herself."

But perhaps the devoutly religious O'Connor would recognize the earnestness in the absurdity. Surely of all people she could see that the flagrant freakiness is meant in its way to be an alignment of faith—not a fragile kind of belief that dissolves into the ether outside of the church sanctuary, but a clear conviction that holds up under the hard, grotesqueness of human nature.

Anyone who has attended the parade knows that when Father Michael Chaney preaches "Where's all my sweetness gone?" as the afternoon melts into the long shadows of the Cathedral of St. John the Baptist, the plea is not satirical but sacramental, a heartfelt testament to the mystery that binds us here together under heaven.

But back to the gorilla. A guy in an ape suit shows up in the short story "Enoch and the Gorilla" and again in the novel *Wise Blood* as Gonga the movie star, though his scenes are brief. Christine says the primate costume was embraced as a symbol that could be easily represented in the parade, along with the prosthetic leg in "Good Country People."

However, as you may recall, Flannery's gorilla is kind of a dick. He tells Enoch to "go to hell" when they shake hands, and his mean response provokes Enoch to stalk him around town, beat him up and steal his simian identity.

On one hairy hand, I can empathize with the gorilla's bitterness, as I know a little something about wearing a full-body fur costume in the heat before the advent of fancy sweat-wicking under armor. Also, Enoch is pretty annoying and definitely creepy, especially when he is fleshed out more deeply in *Wise Blood.*

Yet it would be wholly inappropriate to embody a literal performance of the literature and have some parent smack me upside the head with a mannequin leg. So I continued to dig for my motivation.

I sought deeper analysis of the character from Michael Schroeder, an English professor at Savannah State University who also happens to be the Vice President of the FOCCH board. "I guess that means I'm in charge of vice," he laughs.

With a good teacher's deft way of teasing out coherent thoughts from dull minds, he led me through a short discussion on what the animal imagery might represent.

"Many of O'Connor's human characters act completely out of

impulse," Professor Schroeder reminded me. "And we know that she was very faithful. Do you think there's a connection?"

We bantered about basic instincts and the longing for spiritual redemption, about how crassness and even violence doesn't preclude even the worst sinner from turning towards heaven, as we witness in the denouement of *Wise Blood.*

I scratched my head and snacked on a banana, working out how free will is still the only thing that separates us from the apes.

The evolution of the soul is a topic we can explore more directly in the posthumously published *A Prayer Journal.* Devoid of the signature sardonic vinegar in her fiction, this slim volume of letters to God reveals the purity of Mary Flannery O'Connor's lifelong dance with devotion and doubt of her own spiritual worth.

"I don't want to fear to be out, I want to love to be in," she writes of hell and heaven. Though she is referring to the supernatural realms, this might also speak to our need to belong, to feel at home in a world that so often seems dangerous and unfair and just plain mean.

So while the patron saint of Southern freakery might offer an appalled arched eyebrow were she to glance down upon Sunday's colorful kooky pageant, I hope she would also see the camaraderie, the goodness, and the inclusion carried out in her name.

It might be as hot and humid as a sinner's armpit on Sunday, but I will rejoice as I don the fur suit, not as a penance but an honor.

And though I forsake Gonga as inspiration, I cannot promise that I won't break out the cheerleading moves.

Tower Feist

There it is, a great green monolith rising like a tectonic plate pushing out of the earth's crust. In this flat city of few views, its 12 stories might as well be a mountain. My urge to climb it is primal, as if I am a giant gorilla instinctively seeking out the highest point to survey my surroundings.

Except instead of scaling the windows, I plan to take the elevator.

Love it or revile it, you can't deny the drama of Drayton Tower. All clean lines and cool glass, it has dominated the corner of Liberty and Drayton since 1951, when father-and-son architectural team Cletus and William Bergen slapped sleepy Southern sensibilities upside the head with their chromed concrete box.

Originally built to answer the call of the 1946 Veterans Emergency Housing Act, its European-influenced International Style was meant to convey progress and slick modern living. But the city's nascent historical preservation movement decried the sparse design as soulless, aloof as an android in reflective sunglasses amongst the lacy porches of its elderly Southern neighbors.

The tower had not aged well in the last decades, many of its 4000 Solex windows broken or replaced with Plexiglass, giving off the impression of a once-handsome gent who had lost his dignity and most of his of teeth. Its cantilevered portico was edged with rust, one end of its ground floor commercial space boarded up.

When the building turned 50 in 2002, it was entered into the National Register of Historic Places, much to the chagrin of its detractors. But bigger minds saw its value as part of Savannah's overall story.

"People need to understand that this is a great example of International Style, one of the only ones in the South," Historic Savannah Foundation president Daniel Carey reminded the haters.

"History, like architecture, is a continuum. You don't just pick the parts you want to preserve. The tower should be, even begrudgingly, embraced."

That means a hug for the tower's "trailer park in the sky" days when rent was cheap, as well as its floundering redevelopment by DrayProp, a group of businessmen who acquired the tower in 2005 for $8.35 million and sold it a few years ago to New York-based Flank, Inc. for $3.8 million.

I called Flank principal Ken Copeland to ask how it feels to own Savannah's most maligned edifice.

"We see a huge opportunity here," explained Copeland carefully. "The whole mid-century, *Mad Men* aesthetic is enjoying a comeback, and once our redevelopment is finished, people are going to see the beauty in this building again."

He admitted that there was a "decent amount" of work to be done to make 100 plush one- and two-bedroom units out of the mostly raw space, but promised by the next spring it would be transformed into a "modern, luxury apartment building."

Flank plans to market big city amenities to its new tenants: Concierge, 24-hour doorman, the works. The commercial spaces downstairs, occupied by Byrd Cookie Co. and ROBS salon, will surely fill up once again. It's going to be fancy, y'all.

Which means is if I ever want to take in a renegade vista from the top, I'd better get in before the construction crews.

I have a real estate groupie friend who spends many evenings exploring our city's urban rooftops, because as I can relate, sometimes a girl just needs an eagle eye view of things.

More than a decade younger than me and unencumbered by familial responsibilities, my friend has spent lots of time roaming Savannah's forgotten places. She's driven around the ancient racetrack on

Hutchinson Island and laments that creepy old Candler Hospital is no longer accessible since its reclamation as Savannah Law School.

She can slip through small spaces and bullshit her way out of just about anything, making her the perfect guide of the unfinished top floor of Drayton Tower. Since she is accompanying me on this gonzo journalistic fantasy, I shall heretofore refer to her as Lazlo.

We meet just before sunset on the longest day of the year under the tower's shadow. Through the lobby doors, Lazlo and I see the restored lush walnut paneling and stunning art-deco light fixture, exhumed during DrayProp's hopeful attempt to restore the building before the economy tanked.

But Lazlo's friend who lives in the tower does not answer her text.

Ever the resourceful one, Lazlo mentions something about picking the lock. Not sure if she's serious, I point to the security cameras and whisper I'd rather use my gonzo Getting Arrested Adventure column on something more poignant than trespassing.

We leave the lobby and walk around back, where an older gentleman is standing next to an open door. He introduces himself as Kenneth, a resident of the fifth floor, and waves a notebook at us.

"Y'all got a pen I could use?"

I hand one over, explaining that my associate and I would like to go up and look around.

"Well, come on in!" he cries, and begins busily scribbling numbers in his book.

As Lazlo and I start down the hallway, Kenneth calls after us.

"The right elevator's only for Jews, Greeks and Italians. And Sicilians. Other one is for whites and blacks."

Lazlo and I look at each other. Kenneth must've been living here a long time.

"We'll take the service elevator," Lazlo calls back.

We turn the corner, and I realize he didn't give me back my pen.

The service elevator groans its way upward, and it occurs to me that taking a creaky elevator to an abandoned construction site 12 stories off the ground may not be the wisest choice I made this week.

Still, as I supposed, the view is stupendous. The space is naked and wide, the windows dusty but unfettered. The sun has melted into the horizon behind the Talmadge Bridge, the lights along the river beginning to blink on. We walk around and around the open concrete floor, taking in 360 degrees of Savannah.

Looking out onto the spires of St. John the Baptist Cathedral, I spy a gorgeous hidden rooftop garden along Drayton. Below the bustle of downtown is ensconced in leafy canopy. All above is quiet and serene.

Actually, it's a little too quiet. And it's getting dark.

"Did you bring a flashlight?" I ask.

Lazlo informs me that flashlights are for sissies but scoots back to the elevator anyway and punches the button. Nothing.

"This is the point in the horror flick where the two plucky protagonists get raped by zombies," I tell Lazlo.

She pokes the button two, three, four more times. The elevator stays mute.

"Oh that happens sometimes," Lazlo says breezily, crossing the cavernous space. "We'll just take the stairs."

No, we will not, as apparently the new owners have just put a shiny new padlock on the door to the stairwell.

Lazlo shakes her hair. "No big deal. Just call your husband. Kenneth can let him in."

My head begins to sweat. I would rather spend the night up here with the spiders before I'd call my husband. My dear spouse can't comprehend my King Kong compulsion for great heights and is not impressed about my intimate knowledge about the Mickve Israel bell tower and the fact that there is no bell. Mark doesn't even like me riding my bike at night, but he knows he cannot keep an adventurous spirit down. He was particularly non-plussed about this particular exploit; in fact, the last thing he said when I left was "If you get into trouble, don't call me."

So even if we don't get raped and eaten by monsters, it looks like Lazlo and I will be starving to death on the top floor of the storied Drayton Tower.

I make a promise to my Maker that if I get out of this one, I'll take up a collection at synagogue for a bell. I start thinking I ought to write my last will and testament. Except, of course, I don't have a pen.

Just then, we hear the exhausted grind of the elevator. Lazlo grins like she knew it all along. "You weren't really scared, were you?"

I will admit here that yes, yes I was. And I may be cured of my urge to climb to the tops of abandoned buildings. At least at night.

As we step out into the posh lobby, Kenneth is sitting on one of the deep couches, still at work on his columns of numbers. He eyeballs us.

"You came down the wrong elevator," he says, tapping my pen on his knee. He holds it out, ruefully.

I don't imagine that Kenneth, who seems harmless but possibly very medicated, will continue to live in Drayton Tower after it's spruced up to its new glory.

"Keep it," I say.

Lazlo and I head across the street to McDonough's for a beer. I look back up at the tower, pocked with the light of its few current residents, glad to have a tiny piece of its once and future story.

June 26, 2012

3 CHARACTER STUDIES

Savannah might have its staid Southern social mores, but that doesn't mean it doesn't welcome the weirdos. There's a long tradition of tolerating eccentrics and outliers around here, probably because gossiping about other people's quirks is a practiced form of entertainment. But it's the ones who take risks, follow their dreams and listen to the voices in their heads that create and build the most momentous things. In fact, this town owes it all to a cast of characters who make no apologies for being exactly who they are doing exactly as they see fit—sometimes it even makes them famous.

High Society with the Duchess of State

If you're to believe the party poopers, Savannah society is a notoriously hard nut to crack.

They will tell you this city's ruling class is a rarefied bunch, their rosters of splendiferous holiday galas, opulent charity balls and swank oyster roasts an impenetrable cloister for most of us peons. To make those hand-scripted invitation lists, your relatives either stepped off the ship with General Oglethorpe or you're dripping in enough new money to allow the tacit overlook of your less impressive origins, dahlin'.

Those of us who arrived with the dust of other places on our bourgeois heels can forget the exclusive supper club invitations and gin-and-tonics at the Yacht Club. But like the great sage Groucho Marx, there will always be those who don't give a flying fig about being a member of any club that would have them as a member.

Besides, why waste time or risk mussing your dress trying to climb the wrought-iron gates of high society when you can forge your own?

"Savannah can be whatever you make it, honey," counsels Alexandra Trujillo de Taylor, a self-styled socialite who operates independently of any such prescribed snobbery.

The dazzling downtown doyenne has been cultivating guest lists for almost 20 years, her parties so legendary that invitations are coveted by even the most cerulean of bluebloods. But it's not your stock portfolio or your daddy's surname that gains entrée.

"I've always thought such things were absurd!" exclaims Taylor. "I've always wanted to meet everybody. Who cares about backgrounds? The most important thing is, *are you interesting*?"

Well, are ya, punk? My own appeal was put to the test last week after receiving a raised-print invitation via snail mail for Taylor's quarterly tea party.

I RSVP'd quickly as proper party etiquette dictates, and also because I've heard that La Taylor is appalled by the proliferation of what she refers to as *mannures*—"modern day manners meets manure." The common Savannah practice of not responding to a party request until the last minute gets a *tsk-tsk* and a Sharpie through your name next time around.

Though this consummate hostess doesn't feel beholden to any other staid Southern conventions, her airs are no less aristocratic. Taylor even rocks her own title: The Duchess of State, bestowed upon her when she regularly hosted parties for the Savannah Philharmonic at her single gal apartment on State Street back in the late 1990s.

With a passionate flick of a bangled wrist, the Duchess clarifies that those famous fêtes were not for symphony patrons but exclusively for the musicians, "to give something back for their incredible talent."

"Where I'm from, we pay homage to the artist," she sniffs. "Besides, they are symphony musicians, so it's instant black tie!"

Raised in Mexico City in a traditional household where formality ruled ("You didn't come out of the bedroom until you were fully dressed,") Alexandra learned to let her hair down in the deep South while spending her summers with her uncle Fernando, who had defected from macho Mexico to Chattanooga to become a hairdresser. On one trip she visited a sister in Savannah and was reminded of the *circuitos* of Mexico by the green squares and slow pace, and so decided to adopt the myth and mystery of the Garden as her own.

The Duchess dialed back her nightlife and moved a few blocks uptown after she married her Duke, Daniel Taylor, ten years ago, but she's far from given up her inclinations to entertain.

The invitation for the tea party—emblazoned with Her Royal Highness' own crest—commanded that winter hats were *de rigeur.* Wearing a hand-felted wool bowler my mother brought me back from her recent trip to Estonia, I knock on a jet-black double door on a block of meticulously restored Victorians and languishing tear-downs. I'm greeted by the Duchess herself, resplendent in a cream-colored Chanel dress and matching ostrich feather pillbox hat.

"*Dios mio*, what a fetching chapeau!" she declares as she kisses both of my cheeks. "*Vene, niña*, come meet everyone."

She styles these seasonal teas straight out of her Mexican childhood, when her mother and her friends played cards and gossiped until the men came home from work. Though she and the Duke host their own supper club for couples, these afternoons are for women only, plus "a sprinkling of the gays." (Adorable SCAD fashion student Antonio Tombari was exempted from headgear in lieu of a striped bowtie.)

Some guests she's known for years, like Christy Cook, who the Duchess once charmed into throwing a small cocktail party at the mansion Christy used to own on Gaston Street for 250 of her closest friends. Others, like 20-something stylist and make-up artist Lady Katherine Taylor, she met yesterday.

"Isn't she gorgeous?" exclaims the Duchess when I inquire about the lovely girl posed on the leather loveseat attired in a purple crushed velvet coat and Amy Winehouse eyeliner. "I just picked her up at Habersham Antiques. She was wearing a full-on opera chignon at two in the afternoon! I had to know her."

Present most always at of the Duchess' social gathering is her dear friend Lily Lewin, as blond and lissome as the Duchess is stately and brunette. Lily, an accomplished photographer, is married to Dr. Lucas Lewin, a Southcoast physician and honest-to-God count from Madrid, which makes her an honest-to-Goddess countess. It is pure charm to hear the Duchess and La Condesa cooing to each other in Spanish—a Castilian version of *AbFab*'s Patsy and Eddy, only sober.

However, these *mejores amigas* admit to some alpha female sparking when they first met.

"We were like two tarantulas in a box," giggles the Duchess.

"Now I'm the only one who can talk back to her and not lose my head," deadpans La Condesa.

Verdad, the Duchess' temper is as legendary as her parties. She might be inclusive, tolerant and welcoming of the eccentric, but doesn't mean that there aren't rules: First and foremost, follow the dress code. Also, no cell phones at the table. And unless you want the Sharpie through your name, do not ever, EVER, go in the kitchen.

"It is where the magic happens, *niña*. Don't ruin it!" she warns as she blocks the doorway. She later explains later that in Mexico, guests do not mix with the help, though she stresses that her beloved longtime housekeeper, Bartola, is part of the family.

As for the sumptuous spread, the Duchess cooks it herself: Smoked salmon with dill sauce, lemony orzo, and, from a lustrous antique tureen, the secret tomato soup recipe from SoHo South Café, bequeathed by a former chef with the oath that it would never be revealed.

For dessert, there are four kinds of loose tea in delicate pots and a homemade pear tart, courtesy of La Condesa. Everything is served in the shell pink dining room on fine china, an always-rotating collection that inspires the Duchess to design her parties "from the plate up."

Her signature aesthetic is eclectic elegance meets high drama, spilling over into the other rooms of *la casa*: She and the Duke have commissioned enormous portraits of themselves by local artists, most notably the royal pose above the mantle by artist Alexandro Santana and another by Jason Zaloudik in the upstairs bedroom-turned-dressing room, refurbished with racks on three walls to accommodate her Highness' fabulous wardrobe.

In her spare time, Alex (as some are brave enough to address her) lends her interior design talents to others and keeps a booth at Habersham Antiques to repurpose her clients' cast-offs. She documents her latest projects and outrage at *los mannures* on the Duchess of State blog and has occasionally been known to dish deliciously on some of our small-town scandals. She also relentlessly promotes her favorite people (we first met when she suggested I write about chocolatier Adam Turoni the minute he opened on Broughton Street), and those who benefit from her patronage affectionately call her their Mexican Fairy Godmother.

As far as the exclusive codes of the mythical Old Savannah gentry go, they don't intimidate the Duchess in the least.

"I don't even know what that tastes like. Tell me something new. If not, move it along," she dismisses with a wave.

Perhaps this is the future of Savannah society, self-defined in its glamour and generosity, unburdened by any dusty pretensions.

My afternoon in the Duchess' court ended too soon, and I can only hope my Estonian chapeau and relentless questions were deemed captivating enough to be invited back. At the very least, it's motivation to keep my *mannures* under control.

Which reminds me: If you'll excuse me, I have a thank you note to write.

Dec. 18, 2013

Miriam Center and Me!

I've got a birthday coming up, which is always an opportunity to obsess about the ephemerality of this one-way road trip.

This year, however, I'm swearing off my usual macabre preoccupations with life's fleeting journey. Now that I've finally burned through the formidable reserves of my youthful angst, I figure I might coast on the plateau of middle age for a nice stretch before any sign of a final destination looms in the headlights.

But it looks like I picked the wrong week to stop fretting over my mortality, 'cause right out of the gate, Miriam Center wants to talk about death.

It makes sense, really. The legendary local has never been one for social small talk, catching you up in her level gaze to tell you exactly what's on her mind. And we are on our way to Bonaventure Cemetery, after all.

Plus, she just turned 90, a milestone not too many folks stick around to see.

"It's a long goddamn time to be alive," agrees Miriam amiably as she slides into my old Mercedes and slams the door. "But I'm not afraid of what comes next. Are you scared of dying?"

I laugh nervously and mumble something about trying not to get us killed in the afternoon traffic snarl on Victory Drive. We cruise past Bonaventure's wrought iron gates to the back, where the tallest trees sweep the tops of the oldest tombs with their sleeves of moss. With her red lipstick, leopard scarf and Holly Golightly sunglasses—the style trifecta of timeless Hollywood glamour—Miriam stands out like a rose in a wheat field.

"It's fucking ridiculous the way people pretend they're not going to die," she says as she strides through the somber gray and green hues. "We're all gonna be under these stones one day. We should talk about it."

She points out this family name and that, telling of Savannah scandals long forgotten until we arrive at the burial plot of celebrated songwriter Johnny Mercer, her good pal who passed away in 1976. They both grew up in Savannah, but they didn't meet until in 1963, after she was married with children and he was already an Academy Award-winning superstar.

She sings a few bars of "Tangerine," dusts off the engraved marble bench with the palm of her hand, plops down to tell me the story.

"I sat on his lap at a party. He started singing to me one of his songs, 'you must have been a beautiful baby...but baby, you got a fat ass!'" she finishes with a cackle.

After Johnny was introduced to Miriam's tush, their snappy rapport deepened when he moved back to Savannah from Hollywood to care for his ailing mother. She was still mourning the death of her 15 year-old son, Henry, from a brain tumor. When Johnny announced he was terminally ill with the same fate, their relationship became profoundly devoted, though always platonic.

"He was just an extraordinary man. We would just talk and sing and laugh and cry," she remembers, tracing his likeness carved on the bench. "He could also be a real shit when he was drunk."

Looks like I picked the wrong week to quit cussing.

One of Miriam's many charms is her gleeful swearing—she could definitely teach a sailor a thing or two—and I find this delightfully contagious as we kibbitz. As we f-bomb the hell out of the early afternoon graveyard hebetude, I marvel that couched in the rounded vowels of Miriam's elegant Savannah drawl, profanity somehow comes out sounding musical.

Musicals are what made Johnny famous, of course, and we're here to pay homage to Mr. Moon River in advance of this week's production of *Johnny Mercer & Me!*, Miriam's original play about their huckleberry friendship. Skylark fans adored it when it was last onstage in 2012, and it's being reprised for one night only at the Lucas Theatre.

Presented by the Savannah Community Theatre and directed by native thespian Tom Coleman III, the show stars longtime Mercer impressionist Jeffery Hall and lovely vocalist Regina Rossi Valentine in the titular roles. All proceeds go to Senior Citizens, Inc. save for $1 that goes to the historic preservation of the dreamy art deco Lucas.

Weaving the stories she wrote with the help of late Savannah State professor Dr. Ja Jahannes, the musical features 16 Mercer tunes that illuminate a turning point in Miriam's life. She had just hit her mid-40s, and she didn't know yet that her best adventures were yet to come.

That was when she started her own real estate business and was instrumental in the construction of the Civic Center. The unapologetic liberal ran for city council twice and was appointed the first female director of the MPC. She wrote a novel, *Scarlett O'Hara Can Go To Hell*. In the 80s, after her two remaining sons, Tony and Scott, were grown, she divorced her husband, Leo, bought a convertible and sped off to California.

There she had a spiritual awakening that led her from white-robed cults to Transcendental Meditation to a degree in spiritual psychology from the University of Santa Monica. Finally, her West Coast journey brought her all the way back home, though hardly the same woman.

"There are so many aspects to a person, and most of us never even scratch the surface of who we are," she says thoughtfully as we walk back to the car. "I'm so glad I've had so many experiences."

It's no wonder that Miriam has no problem standing up to death. She's always followed her buddy Johnny's admonition to "Ac-Cent-Tchu-Ate the Positive," and if that doesn't work, fill the days with wine and roses.

And carbs.

"You know what sounds good?" she says as we pull away from the cemetery. "Krispy Kreme. Let's stop and get a box."

Dammit, looks like I picked the wrong week to quit gluten. (Again.)

As we devour glazed old-fashioneds at her kitchen table, she tells me about growing up the daughter of immigrants from Belarus and being ostracized from the sororities at Savannah High for being Jewish.

"I didn't care," she says, tossing her shoulders with a mischievous grin. "I was popular with the boys, and that was all that mattered."

She voted for FDR for his last term and is thoroughly disgusted with the current state of political affairs.

"If Trump gets elected, I'm fucking moving to Italy," she says, daintily licking her fingers.

I note that the only thing on the kitchen counter is a bottle of gummy vitamins. She responds that the secret to her vitality is to avoid "all those damn medications they're always trying to shove down old people's throats."

"That, and good sex," she adds with a raised eyebrow as longtime paramour John Patterson strolls in the door.

John gave her an exquisite triangle-shaped ring from ZIA jewelers on Broughton Street recently, but she hasn't gotten around to setting a date for a wedding.

"I said I was engaged," she giggles. "I didn't say I was gonna get married!"

She sees Thursday's show as a warm-up to the only item left on her bucket list: To take *Johnny Mercer & Me!* to a New York stage. "Other than that, I've done everything. I've already lived forever!"

I'm considering the math that Miriam is exactly twice my age when she pushes away her plate and trains her twinkling peepers on me. "So? Are you scared of death?"

Not as much as I am of not living, I tell her.

"Well then, you should have another donut, dahlin'," she nods.

I help myself. We all end up at the same rainbow's end anyway. The only real wisdom that makes any goddamn sense is to go ahead and enjoy the ride.

Sept. 21, 2016

Lunch with the Romeos

My father-in-law called me up last week in the middle of the day, which was odd.

First of all, he usually avoids me during work hours lest I chase him down with a request to carpool a gaggle of yammering Girl Scouts. Second, ever since he finally bought a smart phone he has become an obsessive texter.

But even weirder than hearing his voice on the line was his request:

"I want to take you to lunch at the Savannah Golf Club with the other Romeos."

Mystifying. As far as I know, this recently retired oncologist has never played golf in his life.

And though he is a very nice-looking man, I think the nurses who worked with him through 40 years in practice would agree that no one but my mother-in-law would ever classify him as a "Romeo."

After I asked him if he was planning to pawn me off so he could make way for a newer model of daughter-in-law, maybe one that didn't crab at him to quit texting at the dinner table, he explained that "ROMEO" is an acronym for Retired Old Men Eating Out.

This still sounded slightly dangerous, but I'm never one to turn down a free lunch.

Turns out this was no ordinary group of guys eating chicken fingers and complaining about their prostates. While some ROMEO clubs veto women, the Savannah Romeos allow female guests to join their monthly gatherings to eat and listen to a program of local interest, ranging from science to history to poetry and everything in between.

On the bill for this day was bestselling author Jonathan Rabb, with four historical novels to his credit and another in the works. A former political theory professor at Columbia, he's now on the writing faculty at SCAD.

I suspected my father-in-law invited me along because he was hoping that Rabb's literary proficiencies would inspire me to push out a book of my own. Regrettably, writing bestselling fiction isn't contagious, but it's always a delight to hear the witty and self-deprecating Rabb speak on any topic.

As we lunched on asparagus, rice and salmon accompanied by pitchers of sweet tea, my father-in-law whispered the names of the gentlemen and few ladies in the room. Most were dressed elegantly in smart ties and crisp suits, the attire of a bygone era when eating out meant always meant wearing one's best, though hearing aids and canes were now popular accessories. And iPhones. Who knew so many old folks were fond of texting at the table?

I already knew a few of these famous Savannah faces from their many accomplishments: Philanthropists and art collectors Don and Kay Kole. Real estate developer and Leadership Savannah founder Ed Feiler. Shoe manufacturer and mystery novelist Larry Wagger, who released his first book last year at the age of 93.

At the next table sat Dr. Harold Black, still practicing dentistry after 50 years and a pioneer in treating sleep apnea. Across the room was Dr. Murray Arkin, former chief of staff at Memorial Hospital, who treated thousands of Savannahians from 1958 to 2005.

I passed the salad dressing to legendary architect Eric Meyerhoff, whose firm penned the plans for dozens of civic projects, including Rousakis Plaza and City Market, and who personally designed the stunning bronze WWII monument on River Street unveiled in 2010.

Even a greenhorn like myself could tell that this was no ordinary gathering of retirees. This was Savannah's greatest generation, people who spent the prime of their lives in service to their community and haven't let small details like being hard of hearing or aching joints stop them from engaging. They're what my people call real *machers*—big shots with indefatigable reserves of leadership and integrity, the kind of people who get stuff done.

Rabb obviously understood the sum of significance in the room because he offered the highest tribute imaginable from a writer: A reading from his work-in-progress, heretofore not heard by anyone but his agent and his lovely wife, Andra Reeve-Rabb.

If you're familiar with *Second Son* or any of Rabb's other novels, you know that place plays as prominent a role as his characters. Set in 1947, the first chapter of his new book describes a Savannah few remember, a bustling West Broad Street (now MLK Boulevard) and Broughton Street, where every storefront was a family-owned business.

It was a time when many of the folks in the room were in their teens and early 20s, just beginning to make their way in the post-War world. In fact, Rabb interviewed many of them to get the historical details just right.

These Savannahians and many more their age spent the next six decades having tremendous impact on the city. They are the people behind the hospitals and museums, the mid-century development and historic preservation, the foundations and charities. And they still possess the same grace that impels a person to put on a tie or the good gold earrings for lunch on a Wednesday.

Maybe my father-in-law just wanted to spend some quality time together, but he and his friends provided a humbling lesson on just how much a person can do with one life. When the Savannah we know now has progressed into its inevitable future, I hope we've have given a tenth as much when it's our turn to be ROMEOS.

Or as I personally aspire to become, a WOLFDOG. That'd be *Weird Old Ladies Fabulously Dining Out Gratis*. Yes, I made it up. Not as catchy, but I hope to make this free lunch thing a habit. But no matter what we call ourselves, may we also cut a well-dressed figure, and most importantly, still have the wherewithal to text the grandkids from the table.

Feb 14, 2012

The Stars According to Bobby Zarem

It's 3 p.m. on Yom Kippur afternoon, and the first thing Bobby Zarem does when I walk into his Ardsley Park living room is offer me a piece of chocolate.

"Oh that's right, you're fasting!" he says apologetically, pointing me to a chair instead.

I look at the candy longingly and sit down, determined to stay focused on interviewing the legendary publicist in time for Savannah Film Festival season, even with a grumbling stomach. I'm probably already a heretic for working on the Day of Atonement anyway, but I'm in good company, since Bobby confesses he hasn't observed Jewish holidays since he was a little *pisher*.

"I used to sneak out of synagogue services at the BB Jacob to get an egg salad sandwich," he laughs, slapping his knee.

God must've been in on the plan, 'cause those egg salad days were the fulcrum of the maven Bobby Zarem was to become.

After an illicit snack with the other Hebrew school dropouts on the holiest day of the year, he'd head over to the Weis Theatre on Broughton to take in the latest Errol Flynn or Rita Hayworth flick, seeding an unstoppable passion for the transformative power of the silver screen. Most of us can relate, but the remarkable thing about BZ's love of movies is how it grew into a 55-plus year career of making audiences love them, too.

Born and raised in Savannah, he followed his older brothers on the nice Jewish boy path to Andover, Yale and then New York City, where there was a short-lived gig on Wall Street before he chucked the idea of law school.

"If I had to spend one more morning waiting for the subway, I was going to jump in front of a train," he recalls with a grimace.

Providence provided a dream job at a PR agency, and so BZ began honing the art and craft of creating stars. Countless household names—including John Travolta, Ann-Margaret and Arnold Schwarzenegger—owe their professional arcs to Bobby Z, who snared the editorial attentions of *Life* and *Time* with earnest eight-page pitches and handwritten thank you notes.

"I would have a vision for every person and project, and I knew what would attract people," says the man *Newsweek* once dubbed "Superflack" after he filled a New York subway station with 500 celebrities and VIPs for the premiere of the Who's *Tommy*. (Turnabout for that shitty stock broker commute, no doubt.)

Another columnist once described him as "more connected than a set of deluxe Legos," but his ability to network also extended to places. He claims the "I Love New York" campaign that brought the city out of its terrible tourism slump in the 70s, and his small Southern hometown has received its share of press over the decades.

"I realized how fantastic Savannah was, but the rest of the world didn't know it. So early on in my career I started getting column items and stories in New York and international papers," he crows, citing mentions of the Hostess City in the *NY Times*, *Vanity Fair* and the *Paris Herald Tribune.*

And of course, there's the Savannah Film Festival, which he helped SCAD launch into the stratosphere by using his Legos to bring big names to town every October for 15 years. In 2010, the same year he moved back home for good, life made one of those amazing circles when he accepted the festival's Lifetime Achievement Award onstage at the Trustees Theatre—formerly known as the Weis, where he'd ditched Torah study for matinee idols all those years ago.

His partnership with the festival ended in 2014, but the BZ machine continues to thrum.

As I sit drooling over the box of chocolates, he takes calls from Page Six columnist Richard Johnson and negotiates a cameo on the *Bravo* reality show *Southern Charm* as assistant Jeremy Scheinbart handles the Comcast rep here to fix whatever's wrong with the cable.

While he's no longer the manic nightcrawler depicted by Al Pacino in the 2002 film *People I Know*, BZ still goes to the movies a few times a week and plans to take in a screening or two at the festival. He's on the phone constantly—the same landline his parents installed in the 1930s—stoking relationships near and far, though these days he's less of a star nebula and more of a bona fide planet.

Celebs like Michael Caine and Eric Idle come to visit on the regular, and Savannah folk of all ages gravitate to him for his stories and—admit it!—maybe a sprinkle of that famous stardust. (I mean who *doesn't* want to sit next to Gerard Butler at Mrs. Wilkes?)

But the real reason people love Bobby Zarem is because he's still wicked fun to be around, gossiping with unadulterated glee and introducing people to each other with genuine eagerness to see what comes of the connection.

His orbits were in full effect on the recent occasion of his 80th birthday at the Tybee Island Social Club. Owners Sarah and Kurtis Schumm tended a spread of Lowcountry Boil and steamed oysters as childhood buddy and car czar Dale Critz shook hands with Londoner Charles Frazier, circled by power couples India and Robert King, Karen and Kurt Oelschig and Drs. Carmela and Chris Pettigrew.

Savannah Philharmonic conductor Peter Shannon lounged on the patio next to actress and Tybee resident Diana Scarwid while nephew Robbie Zarem waxed on about fuel cells with Foss and Chris Hodges. Overseeing hostessing duties were Beth Vantosh, Lisa

Kaminsky and Karen Guinn of the group of doting women I like to call "Zarem's Harem."

As the couple of hundred other guests schmoozed, the honoree sat in the middle of the room, grinning from one tuft of white hair to the other.

"It was the 'who's who' of my Savannah, my world, even if some people couldn't make it," he reflects a week and a half later as we sit in the living room, pointing out the birthday bouquet sent by Catherine Zeta-Jones and Michael Douglas on the coffee table.

All around his childhood home is the evidence of his world, from signed movie posters to framed photos of him with Tom Hanks and Christy Turlington. Also on the wall is a glowering portrait of the publicist as a young man painted by his late brother, Danny Zarem, the famous stylist credited for inventing men's casualwear.

His other brother, Dr. Harvey Zarem, a renowned Hollywood plastic surgeon, passed away in 2015. The youngest Zarem *mensch* carries on, insisting that he's already planning his 90th birthday party.

"I feel like I'm finally reaching puberty! I'm serious!"

If you've ever hung out with Bobby Z, you might recognize some items missing from this tableau. But the thing about interviewing publicists is they're very clever to tell you what's off the record. Cross him and he'll see you next Tuesday, if you catch my drift.

But all anyone really needs to know is that though Bobby Zarem may have exchanged the Hamptons for Tybee Island and Elaine's for Circa and Cotton & Rye (and The Grey and The Vault; seriously, don't ask him to pick a favorite restaurant), his star is shining bright as ever.

As I'm leaving to get back to synagogue and finish atoning for the year's sins, I ask him if he wants a ride, just for giggles.

"Nah, what for? I don't have a single regret," he chortles, eyes twinkling. "But here, take some chocolate with you. You might want it for the movies later. You're going to the movies, right?"

Oct. 16, 2016

Bugg Blow Tells It Like It Is

As a rule, if someone shows up late to an interview, I'm gone.

I'm a busy lady, and if we've agreed on a time to talk, I don't take kindly to being left hanging.

I sent my interviewee a text at ten past the hour and haven't heard back. My friendly server at Carey Hilliard's asks once again if I'm going to order. I'm table-tapping out the Christmas music blaring from the speakers when a return text pops up:

Sorry got stopped by the police—on da way

Five minutes later, local rapper Bugg Blow slides sheepishly into the booth with another apology. "I guess my car windows are tinted too dark."

"Do you get pulled over a lot?" I ask.

"About four times a week," he shrugs and orders a lemonade.

"Driving while black?" I joke clumsily to break the ice wall I forged in my snipey text.

He laughs. "Yeah, pretty much."

I invited Bugg to lunch after I saw some of his astute posts about the killing of 12-year-old Keith Passmore. As a young black man, he'd wondered if the fact that Passmore was white affected how his death was reported. In his comments, Bugg asserted that Passmore was shot in a drug deal gone bad, and the media's presentation of him as a freckle-faced innocent persisted in a way that it never would have if he'd been black.

Online, Bugg defended his position calmly amongst the finger pointers and the know-it-alls. While there has been no confirmation of Passmore's involvement in drugs, I appreciated Bugg's tone: He wasn't accusatory, just thoughtful, applying the kind of courtesy and courage that every Facebook troll ought to emulate.

With the embers of Ferguson still aglow and Savannah's new police chief calling in the Georgia State Patrol to help deal with all these shot-up children, online civil discourse has had it rough lately. So much of the conversation has been revolving—and some might say devolving—around race, specifically on the depiction and perception of young, black men.

I've been in this business long enough to know that everyone has a story, and no one can be reduced to a stereotype if you listen.

But as empathetic as I believe myself to be, the fact is that I am not young, black or a man. And though I enjoy friendly acquaintance with some lovely young black men, I don't ask them about being young black men, because that would be weird and rude.

Bugg Blow, however, seemed like he wanted an opportunity to clarify what it's like to be a young black man in Savannah, perhaps the kind easily stereotyped.

I didn't think hearing his story could change the way we handle our crime crisis and our criminals. But talking over a plate of fried shrimp didn't seem like a bad way to start.

Dressed in gray pants and pink and purple kicks, he introduces himself as 23-years-old, a hiphop artist with three songs in heavy rotation on E93 and managed by DJ Mike Fresh.

"The radio don't pay, but the shows do," explains Bugg, ticking off a roster of recent gigs in Jacksonville, Statesboro and Claxton. "It's enough money to keep me out of trouble."

But he matter-of-factly offers that this is a fairly new development. Raised on West 53rd Street by a single father who kept his kids fed by running low-grade check scams, Bugg (he doesn't divulge his real name) dropped out of Savannah High and eased right into the local illegal economy with the help of an uncle who's now doing 15 years for homicide.

"In Savannah, there aren't any gangs. It's not like you think. It's just a bunch of kids who've grown up together. At 15, I was living the life, selling weed, robbing people, toting guns—doing the same thing that little guy was doing," he says, referring to Passmore, whose Facebook page showed a photo of the 12-year-old with a gun in his waistband before it was taken down. He compares that to the killing of his friend Tre Walker in 2007, who was shot in the head walking home from school and vilified in the media as a thug.

Bugg says he doesn't know who killed Passmore but understands the kid's ambition, invoking the term "street struck."

"You're a kid and you see the people pulling up in your neighborhood with the nice cars, and that's what's going to get the girls, that's what's going to get you the nice outfits. That's what that kid was, street struck."

It's a pretty common condition in Bugg's neighborhood. He says he's not justifying any crimes, but he wants me to appreciate that when you need money to live and there's a chance to sell drugs, you take it.

Or you don't. I point out there are other, legal ways to make money.

"Like what? Get a job for minimum wage at McDonalds?" he wonders. "You can but that don't support you."

Since drugs appear to be at the crux of it all, I ask him if he thinks things would change if weed was legalized.

"I think it would make things worse. If they legalized weed, people would have to do something else to get by. They'd have to sell guns."

We talk a bit about how deeply rooted the dysfunction is and how everyone is his neighborhood knew that former police chief and recent convicted felon Willie Lovett helped along the cycle.

Bugg is also a dad and speaks proudly of raising his 15-month-old daughter. He doubts that anyone will ever come forward to help solve the murder of 2-year-old Kiki Smalls, shot while sleeping, because even with promises of anonymity from the police, the fear of retribution reigns.

"Everyone is involved, and no one wants it to come back on them," sighs Bugg.

He touches on this culture of silence on his track "Heaven and Hell": *Rest in peace Tre/ Rest in peace Tyrell/Before I snitch I'd rather slit my wrists and burn in hell.*

Halfway through our conversation, a tall, broad-shouldered black man sits in the booth behind Bugg and whispers in his ear.

"Who's that?"

"He's with me," says Bugg.

"Is he, like, your bodyguard?" I ask.

"More like a life coach," says the man, who introduces himself as Jay. "I keep him on right track, make sure he's not saying anything dumb."

"How'my doing?" grins Bugg.

"Great," I say.

"Pretty good," agrees Jay.

After a little cajoling, Jay joins us in the booth. He's 26, softspoken and back in Savannah after graduating from college. He'd like to become a physician's assistant, but that means more tuition money, which he doesn't have.

"There's not much out here for educated men and women in Savannah," says Jay. "You're a young black man and you come back home after going to school, what is there? There are people trying."

I nod, tentatively offering that many Americans, regardless of race, have the experience that persistence and hard work just aren't enough. After all, *Breaking Bad* was about a middle-aged white guy.

"I think people want to help," I tell them. "What do you think would help?"

Bugg thinks for a moment. "Depends on what your goal is. Do you want to stop crime? Or do you want to help? If you're trying to stop crime, you're going to start a war. Because you're trying to stop how people are making a living."

Jay thinks raising the minimum wage would provide some incentive. "Crime happens because people need money. Better opportunities would mean less reason to participate in criminal activity."

We riff for a while on that, and I ask these two gents what they believe are the obstacles to their success. Although we began by talking about racial biases, Bugg doesn't think that's the real problem, and maybe his point all along is that while young black men may be unfairly represented, everyone is susceptible to a life of crime.

"I don't think it's racism," he muses. "I don't think it's about color. I think it's about your level of life, the bracket you're in. That's very hard to change."

Jay nods in agreement.

Our fried shrimp has gone cold and the lunch hour has long past. It seems like a good time to give up our booth and get on with life: Bugg Blow has shows lined up and a new mix tape coming out in January. I'm rooting for Jay to figure out the financial aid maze for his next degree. I thank them for the opportunity to ask them a bunch of rude questions.

Though we haven't solved a damn thing, I feel like a little more space has been scraped out for me to understand the complicated little city where I live. With my hand on my heart, I pledge to keep listening.

Dec. 3, 2014

The Beach Bum Behind the Pseudonym

At first, I felt a little lost amongst the fancy flip flops and Lily Pulitzer sundresses. My usual Tybee Island uniform is a frayed pair of board shorts left over from my husband's teenage years and a striped bikini top I snuck out of someone else's Goodwill bag, allowing maximum sun soakage and ease of waveplay.

Mostly, this is *alllll good* anywhere on Tybee, a place where just tucking in your shirt makes you seem overdressed.

But *New York Times* bestselling author and chick-lit superstar Mary Kay Andrews was on the island to sign copies of her new book, *Spring Fever,* and as the cozy rooms of antiques-and-curio shop Seaside Sisters filled with nicely-dressed ladies sporting tans and pedicured toes, it occurred to me I could have maybe cleaned up a little. Or at least put on a bra.

I tried to find a fly's spot near a wall to observe, but Seaside Sisters' friendly owner Susan Kelleher plunked me down on a sea green telephone chair from the '50s, two feet away from Ms. MKA herself. "Make yourself at home!" she commanded as she rushed off to oversee book sales.

One by one, polished women of all ages approached the signing table, clutching copies of the new hardcover as well as worn paperbacks bearing the titles of older MKA novels, including *Savannah Breeze,* which features our offbeat little island. Though they seemed to share a certain affinity for floral patterned Vera Bradley purses, fans revealed themselves to be from all over: Ohio, California and even Canada, many confessing a little breathlessly, "I came to Tybee because of your books."

One middle-aged lady sheepishly apologized when a small sprinkling of the beach fell on the table when she handed over her book to be signed.

"They're beach reads," chuckled Andrews. "You're supposed to have sand in the pages."

Though her new book debuted at #5 on the bestseller list, there's something distinctly unpretentious—and therefore Tybee-esque—about Mary Kay Andrews. She laughs loudly and often, and doesn't try to hide that she's really Kathy Hogan Trochek, a former Georgia newspaper reporter with a weakness for garage sales. The pseudonym is a mash-up of her kids' names. When asked how to address her, she shrugs, "I answer to anything."

It's this same comfy camaraderie that's driven her success. I tend to dismiss "chick lit" as a contrived gender-directed marketing tool and therefore to be avoided at all costs, much like pinchy high heels and Spanx. But I've thoroughly enjoyed MKA's Savannah series—recognizing local spots is always exciting, and she skewers Southern weirdness as if she keeps a bayonet next to her laptop.

Anyway, hers are not cheesy romance novels, she assures me a few days after the book signing, when I get the chance to chat with her in Kelleher's perfectly shabby chic living room. Hell-to-the-NO on shirtless dudes with long flowing hair on the covers. The most important relationships in these stories are between friends.

"My protagonists are women who reinvent their lives," says Mary Kay/Kathy, sipping a sparkling water. "There might be a romantic angle, but it's not so much about whether she gets the guy, but does she get the life she wants?"

We talk about how she's invented the life she wants: Quitting journalism 20 years ago to write fiction so she could be home with her kids, holing up at the beach to write a book a year and feeling a whole new level of success after shedding 55 pounds. Mostly we marvel how Tybee has changed since she first saw it as a newlywed in 1976.

"Tybee was very rundown at the time. St. Petersburg, where I grew up, sand sparkling, turquoise water, that was my idea of a beach," she laughs, crossing her pretty green flipflops.

"But the more I was here, the more I liked it. It's not Hilton Head or St. Simons Island, but it has this funky, laid-back vibe. It's Everyman's Beach."

She bought a cottage soon after her husband's career took the family to Atlanta, and fixed it up with antiques and a fresh coat of paint, not unlike one of her characters. (She admits being addicted to "house porn," those gorgeous interior design magazines featuring pretty, uncluttered houses.)

"I think whatever beach you grow up on is the beach that's most beautiful to you," sighs the author who could probably sun on the French Riviera if she wanted, yet escapes to Tybee every chance she gets. "But there's something to be said for location. It's only four hours door to door."

She, along with her cadre of Tybee girlfriends including Kelleher and Mermaid Cottages owner Diane Kaufman, have watched the island evolve into much more than "a drinking village with a fishing problem." It wasn't too many years ago that a disgusting snake of beer cans and dirty diapers used to sit on the shoreline every afternoon to be taken out with the tide. Now, beach sweeps and "leave only your footprints" campaigns help remind Everyman (and woman and child) to pack out their trash.

Though drinking remains a popular pastime (the new Wet Willie's is always busy), more restaurants have popped up where you actually have to wear shoes. Perhaps this reinvented image will make in an appearance in a future novel; Mary Kay Andrews does have a contract for a fourth installment in the *Savannah Breeze* series.

For the moment, however, it's just Kathy Trochek who is sitting on a lovely white couch looking out into the mouth of Lazaretto Creek. Even though the water might be cloudy and that damn Geico plane buzzes far too often and there's still plenty of garbage to pick up when the tide goes out, we agree that it's always a good day to be at the beach.

I look down at my ugly old board shorts, still dusted with dried salt from the morning's paddle session. We toast our seltzer waters and hope no matter how tony Tybee gets, it'll still be Tybee, after all.

July 10, 2012

Sign o' the times: RIP Leonard Miller

One chilly morning years ago, I was riding my bike to work through Daffin Park when I came upon the strangest of visions.

There at the roundabout was a large black man leaning up against a beat-up van, singing in a velvety baritone. The trees framed him in a curtain of moss, and a ray of sunshine had broken through the mist, bathing him in a heavenly spotlight.

"Praise be to God on this beautiful day!" he bellowed, nodding to me in greeting as I slowed to a stop.

"Hi," I said, blinking hard, trying to decide if this was a holy visitation or that I just hadn't caffeinated properly.

"Hello," he intoned with a toothy smile.

We stared and grinned at each other for a long minute, then he returned his gaze to the sky. I took in his weathered hands and cut-off jeans and concluded that angels probably don't wear orthopedic shoes.

"Ok, well, have a good day," I said, pushing off.

"Oh, yes, ma'am, I will," he laughed, turning to fiddle with the equipment in the back of his van. He resumed his song, and his melodic voice floated above me all the way to Grayson Stadium.

That was my first close encounter with Leonard Miller, the legendary sign painter and self-taught artist who passed away last week at 59 from complications caused by diabetes.

I had long heard of this prolific local talent, and after our exalted meeting that morning in the park I began to notice his work everywhere.

The man and his van got around, and his signature looping script graces buildings and businesses all over Savannah and beyond: The iconic clown at Bradley Lock & Key, the window dressing at Sekka Bikes, the list of ice cream flavors at Seaside Sweets.

Our whole family became big fans of Leonard (pronounced "Le-NARD," he'd remind you firmly,) and my kids have learned to recognize his handiwork.

"There's a Leonard!" they squeal every time we discover a new instance of his perfect freeform lettering. One time we ran into Leonard himself on Tybee Island eating a meatball sub at Nickie's 1971, and you'd have thought he was a YouTube star the way they fawned all over him.

While some companies are all about slick marketing campaigns and "brand identity" these days, there have always been plenty of small business owners who preferred Leonard's simple signage. He started making signs for Belk's in the '70s when he got out of the Air Force and struck out on his own soon after. Some folks remember when you'd have to leave a message at a beauty parlor if you wanted to hire him and wait for him to call back.

"He could sit down with a pencil, and ten minutes later he had painted what you wanted, completely freehand," reminisces Gerald Schantz, who commissioned him to decorate Gerald's Pig & Shrimp restaurant on Tybee Island with several dozen quotes by Einstein, Gandhi and a couple of Leonard originals. (Our family favorite: "It doesn't cost anything to be nice.")

"You never knew when he was going to show up, mind you, but he always did a marvelous job."

While he lent his sonorous vocals at church services and early morning raptures, his clients knew him for his sweet-as-tea disposition and his habit of whistling as he painted a wall or meditated on a new project.

Leonard also constructed large-scale outdoor mobiles—there's one weathering outside Coach's Corner on Victory Drive—and could camouflage a shipping container with foliage so realistic it disappeared.

Other works have also disappeared, but not in a good way. Many businesses have closed over the years, taking with them the primary-hued murals and wall-mounted menus. Other masterpieces have simply been painted over or torn down to make way for the next hotel or chain store.

There has been a focus in the last decade of the importance of documenting and preserving the tradition of African American sign painting, examined through the lens of Leonard and other Savannah "wall dogs," notably Jimmie Williams and William Pleasant, Jr., who has been honored with a permanent piece in the Smithsonian Insitute's National Museum of African American History & Culture. Their work was heralded in 2004 with a photography retrospective at the Beach Institute and a 2010 lecture delivered by anthropologist Susan Falls as vital representations of a rich culture and history. In spite of such attentions, however, the wrecking ball of commercial progress continues its slow erasure.

But perhaps slower on Tybee, where Leonard was especially

revered for building intricate sandcastles, earning him the sobriquet "The Sandman." While those arches and moats are gone with the tides, his murals and script still decorate some of the island's toniest homes, thanks to his friendship with award-winning interior designer Jane Coslick. After seeing his work in Savannah, she brought him out to the island to paint zebra-striped garage doors and wall art in her trademark beachy bright hues.

"He had no idea how fabulous he was," laments Jane. "He would never say, 'I can't do that.' He'd say, 'let me think about that for a minute,' and then he'd figure it out. He was brilliant."

Coslick's chic designs make regular appearances in glossy coastal shelter mags, and she made sure Leonard received print credit whenever one of his painted windows appeared in *Cottage Style*. When she found out that Leonard also crafted vibrant scenes of the beach and shrimp docks on pieces of plywood, she encouraged him to sell them at the Isle of Hope Art Show.

Original Leonard Millers now hang in some of the South's most impressive art collections, though his most visible legacies can still be found on the city's streets.

"You can't really understand Savannah without knowing about Leonard Miller," says SCAD professor and writer Rexanna Lester, who uses examples of both his signs and fine artwork to deepen her ESL students' insight into their adopted home. "He drew the city in ways that captured life here that no one else could."

Yet for all his breadth of talent and local fame, Leonard Miller remained humble and unabashedly devoted to the higher realms. He lived with his parents throughout his life, and all who loved him were constantly scolding him for undercharging for his services and his artwork.

"He was not concerned about money," sighed the Rev. Lee Wright at Leonard's funeral last Monday. "He was most interested in using the talent God had given him."

The passing of Leonard Miller is indeed a setback in the battle against gentrification and corporatization, a harbinger of a future when the plywood signs of Savannah's poorer and lesser-known neighborhoods will fade away.

It's also, more simply and sadly, the loss of one of our greatest characters, a gentle giant who never once let the devil find his hands idle. I can almost see him now, painting the halls of heaven and whistling while he works.

Jan. 20, 2016

The End of the World with Jane Fishman

Maybe it wasn't the best idea to go looking for comfort on the darkest day of a very dark year from another misanthrope.

"It's cold and miserable and I want to throw up," Jane Fishman informs me when I knock on the front door of her Parkside bungalow.

"Yeah, well, perfect weather for this dumpster fire of a year," I growl back, brushing the dots of mist clinging to my coat.

We both laugh, because being mildly depressed during winter is such a cliché, as is already the term "dumpster fire" to refer to 2016.

Jane doesn't do clichés. She prefers—nay, *champions*—unconventionality both in her writing and her other favorite endeavor, digging in the dirt and planting stuff. The two converge once again in her latest book, *I Grew It My Way: How Not to Garden*, a hilarious, informative collection of local herbal lore and urban horticultural adventure that heralds appreciation for nature's overlooked gifts.

I figure I've brought the perfect offering, a few Meyer lemons purloined from the ungated backyard of a vacant house on my block. Or not.

"Oy, I'm up to my ears in citrus!" she says as she adds the deep yellow orbs to a basket overflowing with oranges and grapefruits. "The orchard over on 38th Street is going nuts."

We head towards the kitchen, Pavarotti hollering from the record player.

"Maybe your mood would improve if you didn't listen to opera in the morning," I suggest, taking in the dining room table full of partially-wrapped holiday presents and Ossabaw Island indigo seeds ready to be sorted.

She shrugs and squeezes me a glass of orange juice from her grandmother's ancient steel countertop contraption, a pulpy shot of straight-up sunshine.

"There, that's better, isn't it?" she says after we toast, the twinkle that's been temporarily robbed by the dreary weather returning to her eyes.

I saw that same sparkle the first time I visited Savannah—*exactly* 20 years ago this week, come to think it—when the dear lady who would become my mother-in-law, God rest her sweet soul, dragged me over to meet Jane at the synagogue social hall. My future MIL thought it remarkable that she now knew *two* newspaper columnists (back then I was a cub scout at Northern California's *Pacific Sun*, one of the country's oldest altweeklies) and seemed a little star struck by Jane, who shook my hand, bemused.

I remember thinking that any town that can deal with a sassy Jewish woman writer is my kinda place. When I tell Jane this story, she giggles. "What the hell was I doing at Mickve Israel anyway?"

When I moved here for good a decade ago, it never occurred to me to wonder if Savannah was big enough for the both of us. Instead, I read her books and columns religiously ("oh my god, stop it with the religion already," she groans, rolling her eyes) and basically followed her around (not easy, since she likes to hide out in three different gardens around the city and sometimes on Ossabaw Island.) I still haven't figured out how to grow a banana but I did pick up a mysterious, three-pronged jumping lily at one of her bi-yearly plant swaps.

Jane rides her bike everywhere and wears blue nail polish to cover the crud under her nails. She spends her Social Security checks on local art and healed her own broken kneecap with a paste made from a comfrey plant growing in her driveway. She once got arrested for keying a street sweeper and had to do 40 hours of community service pulling weeds at the Bamboo Farm.

She is the eccentric, DGAF auntie my children always needed and probably the closest thing to a mentor I'll ever have.

"Oh *pssssht.*" Jane waves off my sentimental drivel and hands me a cup of sorrel tea made from the deep red petals collected from the sprawling bush on the city-owned side of the back fence.

We sip the hibiscus-flavored brew and talk shop instead. We're both best motivated by deadlines and agree wholeheartedly with Dorothy Parker, that grouchy scribe supreme, who put it best: "I hate writing, I love having written."

Jane must love the past pluperfect tense a lot, because she's already working on two more books, *Something about 70*, which promises to be a *most* unconventional treatise on aging, and an homage to her late mother, *When Did You Get So Jewish?*

"My mother always thought it was hilarious when I started putting Yiddish in my columns," she recalls. "Who knew people would think being Jewish was so funny?"

We get all subdued again as we consider that might not be the case in the coming alt-right assault on the media and beyond.

"Let's go see the chickens," she suggests.

We visit for a few minutes with her menopausal girls, who are only giving up a single egg every other morning between them these days. Then we head out the back gate to the lane, where Jane has fashioned an amazing garden in the strip of earth between the wooden fence and the garbage truck route.

Frilly skirts of kale, crowns of broccoli, sweeping fans of collards are lined up in surprising order (in her book, Jane loves to brag about how disorganized she is) next to turmeric shoots and garlic toes pushing up green stalks. This incredible winter bounty is fed by composted heaps of broken egg shells and carrot ends moldering into magic a few yards down, waiting to be shoveled and spread directly onto the ground.

"I hate raised beds. They remind me of coffins," she grumbles, pulling a stray weed in an area marked off by a Barbie leg.

That sets off my misery again, flooded with frustration about Savannah's pernicious problems and the heartbreak of Aleppo and watching Clown Voldemort and his Sinister Council of Ignoramus Deatheaters usher in the end of the world.

"Oh, Jane, what are we going to *do*?" I cry, feeling the cloak of darkness hovering above in the slate-colored clouds.

She hands me a comfrey leaf. "We wait until spring."

This is the solace I've come for, I realize as she continues to poke her blue nails around the plants, humming with contentment.

It's exactly what I needed to hear from the wisest person I know on the darkest day of a very dark year: That nature always comes through no matter what, and the days only get longer and brighter from here.

Dec. 28, 2016

4 CIVICS LESSONS

Local government and urban planning might sound like an interminable snoozefest. But the current state of the city—the good, the bad and the ugly—is built on public policies and zoning ordinances that have the power to create prosperity or destroy neighborhoods, so pay attention to the small print. While it's tempting to take boring things like infrastructure and sanitation for granted, fascination and scandal await if we stop to ask questions about what happens when we flush the toilet and where the Talmadge Bridge got its name.

Tourism: Balancing Journey and Destination

Oh my heavens, y'all, we are so lucky to live here.

That's what the nice lady from Michigan told me breathily as we chatted in line at the Savannah Book Festival last Saturday. Betty had traveled thousands of miles in horrendous weather to spend time and money in our lovely city, and she and her best friend, Karen, were having a ball.

They honest-to-God squealed when they found out I was a local, peppering me with questions about where they should eat lunch and whether they ought to take home a few clumps of Spanish moss in their suitcase.

Naturally, I turned up the Hostess City charm, marking up their map and recommending they leave the moss alone unless they wanted to be scratchin' themselves silly for the rest of their stay.

I may have laid on the Southern accent a little thick, but in the sparkling sunshine of Telfair Square, it didn't feel like an act.

I love Savannah, and I love sharing it with others. Most of the time.

Of course, there are those moments when residing in a wildly popular tourist destination makes a person cranky, like when you've been searching for a parking spot for 45 minutes and now you're stuck idling behind a horse-drawn carriage as a gaggle of Girl Scouts makes 10,000 Instagram posts of the Mercer Williams House.

Or when a bachelor party rents the Airbnb next door and you're up 'til 4 a.m. listening to the groom puke in the azaleas. Or watching another 12-story corporate hotel monstrosity gobbling up downtown parking places and views of the sky.

While it's wonderful to live where so many people want to visit, it definitely has its share of headaches. But Betty and the other purported 12 million visitors a year are an indubitable anchor our local economy, and their $2.6 billion of annual direct spending revenue buys a lot of ibuprofen. Tourism is also the single largest employment sector for the region, and those new hotels will create thousands more jobs—though not everyone believes that to be beneficial in the long run.

It's a tricky business, this balancing act of maintaining a good quality of life and showing our guests a good time. And we're certainly not alone, promises award-winning journalist Elizabeth Becker. In her bestselling *Overbooked: The Exploding Business of Travel and Tourism*, she examines the $6.5 *trillion* global industry and how other hotspots handle the inevitable issues of oversaturation, regulation and degradation. According to her, Savannah is actually doing a pretty decent job.

Becker gave a series of well-attended public talks recently, regaling diverse audiences from the grassroots Emergent Savannah to the tonier Downtown Neighborhood Association with her favorable assessments:

First of all, we are undeniably gorgeous. Also, our short-term vacation rental ordinance may not be perfect, but we're ahead of the game in that at least we have one.

Most importantly, we know how to say "NO" to bad ideas.

"I've not found another city that was so against cruise ships," she said of our kibosh on a 2013 proposal. "I mean, look at the mess Charleston made. It's rare that a city learns from other cities' mistakes."

(I know y'all are grinning right now; we love it when we're compared favorably against Charleston.)

Becker admonished us to conduct a saturation study lest we end up like Venice, where vacation rentals have swallowed the ancient real estate market, leaving only 60,000 permanent residents in a fragile city that hosts 24 million visitors a year.

In conversation, she also touched on the challenge of incorporating Savannah's African American and slave history into the metanarrative of the city. That effort is a focus of the recent formation of the Urban Savannah Chamber of Commerce and the African American Tourism

Council.

"The most important questions going forward are, 'who are you?' and 'where do you want to go?' I'm not sure you've figured it out yet," she mused.

We welcomed Becker as an enlightened guru with intimate knowledge of parts of the world most of us will never see. (She counts Phnom Penh, where she was one of the only journalists granted an audience with Cambodian dictator Pol Pot, as a spiritual home.)

But it's important to note that her ideas aren't completely foreign to us.

When developing the city's Dept. of Tourism Management and Ambassadorship in 2014, city staff passed around *Overbooked* as its inspiration for pro-active policies.

"We recognize that we are in a dynamic environment and must be flexible and make changes when needed to protect neighborhood integrity while sustaining the industry," says director Bridget Lidy. "We need to talk about the issues impacting our community and develop strategies to address them."

The hottest issue at the banquet table is how the hospitality industry contributes to a perpetually subpar economic climate for many of its workers. According to some reports, about half of the people with 25,000 hotel and service-related jobs make an average of $8.60 an hour—less than $16,000 a year. Federal guidelines cite a family of four that earns less $24,300 as below the poverty level.

"These are poverty wages," rails former Chatham County Commissioner John McMasters, who has been an outspoken proponent of wage reform in our local hospitality sector. "Each new hotel built will only enlarge our poverty level, so the obvious conclusion is to either stop building hotels or find a way to raise wages. We are digging the poverty hole deeper and deeper while our quality of life degrades from the onslaught of increasing tourism."

McMasters has proposed to raise hospitality wages two dollars an hour, an idea fast gaining populist support, though the business sector scoffs at such government-mandated sanctions.

Since we're about as likely to stop building hotels as we are to stop frying shrimp, an increase in 10 percent of the city's paychecks could and would dramatically cut the city's stubborn 28 percent poverty rate—and by proxy, reduce crime motivated by generational poverty.

From her world-sized view, Becker suggests the way for workers to advocate for better compensation is to organize. But that's a difficult edict, as just breathing the word "union" around here gets people all huffy. Georgia's despotic "right to work" laws keep unions weak anyway, and state legislators voted down a minimum wage increase last year.

Can Savannah create a more livable wage for its hospitality workers on its own? It seems to be trying. The City has introduced the West Downtown Urban Redevelopment Plan, which gives incentives to downtown businesses to hire from the poorest neighborhoods and pay at least 25 percent above the $8.60 average—an increase along the same numbers as McMasters' plan.

Participation hasn't quite caught on with big box boys, and city-directed negotiations among all the stakeholders would and should give the program momentum. Others maintain that tourism's low-paying gigs are an unfortunate but necessary evil.

"Look, this is the service industry, and a lot of its jobs are for housekeepers and dishwashers," says Tourism Leadership Council director Michael Owens. "But those jobs can lead to a true and real career path if someone wants to work."

Owens advocates for better training so that more minimum wage workers can move up the ladder, citing the example of the current general manager of a prominent hotel franchise who grew up in local Section 8 housing and started work at 16 in the back of the kitchen.

"Every industry has to have bottom rungs. If you want to change how people move up, our focus as a community must be on education and skills," he says.

So how do we empower a capable, enthusiastic workforce while recognizing the reality of the free market?

If Paris can figure out how to shuttle 7 million people a year up and down the Eiffel Tower, surely our council can draft regulations that prevent the corporate takeover of our tiny downtown without sending the rabid capitalists into a tizzy. Becker assures that it is possible to accommodate travel's big boom without biting the hand that feeds us.

"The key to good tourism is to do your planning for the people who live there," she writes.

For all of her whirlwind engagements around town, after three days in Savannah Becker had yet to enjoy much of the city outside of her Gordon Street bed-and-breakfast. I tagged along as Kevin Klinkenberg of the Savannah Renewal and Development Authority chauffeured her in a wide circle through the historic district and the contrasting neighborhoods, presenting a far more complete tableau than most tourists ever see.

Slicing between blocks of fancy townhouses and blighted bungalows, we discussed how Slowvannah's sleepy urban renewal efforts may have worked in its favor as it inadvertently preserved culturally-rich areas like the historic Cuyler-Brownsville neighborhood through neglect. Klinkenberg and the SDRA are working to invigorate these once-thriving commercial districts and include them in the spoils of Savannah's newfound prosperity.

Still, some of our future plans seem questionable when seen from an outsider's perspective. I have never experienced a longer or more awkward car ride than the detour taken through the blighted west side to the site of the proposed massive arena, which is supposed to bring in thousands more people a day for events.

"Wow, this isn't *anywhere* near your tourist corridor, is it?" murmured Becker.

We were all glad to finally ditch the car and walk through Forsyth Park, where the sublime afternoon had enticed picnickers and basketball players and hammock dwellers out to our jewel of common greenspace.

"It's so beautiful and alive here," she marveled, taking in a thatch of candy-colored azaleas.

It was so gratifying to watch a world traveler like Becker be enchanted by Savannah, and I'd like to think we made as important an impression on her as she did on us. Like every other tourist, she's since left a bed of used linens behind, but her queries continue to ring on:

Who are we, Savannah? Where do we want to go?

I spend a lot of time trying to wrap my head around the complex, diverse nature of that first question, and I still don't know.

But I'll tell y'all, as I sit on a shadow-dappled bench in my favorite moss-draped square listening to the early morning buzz of a city readying for work and play, there's only one way to answer the latter: Nowhere but here.

Feb. 23, 2016

The Dredge RePort

You probably thought I'd forgotten about it.

It's been so long since I've kvetched about the Savannah River deepening, I'm sure it seems that way. But I was merely taking a break from worrying about my most unfavorite civic project to wring my hands over other things. I promise, it's still there, gnawing away at the back of my mind like a rat burrowed in a sock full of peanuts. And a few recent updates have chewed a hole in the toe.

Some of you may be new to my nutty metaphors, so in the words of the inimitable Inigo Montoya, let me 'splain. No, there is too much. Let me sum up:

Last fall, after 15 years of plotting and planning, the U.S. Army Corps of Engineers finally began The Savannah Harbor Expansion Project (SHEP), a 38-mile dredge that will take the current shipping channel from 42 to 47 feet so that the Georgia Ports Authority can welcome the gargantuan new ships passing through a newly-widened Panama Canal, a project beset with its own problems and delays.

Heralded as an economic savior and job creator for the state, SHEP will cost taxpayers $706 million—with nearly half of those dollars applied to environmental mitigation and ancillary measures to keep the river alive and ocean salt out of our local drinking water. The price of progress, you understand.

Over the years, I've spent a lot of words pointing out how few permanent jobs SHEP actually creates and the weak logic of spending that kind of bank and destroying that many acres of wetland for what ultimately amounts to less ship traffic. Not to mention how totally lame it is that the 97 million-gallon freshwater reservoir built by the Corps will have to be maintained with City of Savannah—not state—funds, even though the city receives *not a single dollar* of direct revenue from the tax-exempt port. The Port of Savannah is based wholly in Atlanta and benefits the city *not at all*, save indirectly from port-related private enterprises.

Other than making me extremely unpopular at certain cocktail parties, such criticisms have had absolutely zero impact. Not that I ever expected they would. That wasn't even my motivation; it's just that the hunky-dory spin given to this project makes me uncontrollably obnoxious.

Progress always plunges on: The Savannah River will get deeper "come hell or high water," Vice President Joe Biden told us when he came to call back in '14, and his truth has come to pass. The Big Dig has had its shovels in motion off Tybee Island for quite a few months now, and all is going to according to plan. Well, almost.

Last month, the Obama administration released his 2017 budget recommendation, and it only contained $42.7 million towards SHEP—less than half of what Gov. Nathan Deal has demanded per year to keep the project on track.

Deal, who has already put up $262 million of state funds to fire up the dredges in the outer harbor, railed against the paltry allocation, which he says underfunds the "most critical dredging project in the country." (The other 17 U.S. port projects seeking federal help might disagree.)

No matter, SHEP will continue to move through fiscal 2017 full steam ahead—aided by a $24 million infusion from the Corps' own discretionary fund. However, the 2018 budget is anyone's guess, and with the country in political and budgetary chaos, the U.S.'s lack of cohesive strategy around its disparate state ports indicate that it will not be a priority.

It has also surfaced that several endangered species have been killed by dredges in the Savannah River. Sammy Fretwell first reported in the Columbia, SC newspaper, *The State*, that two Atlantic sturgeon and a green sea turtle had been churned up by the SHEP hoppers since January, and a loggerhead turtle had died during routine maintenance of the channel. The severed flipper of a giant leatherback turtle was also recovered around the same time, though NOAA biologists determined the animal was more likely hit by a ship rather than sucked into the hoppers.

As determined by the National Marine Fisheries' Service (NMFS), the "incidental take" limits allow for a loss of a total of four Atlantic sturgeon over the entire three years of the dredging—which means SHEP has already reached half its limit in the first few months. The project maxes out at three green sea turtles, 16 loggerheads and 11 Kemp's Ridley sea turtles, a highly endangered species that migrates past the Georgia Coast to its nesting grounds in the Gulf of Mexico.

It's something for activists to watch, though it must be noted that in addition to other precautions, the Corps has implemented a trawling net in front of the hopper in order to catch and relocate wildlife. In its biological opinion, NMFS estimates 51 turtles and 20 Atlantic sturgeon will be moved out of harm's way during the project.

"We regret the taking of any species; however, some adverse impacts are an unavoidable result of keeping the waterways open for commerce," writes the infallibly polite Billy Birdwell of the Corps' public affairs office. "We assessed those potential impacts to endangered and threatened species as part of [SHEP's] Environmental Impact Statement."

But even if kills exceed NMFS projections, it's not like SHEP will be shut down over turtle soup. The limits would likely just be amended, as there are bigger fish to fry, as it were. [Note: The Corps released an amended biological opinion in November 2017, increasing both lethal and non-lethal takes due to the unexpected prevalence of the threatened species.]

Over the summer, the Corps awarded a $100 million contract to Florida-based CDM Constructors, Inc. to build the dissolved oxygen (DO) systems on Hutchinson Island and upriver in Effingham County that are supposed to mitigate dangerously low oxygen levels caused by the deeper channel, especially during the summer. (There's that "mitigation" word again. To invoke Inigo again, I do not think that word means what you think it means.)

The DO systems will consist of a dozen domed bubblers called Speece Cones that periodically saturate water with oxygen to prevent the suffocation of fish and wildlife. Such technology has never been used in an open water environment on this scale, but don't worry: The terms of a 2013 lawsuit settled with the Southern Environmental Law Center dictate that the Corps has to prove they actually work before it can start digging down into the inner harbor.

Yet no matter what, we end up with a river that can't survive without iron lungs. Take a deep breath and think about that.

Birdwell says contractors will break ground on the Speece Cone farms very soon, along with another $40 million "mitigative" measure: Thalle Construction Co. of Hillsborough, NC was recently tapped (tell me again how this creates local jobs?) to build us Savannahians that tidy freshwater reservoir upriver at the Abercorn Creek intake, so that when the deeper channel pushes the ocean even further upriver, we're not drinking saltwater.

"The city's treatment plant can use water from the impoundment on occasions when high tides and low stream flow result in higher chloride levels," explains the Corps' Savannah District's website.

The concern isn't just salt in our sweet tea. Studies indicate that high tides are getting higher, and increased chlorides in the water will make it more corrosive, increasing the risk that it could leach lead from some of Savannah's 750 miles of aging distribution pipes. The Corps assured in a 2011 report that this would probably never happen. But it'd be real nice to check again, considering Flint, MI has poisoned its entire population with river water that corroded old lead pipes.

I don't doubt that the hard-working engineers and scientists are doing the best job they can to meet their objective: Get 'er done regardless of drinking water hell or tidal high water. But I still just don't get the cost/risk benefits, no matter how many times that vague "$5.50 returned for every dollar spent" flag gets waved. It's always a shock to find out I'm not the only one.

"I've been in the shipping business for over 40 years, and it doesn't make sense to me either," a high ranking executive in a local import/export business recently told me after swearing on my grandmother's grave that I would not reveal his name.

"The amount of ships that will come to call may be bigger, but there will be less of them—there are only so many to go around, ya know," he pointed out. "What captain wants to snake their way up the Savannah River when they can just sidle up oceanside in Charleston or Jacksonville? Plus, if the federal money doesn't come in, which it probably won't, the state of Georgia cannot afford to do this without a major tax increase."

There's also the matter of the proposed $4.5 billion Jasper Ocean Terminal, to be built on the South Carolina bank of the Savannah River. Last year the Georgia Ports Authority signed an agreement with the State Ports Authority in South Carolina to build the 1,500-acre shipping terminal, which could open as early as 2025.

But why would Georgia want to compete with itself with another, more convenient port right downstream? Our friendly anonymous source opines that it's a stalling ruse to appease the people of Jasper County and the joint venture will never happen.

"The whole thing is smoke and mirrors," he laughs ruefully. "The whole world is going off shore anyway, and more and more ports are becoming automated. So ultimately, that won't create more jobs, but less."

Look, it's all speculation, whether you're betting on the risks or the returns. No one can make the case that the Port of Savannah isn't a vital economic anchor for Georgia, and most folks around here seem to believe that if its growth means some sturgeon get chopped up and our coffee tastes a little salty once in a while, it's worth it.

So I fully accept that nothing can or will turn the SHEP ship around, and that the peckings of this mouthy columnist are just flotsam under the hull.

But it's still a free country, and I can holler into the spray if I wanna.

March 9, 2016

All Hail the Porcelain Throne

As we enter this season of giving and thanks, I must publically praise an often overlooked but highly essential companion of our cushy modern lives: The toilet.

Yes, there are plenty of other worthy contenders (looking at you, root vegetable peeler), but you may understand my devotion as I share the tale of my recent battle with a mighty microscopic enemy, suspected to have breached the walls of my probiotic-bathed intestinal fortress via an undercooked egg.

Though the temptation to resort to the scatological remains nigh, I will simply say that during this time a great war of gastric distress was waged upon my being. Toe-curling abdominal cramps and contorted bloating were followed by complete seizure of all main exit gates.

The invasion was devastating, but I survived the six-day siege. Not completely unprepared, I went through an entire 12-pack of double roll Charmin *by myself*. Our teal-and-yellow-tiled bathroom shall heretofore be known throughout Westeros as the Land of 2,000 Flushes, and I shall forever reign as its undisputed Khaleesi. I owe it all to my throne.

My adoration of the commode became all the more significant after last week's visit to the City of Savannah Water Reclamation Facility. You've probably driven by it on Presidents Street Extension plenty of times, but few besides our stalwart soldiers of sanitation have seen beyond its imposing concrete embankments.

It was a harbinger, really, as the forcible gastroweapon had not yet struck my person. Looking back, I remember feeling a wee bit off when I met Water and Sewer Environmental Administrator Laura Walker. She had organized the treatment plant's first open house in conjunction with World Toilet Day to help us citizens understand and appreciate "the marvel of the porcelain wonder." (I had no idea then how many times I would repeat that phrase over the next six days and nights.)

Not only do our indoor potties bring dignity to our most undignified moments, they're connected to a complex infrastructure that protects us from cholera, dysentery, ebola and worse.

"The United Nations designates World Toilet Day for some very good reasons," explained Ms. Walker, reminding that over a third of the global population does not have a clean, safe, private place to poop. "More than half a million children died last year due to lack of sanitary conditions in their communities. Many girls around the world are in peril when they have to leave the safety of their homes just to relieve themselves."

There are so few things that humanity has gotten right thus far, and certainly municipal sanitation infrastructure is a paragon. You can deposit your foulest mess and push a little lever on your own personal Moon Door and *whoosh*—it is banished.

But of course, we know it doesn't just disappear into the void like a young Rickon Stark. I think it's important to pursue things, even the smelly ones, to their conclusion, so I followed the department's interim director Lester Hendrix into the reclamation plant's, well, bowels.

Mr. Hendrix led me first through the control tower, where sentinels monitor the city's entire drain/flush/sewage influx 24 hours a day, seven days a week, treating 6,745,000 gallons of our wastewater every year. Pointing to the screens, he showed how our offal is removed in several phases using a combination of gravity and biological processes.

"Nature has a way of treating waste," he described, explaining that there is no "magic filter" other than the carefully-cultivated tanks of bacteria that anaerobically break down what we flush down. "Basically, we're doing what nature would do in a concentrated way."

From there, we climbed to see the industrial claw that rakes the first level of solids from the incoming flow, kind of a giant Hungry Hungry Hippos situation, except that those aren't marbles.

A lot of weird and gross things get trapped here, including kids' toys, and Mr. Hendrix implores us to keep everything but the necessaries out of our bowls. (Please quit flushing those godforsaken pre-moistened tushy wipes, because they don't biodegrade, no matter what the nice packaging says.)

The next two phases use gravity to allow the larger particles to settle and, in a feat of closed-system engineering genius, be turned into Class A fertilizer for the Bacon Park Golf Course and Hutchinson Island. The rest continues through a series of reservoirs bubbling with bacterial breakdown.

As we navigated the bulwarks of the cement castle surrounded by moats of halfway-clean gray water, I have never clutched my phone so tightly. The smell was a tad sewage-y but not overwhelming, punctuated by faint whiffs of potpourri. At this point I was beginning to sense the imminent attack of my own infinitesimal invaders, but I could not help but appreciate the magnificence and magnitude of what happens here.

Our tour took us 13 acres closer to the Savannah River, where the reclaimed water gets a quick splash of chlorine (the only chemical used in the entire process) to rid it of any chaos-wreaking bacterial agents before it's released back into the wild. This is a necessity, Mr. Hendrix reminded, since every time you turn on the tap or watch your porcelain throne fill with fresh water, you start the whole cycle over again.

Which brings us to the bi-monthly $1.50 rate hike you'll soon be seeing on your water bill. Some have expressed outrage over this unbelievably modest increase, and Mayor Edna Jackson recently rightfully excoriated its detractors.

People, Savannah's water and sewage *fees are the third lowest in the entire Southeast.* I know so many of us must watch every nickel, but surely, there must be some other cache from which to squirrel *nine dollars a year* to ensure that when you flush your toilet, Mount Ve-sewage-us doesn't erupt out of the bathtub.

The City deserves kudos for being uncharacteristically pro-active by funding needed upgrades to the 20 year-old plant to meet new EPA standards and address deferred maintenance. I can't think of money better spent—especially if a tiny fleck of that funding could go to snazzing up the facility's mural seen from President Street, because some public art memorial to the monumental activities happening within this excremental citadel is surely in order.

As my own personal principality slowly recovers back under my own intestinal domain, I encourage all of us to include our humble ceramic companions in our expressions of gratitude this week.

Just maybe not at the Thanksgiving dinner table.

Nov. 26, 2014

Welcome to the State of Poverty

Let's pretend that we're in the top 1 percent. What shall we do today?

Fly the Gulfstream jet to Cannes for the weekend? Host a Super PAC hunting party? Kick it on a yacht with gold-plated toilets while a staff in full livery feeds truffles to a stable of dressage horses?

Fun, right? Now let's take off those Gucci loafers and pretend we're in the bottom 25 percent.

Oh, please. Who wants to fantasize about being poor?

Apparently, plenty of us. Over a hundred people signed up for last Thursday's Poverty Simulation at the Civic Center, which goes to show that empathy *can* be as interesting as an offshore bank account. Only about half of those actually arrived due to some terrifying weather, but Step Up Savannah proceeded.

The quarterly community action event—open to the public—is just a small part of Step Up's arsenal against poverty, which also includes job training, benefits assistance and collaboration with over 80 other local social service organizations.

I've been curious for years about these poverty simulations, not because I think imitation destitution sounds like a good time, but I wanted to dig into notions about Savannah's persistent poverty problem: The rate has hovered between 24 and 26 percent for over a decade.

Why, with so many services available, are over 34,000 of Savannahians still poor? Will cutting welfare fix America's budget ills or choke a necessary part of a civil society? How possible is it really to pull oneself up by one's tattered bootstraps?

Data released this time last year revealed that one in four Savannahians subsists under the poverty line, defined as a yearly income of $22,000 for a family of four, up three percent from the last census. Many more hover in the "working poor" zone of under $40,000 a year. But dry numbers don't tell much of a story.

"Statistics don't necessarily stick," says Suzanne Donovan, Step Up's Communication Director. "These simulations help people get it on a emotional level."

After a stern reminder that "this is not a game," everyone broke up into "families" of three or four. I sat down with Nicole Hobbe, a graduate student in mental health counseling at South University, here to learn more about the people she'll be helping in her career. Also in our "home" were Asia Coles, a junior at Woodville-Tompkins High, and Kayla Smokes, a sophomore at St. Vincent's Academy, both Chatham County Youth Commissioners participating as a required part of their community service.

Together we were the Xanthos family, two immigrant grandparents raising grandchildren whose mother was incarcerated for drug use.

Encouraged to mix up our assignments as much as possible, Asia took on the role of Grandma Zelda, a full-time cashier making minimum wage. Kayla was Anthony, the disabled grandfather in his 50s with no high school diploma.

Nicole played 9 year-old Zoe, and I stepped about as far out of my comfort zone as I could as Xerxes, a 7 year–old boy with ADHD described as "a handful."

We were given a packet containing transportation cards, Social Security IDs and a few items that we could hock like a camera and some jewelry. Other families got EBT cards and cash. Everyone had four 15-minute weeks to secure food and pay the bills without getting evicted.

Adding up our resources and our expenses before the call-and-response signifying the start of Week One, we came to the gut-punching realization that we were already $24 in the hole.

"Sell the jewelry, Grandpa," commanded Zoe/Nicole.

Us kids had to attend Realville Public School, where I slipped through the cracks as a behavioral problem because my grandparents couldn't afford my ADHD medication. At the end of the "week," we reconvened to find that Grandpa had pawned our stuff but had run out of transportation passes to go buy food.

"This is stressful," panted Grandpa/Kayla. "Do my parents have to figure all of this out?"

We found out that we could have gone to Interfaith Services for help, and Grandma/Asia expressed frustration that we weren't made aware of available resources. "Plus, it's not fair that the person with the most disabilities is the one with the most responsibilities."

We were learning fast that life's not fair, and even less fair when you're poor. The next weekend brought some relief when an exhausted Grandma/Asia brought home a paycheck, but still no food. At least we were doing better than the Perez family next door, who had planned to sell their TV and fridge but got robbed.

Week Three brought a school vacation, and our grandparents locked us in the house because there was no money for childcare. Still, a drug dealer pushing packets of Sweet N Low managed to get in. Someone from the Friendly Utility Company shut off the electricity because Grandpa had paid the bill too late.

The grown-ups finally brought home food and medication, but we didn't have enough money to cover the mortgage. The problems piled up faster than they could be managed, and we returned from Week Four to find our chairs tipped over. In spite of the hustling, we'd been evicted.

"At least the lights are on," sighed Grandpa/Kayla.

In the debriefing led by Step Up Executive Director Daniel Dodd-Ramirez, we found out only one family had been able to survive the month. Many had resorted to crime, shaking down their neighbors when the money ran out. Others, like Grandpa Xerxes, had spent too much time in the wrong lines and became overwhelmed.

"You can see that people spend an extraordinary amount of time just trying to get basic services," he said, adding that in spite of available resources, obstacles like public transportation schedules, lack of education, unhelpful gatekeepers and "easy" high-interest check cashers keep people stuck in a frustrating whorl.

Dodd-Ramirez explained that the cycle affects our entire society in the form of an undereducated workforce and rampant crime. Take away the umbrella of social services, and we're already there.

I still know as little about the struggles of being truly poor (to paraphrase Russian writer Alexander Solzhenitsyn, "How can you expect someone who's warm to understand someone who's cold?") as I do about how rich people spend their weekends. (Champagne hot tubs? Touring diamond mines? Who knows?)

But I came away from the Step Up simulation with the keen understanding that poverty is everyone's problem.

Savannah's economic issues more or less mirror America's. As wealthy politicians talk dramatic slashes to social services budgets and austerity measures, I wonder if they could fathom even an afternoon of poverty.

`August 28, 2012

A Year of Living and Dreaming with Emergent Savannah

First week into the year, and I've already had two traffic tantrums and eaten my weight in chocolate croissants. So much for resolutions.

Meh, unreasonable expectations rarely lead to success anyway. When it comes to creating positive change, I've decided instead to adopt a new strategy for 2016: Flood my psyche with magnanimous adoration, preposterous possibilities and glorious speculations and see what sticks.

That philosophy seems to be working stupendously for Emergent Savannah. The grassroots advocacy group launched last January with the intention of empowering local citizens to shape the future, a lofty goal in this Age of Apathy.

To get a handle on a workable plan, its first action was to ask Savannahians what we love about and what we dream for our city—and we had to answer not with Facebook posts but Post-it notes.

Organizers set up colorful writing stations at the Sentient Bean and shlepped pads of paper and pens all over town to various festivals, elementary schools and far-flung neighborhoods. Thousands contributed their scribbles, and the sticky squares festooned the Bean until it looked like the walls had been attacked with Tibetan prayer flags.

The low-tech medium not only brought opportunity for plenty of face-to-face interaction, it provided a rainbow of raw data: The Love/Dream Project identified trends that cross Savannah's numerous cultural and economic divides, showing that most of us love Savannah's history, its natural beauty, its diversity, its potential. We all dream of safer streets, better schools, more art, less crime, higher paying jobs, a responsive local government.

"Looking at it from the perspective of our hopes and dreams, we found that we really aren't that different," says Emergent Savannah coordinator Courtnay "Coco" Papy. "So we took that information and have tried to create conversations that matter to everyone."

Coco, along with sculptor Betsy Bull, painter A.J. Perez, photographer Emily Earl and musician Alex Raffray, catalogued those paper declarations and quickly morphed them into dozens of jam-packed events: Emergent Savannah's monthly "Monday Means Community" panels attract standing-room only crowds at The Bean, the longtime community gathering spot that Betsy calls a "beacon of acceptance." (It is also a bastion of delicious baked goods, specifically chocolate croissants.)

The themes of economic development beyond the minimum wage tourism sector and the establishment of a sustainable arts economy came up repeatedly throughout the year. A unique "un-debate" for City Council candidates was roundly lauded as one of the most informative interludes of the local election season.

"There was all this talk about Savannah growing, but we saw what was happening and were not necessarily feeling like we were a part of it," recalls Coco, who returned to her hometown in 2014 on fire for social action and has lent her passion and skills to many other good works, including Deep Center's Block by Block and the Flannery O'Connor Book Trail. "We wanted to understand our place and provide a space for people to learn."

She adds with a grin, "We're trying to make civics sexy."

These artsy types in their 20s and 30s classify themselves as progressives, though they managed to stay remarkably neutral through the fall's super sparky political lightning storm, focusing instead on inclusivity. Recognizing that social connection is arguably Savannah's greatest currency, they sought counsel across cultural, partisan, generational and racial boundaries to build a consensus of Savannah's unheard voices.

They found lockstep with veteran insurgent Tom Kohler, who has helped bridge relationships with some of Savannah's most invisible residents for decades.

"The core idea in my mind was if we keep using the same processes, we're going to get the same outcomes," says Tom, who serves as something of a den papa at the Emergent Savannah clubhouse inside community arts collective Sulfur Studios, founded by busy bees Emily and A.J. this summer. "What we've tried to do is think of new ways to communicate with people, new ways to invite people to meet and be with one another."

Each meet-up centered around an unlikely cast of characters—a mix of artists, activists, politicians, city staff and business leaders whose agendas may not line up on the surface—and the ES activists earned their diplomacy badges by wrangling all of them into the same room. Information architect Brittany Curry traveled from Milledgeville throughout the year to document the action, her markers flying as she channeled choice quotes and cute likenesses into brilliantly hued murals.

The resulting atmosphere has been refreshingly civil in this day of comments-section vitriol and anonymous trolls, though a few gatherings definitely entertained as well as educated. (Oh, did you think discussing the city noise ordinance with working musicians in the room was going to be *tame*?)

Now, a year after interpreting that wall of fluttering paper squares, Emergent Savannah has firmly established itself as a highly relevant entity for anyone who gives a fig about the city's future. The crew is celebrating its first anniversary by returning to the Love/Dream theme for its first Monday Means Community event of 2016.

Emceed by the indie arts queen JinHi Soucy Rand, the evening features reflections from attorney raconteur Wade Herring, proper Victorian preservationist Ardis Wood, food justice maven Jessica Mathis, beloved politico Regina Thomas and teenage poet and recent White House award recipient Andre Massey. (Yours truly will also share a few thoughts about what I love/dream about/for Savannah, which is sort of my favorite topic.)

Per usual, the conversation will continue into the night for those 21+ at the American Legion, where I'm pretty positive all of Savannah's problems will be solved someday.

For this year, the Emergent Savannah action-ists have a bit more structure to work with than sticky notes as they move forward with their mission of inspiring Savannahians to leave their screens for a minute and get involved. They've received fiscal sponsorship under the Educational Media Foundation, which means these hard-working folks can replenish the supply cabinet and maybe receive tiny stipends for their time. (Nonprofit sector, take note: last year's ES budget was under $1000.)

Future programming includes a talk with *New York Times* reporter Elizabeth Becker ("The Revolt against Tourism"), a lively panel on Savannah's LGBT history, collaborative art shows and official town hall meetings with elected officials. The affable radicals also resolve to keep loving, keep dreaming, and "continuing to pack the Bean like sardines."

Yet their origin story still seems like a solid way to start the new year: Instead of feeling guilt for stress eating or dissolving into rage over people's inability to navigate four-way stops, slap every awesome idea you can think of to the wall of your brain and watch what happens.

Jan. 6, 2016

A Tale of Two Horror Shows

Shudder at the bloodcurdling screams. Cringe at the zombified inmates. Witness the scenes of torture...if you dare!

Oh, come ON, *why so serious?* It's all part of the frenzied fun at Panic in the Pen, the haunted Halloween thrillfest giving out goosebumps at the old county jail on Montgomery Street through Halloween.

Wait, did you think I was alluding to something else? Perhaps the viral video depicting uniformed deputies tasing a barely-conscious young man in the testicles while he was he locked in a restraining chair, where he was found dead a few hours later?

I can see how you might make that mistake. After all, both events feature terror and gore, both happen inside a local jail and both are brought to you by the Chatham County's Sheriff's Office.

Of course, there are obvious differences. One takes place in the current holding pen on Chatham Parkway, the other at a disused facility downtown. One has cost taxpayers hundreds of thousands of dollars in court fees; the other is raising funds for charity. One is real, the other is pretend.

To conflate the two is what the director of public affairs for the Sheriff's Office calls "a heckuva stretch."

I guess I've been doing too much yoga, because Matthew Ajibade's death is what came immediately to mind when the first Panic in the Pen press release circulated in September. It promised "all sorts of doom and gloom" and "maybe even a clown or two ... remember killer clown, John Wayne Gacy???" *[sic]*

Some thought it a bit unusual that a law enforcement agency would host a chamber of horrors at the ol' prison when two of its deputies had recently been indicted for killing an inmate and seven more fired over the incident. Also, that namedropping a raping serial murderer was a selling point.

What's next up on the Docket of Inappropriateness, we joked, a Holocaust Easy-Oven Bake Sale? How about a firecracker show for the Boston bomb victims?

But it wasn't until the video of Ajibade being beaten and tortured was released during the recent trials of former deputies Maxine Evans and Jason Kenny that the terror-in-the-clink concept moved beyond simple poor taste to flat-out bad judgment.

As the sickening clip lit up national news sites and social media, I reached out two days before the haunted jail preview to see if the Sheriff's Dept. planned to release a statement acknowledging the painful parallel.

I did my best to clarify that the aim of my query was not to vilify anyone involved in the Halloween show. Rather, I saw it is an opportunity to broker a conversation about police brutality and our broken justice system—and perhaps help temper yet another national PR disaster for the city.

"Not sure how ANYONE can be outraged by a 20 year old unused county facility being put to use to raise money for 2 kids groups and wounded warrior[s], *[sic]*" came the emailed response. "This event has been planned since last June and is giving kids an opportunity to earn community service hours."

I would never want to diminish the charitable aspect of the event and applaud any opportunity for volunteer work, even if it entails shrieking in people's ears and carrying around your own intestines on a plate. Funds generated from Panic in the Pen benefit Chatham County Explorer Post 876, Chatham County Youth Commission and the Wounded Warrior Project, three important local organizations that create opportunities for our kids and provide vital services to our soldiers.

But I wouldn't be doing my job if I didn't point out what seems to be a serious case of cognitive dissonance.

I have been following the Ajibade case from the beginning, which began when the 21 year-old Nigerian-born SCAD student was arrested on New Year's Day on a domestic violence charge. According to reports, his girlfriend begged police to take him to the hospital, giving the officer a bottle of medication used to treat Ajibade's documented bipolar disorder.

Instead, he was taken to the Chatham County jail, where he became combative and broke a deputy's nose. He was then wrestled into the restraining chair and a spit mask placed over his face. He was still wearing it when he died.

Last Friday, a local jury acquitted Evans and Kenny of involuntary manslaughter, though the lesser charge of cruelty stood for Kenny and his perverse use of the Taser. Evans could face jail time for perjury.

Reports of the not-guilty verdicts in Savannah—along with the video—rose to the front page of dozens of international websites and garnered thousands of comments, many professing shock that jurors didn't see the violent video as sufficient evidence to convict the deputies.

Ajibade's family wasn't nearly as surprised. "I knew that that same system that failed Mathew would not be the system that got him justice," cousin Chris Oladapo told NBC News. "We expected nothing, and we got nothing."

"Disappointment requires a conflict of expectation," echoes attorney Mark O'Mara, who is representing Ajibade's family. He calls the assistant DA's performance in court "subpar prosecution from start to finish" and that the handling of the case indicates a "serious institutional unawareness" in the Sheriff's department.

O'Mara is filing a civil suit on behalf of the family later this month against the county as well as its contracted healthcare provider, Corizon Health, and several individuals including Evans and Kenny. The lawsuit will seek punitive damages as well as demands to overhaul the deputy training program.

"Matthew Ajibade was deprived of his federal and civil rights and suffered at the hands of this department," says O'Mara. "With that kind of systemic incompetence, it will happen again."

After the verdicts were released, I called the department again to discuss Panic in the Pen, described as "super *super* scary" by a couple of last weekend's attendees.

The PR rep explained that the fundraising event had indeed been planned for over a year, though the original venue was outdoors. Concerns about the weather led the organizers to tap the abandoned jail as a possible locale, spurred by the popularity of *The Walking Dead.*

The rep said that hundreds of dollars and hours have been donated to produce the event, and finding genuine old guard and inmate uniforms inside sealed the deal. (Authenticity—yet another disturbing selling point!) She reiterated that any scenes of torture involve inmates restraining a guard, not the other way around.

The planning committee also brought in a paranormal investigation team to validate purported ghostly activity in the jail, imprinted by the many "murders, suicides and natural deaths" of prisoners within the concrete walls.

"But you don't see any connection between those tortured souls and Matthew Ajibade?" I pressed.

Wrong question. "What is wrong with you? Were you not allowed to have Halloween as a kid?" she yelled.

I replied that it was, in fact, my family's favorite holiday, but that I was honestly trying to understand how the Sheriff's Dept. could not see the irony of its participation in actual torture and putting on a "fun" house that depicts it.

"Well, you and your editor are literally the only people who have complained," she retorted.

I don't doubt that's true, considering the unsettling lack of local outcry over the Ajibade verdicts. But anyone who's familiar with my work knows I ain't skeered of being the lone werewolf in the pack.

Yet I have to wonder: How many others have kept silent out of fear of intimidation by those sworn to protect and serve? Or simply rendered speechless by the abject absurdity of it all?

I know there are plenty of decent folks who will enjoy having the pee scared out of them at Panic in the Pen this weekend, and I sincerely hope barrels of dollars are raised for the good works it benefits.

But after the fake blood is mopped up and the zombies go home, some of us will still be haunted by the screams.

Oct. 28, 2015

Name Shaming the Talmadge Bridge

It's always a relief when it appears in our windshield.

The double-H piers poke into view as we barrel east down the two-lane anxiety attack of Highway 17, past the shabby strip clubs and cavernous fireworks warehouses, and we know we're almost home.

The green river sparkles on either side of the car as we approach the incline, the road so close to the water it feels like we're hydroplaning.

Then we're lifted above the world for a brief moment, taking in the expansive view of where we live, from the church spires and the port cranes to the gold ribbons of marsh and the ominous blue tanks of Elba Island.

A few seconds later, the Talmadge Memorial Bridge drops us into Savannah and safely across the state line, where we ignore the homeless camp inside the cloverleaf and do our best to believe that life is more civilized on this side of the border.

But as we shake our heads and snicker about those rednecks in South Cackalacky clutching their Confederate flags to their tobacco-stained Duck Dynasty T-shirts, let's remind ourselves once again exactly who is memorialized on this shiny, cable-stayed gateway to our fair city.

Obsequiously referred to as one of Georgia's most "colorful and controversial" politicians, three-term governor Eugene Talmadge was a straight up KKK racist who, during the Depression, told President Roosevelt to take his New Deal and stick it where the sun don't shine. He ran his 1946 campaign on a platform of white supremacy, and recently uncovered files reveal that he openly advocated the lynching of black citizens. He was, agree many historians and other modern thinkers, a tremendous asshole.

Yet voters (those who weren't intimidated away from the polls, anyway) kept on electing him, and when the State Highway Board built the Interstate over the river in 1953, they gave it his name. You'd think there would have been an opportunity to correct this embarrassing affront when the original bridge was torn down for the more modern truss in 1991. Instead, the Georgia Assembly passed a resolution to carry on the Talmadge name—and by proxy, his nefarious legacy.

Yup, it's 2016, and Savannah's most recognizable modern icon is still named after Georgia's most recognizable racist (#sorrynotsorry, Lester Maddox). Honey Boo Boo might as well be twerking on the steps of City Hall for the backwards message it sends to visitors and citizens alike.

"We cannot, on the one hand, celebrate the racism of yesteryear and then on the other scratch our heads claiming confusion over the absence of black-owned businesses on Broughton Street, or over the higher-than-national-average level of poverty in the city," admonishes legendary local poet/activist Aberjhani, who wrote a lengthy essay about this ironic injustice and kindly updated his thoughts in a recent email.

Whoa whoa whoa with the political correctness, say the reactionaries. *We've got monuments to all kinds of racist historical figures around here. What's one more?*

As Aberjhani puts it, "there is a big difference between maintaining a Confederate statue that marks an authentic historic site of the Civil War and declaring a major public thoroughfare and landmark as a memorial to someone who openly advocated racial oppression."

Plus, "the wild man from Sugar Creek" ain't from anywhere around here anyway. Eugene Talmadge's kinfolk hail from the Atlanta area, so he's about as locally significant as Jane Fonda in a Falcons jersey.

Yet efforts over the years to change the name of our bridge—to Oglethorpe, to Tomochichi, to *anything* else—have always fizzled.

The most recent one came a few years ago, when an op-ed by the Georgia Historical Society's Stan Deaton sparked a new cycle of outrage. This time, local legislators got on board. Supported by a vocal grassroots campaign, House Reps. Ron Stephens (R-Savannah) and Craig Gordon (D-Savannah) led a bipartisan, racially diverse delegation to the state assembly to submit a bill that would scrub the bridge clean of its bigoted associations.

Guess what happened? Nothing. The GA closed its session without hearing from the delegates—some of whom reported they were browbeaten in the halls by the current generation of the still political and extremely territorial Talmadge family. (Eugene's son Herman succeeded him in the governor's mansion after the Three Governor's Controversy of 1947, and his grandson was a longtime U.S. Senator.)

"One of the gentlemen...was essentially pushing us up against the wall," Stephens was quoted in an April 14, 2013 *Savannah Morning News* article. "How did he put it? He said, 'I'll raise $100,000 just to beat ya."

Those dynastic intimidations clearly worked, though democracy has a funny way of rearing its beautiful head.

"I am still a proponent of changing the name. It's what's best for tourism and the city. It's worth going through the process," vows Gordon, adding that many local African Americans only refer to the contentious causeway as "The Savannah Bridge."

Former mayor Dr. Otis Johnson believes it is no accident Talmadge's name was memorialized on the bridge in the first place, but was a direct response to the Brown vs. the Board of Education decision to integrate public schools by the political power structure back in 1954. Neither was it an afterthought, says Dr. Johson, when the original cantilever truss was replaced with modern spires in 1991 and Talmadge's name came with it, meant to be an insult and a warning to those who would challenge the families that still have a firm fist on Georgia's economics and politics.

Since 2015, an organization called Span the Gap has worked to change the name of the bridge to represent the City of Savannah and its diverse, thoughtful citizenry. Founded by artist Lisa D. Watson and currently spearheaded by local businessman Ron Christopher, Span the Gap has posted surveys and hosted panels to garner support for the cause. A survey last year garnered more than thousands of responses in favor of changing the name, and several hundred people attended event in September, the vast majority it seemed not so much questioning whether or not the name ought to be changed, but how and when already.

Unfortunately, it's not as simple as taking a Sharpie to the green highway sign. The Talmadge Bridge is under the jurisdiction of the Georgia Dept of Transportation, and the change requires a majority vote from both houses of the Georgia Assembly. This action that has thus far been prevented from even reaching the floor of the Gold Dome, in spite of having been championed by city leadership and the Chatham County delegation, members of which were reportedly thwarted from presenting their proposal in 2013 by those opposing the change.

The Savannah City Council recently approved a resolution to rename the bridge, and Georgia senator Lester Jackson, chair of the Georgia Legislative Black Caucus, has promised that he will push the issue during the next legislative session. Though he has warned that it might be difficult to get the entire GA on board with changing the name of one little bridge. But surely there are other communities around the state of Georgia who are challenging the white supremacist narrative embedded in their infrastructure, and a coalition is waiting to be built of the efforts to reclaim the names of schools, highways and public institutions for a more just and equitable future.

"It should not be necessary in 2016 to stage marches across the bridge or have sit-ins on it to disrupt the illusion, or delusion, of normalcy in order to bring about a crucial intelligent change," counsels Aberjhani.

It shouldn't be necessary, but maybe that's what it will take.

It actually sounds pretty awesome: To climb to the apex of that two-mile marvel with our neighbors and friends as the giant ships sail beneath, standing up in the name of connecting Savannah with the right side of history.

April 20, 2016, updated November 2017

5 FORKS, KNIVES & NAPKINS

Who's hungry? Visits to Savannah's finest dining establishments such as Elizabeth on 37th and The Grey mean mouthwatering reports, though they reveal much more than reviews of food. Sometimes the best meals come from the food bank, and maybe over a campfire cooked by the South's most colorful culinarian, Michael Twitty. And let's explore the question of eating lion burger—would *you* eat a Simba sandwich?

A Delicious Ménage a Trois: Me, my man and Elizabeth's on 37th

A single friend recently asked Mark and me what the secret is to a happy marriage. We burst out laughing.

"Hell if we know," we cackled simultaneously.

Truth is, after the day's mad dance of work and shlepping to kids' activities and throwing some kale in a pot for dinner before packing lunches and paying bills and starting the whole process over again, encountering each other in the hallway on the way to bed tends to be a pleasant surprise. "Oh, are you still here?"

So maybe it's staying busy that's kept us grooving along for 14 years. That, and earplugs.

Certain niceties do tend to slip in our life of constant chaos, like closing the door to the bathroom and retaining personal ownership of one's deodorant. Even our anniversary celebrations can get pushed aside in favor of band concerts and science projects and deadlines. We dimly remembered eating takeout out of Styrofoam containers after mattress shopping last year and vowed to do something classier this time, lest we end up falling asleep at the kitchen table after snarfing a box of Chex cereal.

It doesn't get any more special than Elizabeth on 37th. Chef

Elizabeth Terry and her husband, Michael, turned Savannah on its ear with their notions about real estate and cuisine when they opened in 1981, yet the awards and the loyal customers kept on coming. This grande dame of Savannah fine dining has served exquisite, regionally-sourced nouvelle Southern cuisine in its stately Neoclassical/Beaux Arts mansion long before anyone coined the word "locavore" back when hanging around that section of town required pepper spray and a can full of crazy.

Though the couple eventually left the restaurant in the capable hands of longtime employees Gary and Greg Butch to move out West, many locals remember their generosity and mourned deeply when Michael passed away last August.

We'd been to Elizabeth on 37th for our second anniversary, both of us goggle-eyed with new baby sleep deprivation. I wore a dress far too tight and tragically, had to skip dessert. I do recall that we fell madly in love with shaved truffles for the first time that night, a torrid ménage à trois that continues to raise eyebrows amongst our more simple-palated friends.

Though he likes to brag he ate at Elizabeth's (as it's inevitably called) for his senior prom, neither of us have been back for a dozen years. We've been distracted by other restaurants and intimidated by an expensive evening out—especially, as my gifted husband likes to brag, since he can cook almost anything at home. (Unfortunately, we haven't had much luck digging up our own truffles.)

But maybe one of the secrets to marriage is knowing when to splurge.

As we passed through the sublime gardens and massive stone steps leading up to the deep porch, there was a distinct sensation of passing into another dimension, a more genteel place on the time-space continuum that us regular folks normally inhabit.

Beyond the pocket doors of the dark wood dining room, architect Christian Sottile held court at a round table for seven. We shared a group hug with Sundial Charters owners Rene and David Heidt, also celebrating their 14th anniversary. (There must've been a whole lotta lovin' going around that weekend in 1998.) Other tables were occupied by mostly by couples, some as old and elegant as a satin smoking jacket.

Our friend and server Aly Morita had put in a nice word, and the hostess led us to a tucked-away banquette that I immediately deemed the Canoodling Corner. Gary Butch poured us flutes of champagne and described the evening's specials with the unbridled alacrity of an Emory philosophy lecturer. Which, as a matter of fact, sometimes he is.

"Eh, I'm just a waiter," he shrugged, then launched into a fascinating discourse on the nature of reality, peppered with references to Kierkegaard and quantum physics, occasionally stopping to ask, "Do ya follow me?"

Anywhere, my good man.

His pony-tailed brother, Greg, could also be seen working the floor, bustling in and out of the tiny kitchen with Zen-like grace. The brothers have opened the restaurant to a host of altruistic events in the last few years, and it's become a favorite stop for the Tibetan monks when they pass through to create their sacred sand mandalas. I've worked in enough restaurants to know that being waited on by the owner is fairly unheard of, and the Butchs' humble, hands-on dedication has to be one of the reasons Elizabeth on 37th's storied ambience and fine flavors endure.

Oh, and the flavors: Our dinner officially began with an amuse-bouche trio of a tiny puff pastry filled with pimento cheese, a single spicy mussel bathed in tomatoes that had been smoked for hours and a two-bite button of melt-in-your-mouth salmon in wasabi cream sauce. Next came soft local scallops sprinkled with butterbeans and generously doused in that heavenly truffle oil, along with a rich roasted eggplant-shiitake mushroom-red pepper-tomato soup redolent of a backyard garden on a sunny afternoon.

Then came a dish of Sapelo Island clams served with savory miniature madeleines to soak up the sauce, followed by a delicately-dressed salad of greens picked less than a block away.

We could taste the time and love put into this haute cuisine by Chef Kelly Yambor and her husband Jeremy, the power couple that continues the Terrys' kitchen legacy, distinctly Southern without the big-toothed twang.

By the time our entrées arrived, we were already swooning, though the Caymus Pinot Noir may be partly to blame. ("Like steak in a glass," murmured my beloved.)

Finally, almost four hours later, dessert: A divine pecan almond tart paired with a 35-year-old Muscat, warm and cozy as an old leather chair. Yes, it was worth waiting 12 years for another visit to Elizabeth's.

Over coffee, Mark and I promised that we won't let life's celebrations slip away anymore. For less than the price of two meals at a mediocre restaurant, we could come to Elizabeth's again, for no reason at all. We are worth it. So are you.

Perhaps a good marriage is like a fine restaurant, holding an elegant yet homey space and nourishing with what's in season. What universal elements have the Butches mastered to pull off this marvelous balance?

They're not telling, just clearing the empty dishes with a small smile and a gracious bow.

Oct. 12, 2012

50 Shades of the Grey

The blue satin jumpsuit was definitely a no.

I was trying to put together a snazzy ensemble for dinner at Savannah's sizzling new hotspot, and I thought I'd make a grand entrance with my recent amazing score from Gypsy Girl Vintage. But my man took one look and put down the kibosh.

"It's *Wednesday*," he pointed out. "That's more an outfit for New Year's Eve...on Pluto."

After several more costume changes, I settled on an acceptably less-crazy dress and boots. It's just that I was so damn excited about my first trip to The Grey and I needed my look on fleek, OK?

Johno Morisano, the owner of the restaurant/bar built into the stunningly refurbished Greyhound bus station on MLK Blvd., says he has been a tad overwhelmed at the explosive popularity of the place. The buzz has lit up foodie radars near and far, and expectations are high.

Though he professes that his nerves prickle every night before opening, Johno looked chill as a cucumber gimlet as he stood watch over the already-packed dining room, which yes, is as breathtaking as everyone says: The chrome shines, the liquor bottles glint under amber globe light fixtures, the servers saunter confidently among the tables as well-coiffed cogs in a sleek, thrumming machine.

You can run your hand along chipped railings down to the baggage claim-cum-private dining room, one of the many details salvaged from the original station. What couldn't be saved was revamped to the specific glamour of the Art Deco period, that historic architectural sweet spot when form followed function in the most glamorous possible way.

Johno kindly seated us at what he called "the Mack Daddy table," a buttery dove leather booth presided over by a massive Marcus Kenney collage. Along with deep respect for preservation and heritage, Johno has also steeped the Grey in contemporary local art, adorning the walls with works by Betsy Cain, Adam Kuehl and Jerry Harris.

But dear Lord, let's talk about the food already.

Pegged by *Elle* magazine as one of 30 culinary women to watch, Chef Mashama Bailey honed her skills at NYC's award-winning Prune, a tiny joint in the East Village where you don't care that the people in the next table are practically sitting in your lap because you can dip your bread in their parsley shallot butter when they're not looking.

Bronx-born but partly Savannah-bred (she went to the same elementary school as my kids), the Divine Chef M has no time for your gastronomic trepidations and is clearly succeeding in her diabolically delicious plan to get everyone here hooked on eel.

From the spicy eggplant appetizer to the lemon pop palate cleanser, every bite was a marvel. I ordered the whole baked snapper garnished with thin slices of orange that I ate down to the rind. My jumpsuit-hating date practically cried tears of joy into his veal chop, seared crisp and pink as a camellia petal when sliced. And the beef liver polenta; well, I had to be physically restrained from licking the plate.

The craft cocktail menu dazzles; one day I will fill my bathtub with the tobacco-citrusy Radder & Lamb. As for dessert, let's just say the cayenne-flecked peanut butter parfait puts Dairy Queen's to shame.

After occupying our booth for three-and-a-half glorious hours, our impeccable server gently encouraged us to take the party to the bar up front, which is styled straight out of an Edward Hopper painting, except the patrons were all laughing and toasting instead of looking like they wanted to go home and kill themselves.

On a stool sipping an old-fashioned sat none other than Tom Stephenson, former owner of Café Metropole, the beloved eatery that occupied this same space over a decade ago. Back then the aesthetic was a bit more, ah, *bohemian* since he and Clara Fishel had a landlord who allegedly gave no figs about historic preservation, let alone fixing the plumbing.

"I love this building so much," said Tom, swirling ice cubes in his highball glass. "It's so great to see it done right."

It's no secret that Johno—a successful venture capitalist who continues to run multiple businesses in addition the Grey—sunk a couple million bucks into the buy and buildout.

The Grey is truly world class, which bodes well for the rest of the boulevard. The revitalization of the rest of MLK has been a little like Bigfoot—excitedly discussed but non-existent until proven otherwise. But progress is emerging from the bush, and I'm not just talking about the four corporate hotels springing up towards the river. There are a slew of small businesses sprouting in the other direction, including a comic book shop and a craft brew store, with more to come.

"As Broughton and the rest of downtown have improved, we've got more and more people who are interested in this corridor," says Kevin Klinkenberg, executive director of the Savannah Development and Renewal Authority.

He reminds that the SCAD Museum of Art and anchors like Rancho Allegre and Creative Approach are thriving, proving MLK Blvd. a sound investment. Further south, The Guild Hall has taken nerdcraft to the next dimension with its gaming compound and recent annexation of the old Bub-Ba-Q for another restaurant, the Chromatic Dragon.

"They're basically remaking a whole city block," Klinkenberg says admiringly.

But how to bring the affluence all the way south? Where the row bustled with minority-owned businesses 50 years ago, there is now a cavernously empty Food Lion and decaying public housing projects, the once-bustling neighborhood tyrannized by the ogre of the I-16 flyover.

Klinkenberg assures that modification for the highway is slowly but surely making its way through the glacial federal contracting process. When it is finally demolished, it will enable the city to reconnect the streets and gain back eight acres for more development. Twenty blocks uptown, the SDRA is also helping things along with a makeover of Wells Park at 38th St. The City continues to offer a super sweet deferred property tax deal all the way up to 52nd Street.

Can the prosperous, polished glow of the Grey reach that far? Will the aging used car lots and convenience stores give way to the next generation of business owners ready to take advantage of the opportunities? Can our MLK become a boulevard of restored dreams?

It remains to be seen, but I've got a hot satin outfit ready for the celebration.

Feb. 4, 2015

Around the Fire with Michael Twitty

It's darker side of dusk at Wormsloe Historic Site, and as I pick through the saw palmettos along the dirt path, I'm sure we've taken a wrong turn.

"No, it's just a little further," urges Forsyth Farmers Market co-founder Teri Schell as she strides through trees vibrating with the cacophony of cicadas.

I follow behind her clutching my purse and try not to shriek when I realize the mosquito I just swatted off my ear was actually a bat. I soldier on, out here in the shadowy woods to track down culinary historian Michael W. Twitty, for whom Teri and I share a certain fascination. (Fine, call it a foodie crush.)

Twitty has soared to fast fame since he published "An Open Letter to Paula Deen" on his blog, Afroculinaria.com, smack in the midst of Our Lady of Perpetual Butter's carmelized career meltdown. In his letter, Twitty gently reminded that Southern cooking belongs to us all, but it cannot be discussed honestly without acknowledging its origins in Africa and American slavery.

Wise but not accusatory, the post burned a big hole in the internet after the *Huffington Post* picked it up, and Twitty has been up to his earlobes in book contracts and speaking engagements ever since. His forthcoming book, *The Cooking Gene*, chronicles his insights as he recreates the meals of his African ancestors in the places they lived and worked, and his social media reflects humorous musings on cultural equality, food justice and creative uses of sorghum.

I don't know if he's the only gay, black, Jewish culinarian in the entire world, but this gent is definitely my kind of unicorn. I got all groupie-eyed when I found out Twitty was in Savannah to lead a special presentation for the Slave Dwelling Project Conference, and I'd be damned if any dark, scary forest was going to keep me from meeting him.

When Teri and I arrived at the former plantation, we heard the strike of the *djembe* and the traditional rhythmic stylings of West Africa—that happened to be provided by Abu Majied Major and his son, Yusuf, who I had just interviewed the day before for an article about a local African dance workshop.

The universe so does love its serendipity, and several of the themes that I'd been researching all week for that story were being discussed here around the tables, specifically the preservation of slave history in the American South and its incorporation into the mainstream narrative.

As attendees found their way from the conference's main locale at the Coastal Georgia Center, one young woman commented on the mile-long tunnel of massive trees that's made Wormsloe one of Savannah's most famous photo ops.

"It's called an 'oak allee,'" informed Reneé Donnell, a recent grad of UGA's historic preservation department. "All plantations had them. But we rarely talk about the people who dug those holes."

The slave dwelling conference attracted academic historians and archaeologists from around the country, since Savannah is ground zero for slave history and the perfect place to foster Twitty's message of inclusive history.

I kept looking over my shoulder for our celebrity culinarian. Teri whispered that she overheard Twitty was preparing his presentation at the Colonial Life Area, further down the dirt road.

"Might be our only chance to talk to him without a crowd," I murmured. "But I'm also hungry."

We looked longingly at the long line for tantalizing food from Daufuskie Island's own celebrity chef and Gullah cookbook author Sallie Ann Robinson. Then we sighed and snuck away from the tables into the woods.

For a few moments, we are guided by the golden strip of marsh shimmering in the last light of day beyond the trees. Then the curtain of the forest swallows us whole, and we step out of time.

As we trudge, I'm aware how little this land has changed since Noble Jones and his slaves cut its paths almost 300 years ago. My phone and its flashlight are a pocket away, but I don't dare break the spell.

Finally, we glimpse the flicker of torchfire. We make our way across a footbridge towards the tiny wattle-and-daub shack, smoke rising from the chimney.

Suddenly, there he is: A barrel-chested bear of a man tending the hearth, sweating as he preps plates of okra and peppers on the rustic wooden table. He is as grand and gregarious as I thought he'd be, his voice higher and more mellifluous than I'd expected.

"Come in, come in!" cries Michael Twitty, wiping his brow.

Teri and I tuck in to watch as he stirs cast iron pots of Muscovy duck and Gulf Coast lamb neck, heritage breeds raised by Bradley Taylor and Cat Compton on their sustainable farm in Sylvania. Knowing the rest of the conference will appear on golf carts momentarily, I spill out a rush of questions like chicken bones at the feet of a voodoo priest.

Though he studied at Howard University and worked at respected sites including Colonial Williamsburg, the thirtyish historian approaches his discipline not academically but as folk heritage tradition. He remains itinerant, traveling and cooking and educating from the roots up.

"If I was interpreting at an institution or a museum, you'd never hear about me," he declares, placing a three-legged skillet in the fire by its long handle. "This is the way I can connect with people."

Though corporate network types have come sniffing around his campfires looking for the next foodie star, Twitty's not interested in being put in a box as "another black chef doing soul food." His Jewishness also muddies any notion of simple marketability.

"People want uncomplicated narratives," he shrugs. "That's not me."

I can relate. As a Jewish gal with a strong affinity for African dance, I ask about this African-American urbanite's Jewish soul.

"Roads converge," he nods sagely, explaining that he converted to the religion of Moses and Barbra Streisand when he was 22.

"Judaism gave me insight on how to preserve something from generation to generation. It's a leitmotif, the obligation of the transmission of Jewish culture. Therefore, my black identity and my Jewish identity are inextricable."

Unlike this heretic, Twitty keeps a kosher home when he has one. But that's not gonna keep him from Sallie Ann's Lowcountry boil.

"Oh yes, I'm going to get down on this plate of *trayf* right now, forgive me," he laughs, nimbly peeling shrimp from shell in less than a second flat.

We talk about the forced Diasporas of Jewish and African culture and the non-racial notion of "peoplehood," a term often used in Jewish circles to navigate the ever-evolving balance between tradition and identity.

"We are but one race on this planet, but our ethnicities are the diversity," he preaches. "Our differences are valuable."

That's what feeds his passion to protect the culinary heritage of his ancestors. And he'll kindly call out those who insist on fetishizing slave culture and cuisine—or worse, appropriating it without honoring its origins.

"Collards are 'the new kale,'" he snorts. "Please."

This, of course, brings us back to Paula Deen. He holds out hope that her people will contact him one day so he can bring her out to cook biscuits and hamhock around the fire, which y'all have to admit would make some good TV.

"I'm not looking for a confrontation," he promises. "I am about reconciliation, I want to have a dialogue. I want to get people talking about how it all fits together."

With a shake of his wrist, the pan-fried veggies are done. They taste of smoke and spice and the air of the night, echoing with the presence of the enslaved people who likely ate the same dish near this very spot.

"Centuries of stories are contained in a simple meal," reminds our host.

The golf carts appear out of the dark. It's time to abdicate our private audience, and the philosopher chef launches into a new round of his fascinating *schtick* to the arriving group. We part with hugs and calls of *mispocheh*, the Yiddish word for family.

As Teri and I hitch a ride back with the rangers through the woods, it occurs to me that we've reached the Age of Meta: History informs the present as the inclusion of neglected narratives feeds back to our perception of the past. An enlightened future depends on how well we honor our own origins while holding others in the loop.

It's a lot to chew. Can we ever learn to see ourselves as a peoplehood, each one of us a unique stew of culture and DNA, nourishing and nourished by the same complicated, multi-layered human story?

Sept. 23, 2014

Noshes and Naches at the Shalom Y'all Jewish Food Festival

When I was 5, I begged my *bubbe* to show me how to make blintzes.

I loved and looked forward to the pillowy treats stuffed with sweet cheese and smothered with jam and sour cream, but they never seemed to be around very often. While the other neighbor kids went wild for the ice cream man, I went around looking for Jewish grandmothers with extras.

My Jewish grandmother always seemed to prefer reading to cooking, but that didn't stop me from being a *noodge.*

"I don't know, it's very difficult," she said, putting down her book. "And don't give me that sad *punim.*"

I kept pestering her, and a few mornings later she woke me up before dawn, the kitchen counter piled with ingredients. We spent the next hours measuring and mixing, her calling orders as I fetched cookie sheets and spoons and bowl after bowl that she filled with sugar and cream cheese and lemon zest and vanilla. I tried to imitate the way she folded the thin pancakes around the filling, slowing rolling it up into a lopsided package.

Finally, as the sun climbed into the sky, she pulled the lumpy cushions from the oven and placed a plate in front of me. They were kind of rubbery, and the only thing we had to top them with was a half empty jar of mint jelly. I ate half the pan anyway.

"Good, I'm glad you like them," said my *bubbe*, settling back into her favorite chair. "Because I'm exhausted."

It wasn't until I was a grown-up that I realized blintzes aren't necessarily that complicated and don't need to be made in the middle of the night. It's just that my *bubbe* had terrible arthritis and was a raging insomniac.

She passed years ago without making them again, and I never got her recipe. Fortunately, there's a whole *mishpocheh* of other blintze-making *bubbes* (and *zaydes*!) preparing for the Shalom Y'all Jewish Food Festival, taking place this Sunday in Forsyth Park.

Organized and produced by Congregation Mickve Israel on Monterey Square, this yearly nosh-fest invites all of Savannah to *fress* (loosely translated as "stuff yer *punim*") on all kinds of traditional Jewish dishes. Volunteers gather in the synagogue kitchen for weeks beforehand, baking loaves of soft challah, stuffing cabbage, packing matzah balls, and assembling trays of hummus and pita.

It's no accident that I showed up the day they were making my favorite comfort food.

"Everybody has a blintze story," agreed Ina Kuller as she dolloped ready-made pancakes with sweet ricotta cream mixture last week. "I remember watching my grandmother make them. Hers were potato, and she used to deep fry them."

Kuller's *bubbe* grew up in Manhattan but likely got the recipe from *her* granny, who lived in the Pale of Settlement, that war torn strip of Eastern Europe that was sometimes Germany, sometimes Russia, from where millions of persecuted Jews emigrated from in the 19th century.

Perennial volunteer and former CMI president Tobi Hollenberg's story is a little different, but no less cherished.

"I grew up in Lakewood, New Jersey, the home of Golden Blintzes," says Hollenberg, referring to the factory that ships their perfect pillows to grocery store freezer aisles around the nation. "I was always excited to see our town on the box."

Boxed blintzes taste mighty fine, but it's always a joy to know they're made by loving hands right here at home, along with the other homemade sweets at the Shalom Y'all Food Fest: Cinnamon-sprinkled *rugelach*, noodle *kugel* with plump raisins, honeycakes—there's enough Jewish grandmothering to go around for everybody.

Of course, savories are on the menu, too, including sizzling lamb in pita bread, hot potato latkes made on the spot, chicken liver paté and pastrami sandwiches piled as high as your head. It all pairs tremendously well with a Dr. Brown's cream soda or a He'Brew beer and is available to take away or enjoyed in the park as the Savannah Philharmonic performs lively selections from the pantheon of Jewish composers. (A little Gershwin, anyone?)

The popularity of the Shalom Y'all food fest brings plenty of *naches*, which has nothing to do with a Yiddish version of salsa and tortilla chips. To "*shep naches*" means to take pride, and an expected attendance of more than 10,000—one of Savannah's largest gatherings—is nothing to sneeze at. Funds raised go directly towards programming, including the Backpack Buddies project that sends more than 100 local kids home with food every weekend as well as interfaith activities like the community Thanksgiving dinner next month. Also benefitting is the Second Harvest Food Bank, which will have collection points throughout the festival and will receive a portion of the day's proceeds.

As the festival enters its 28th year, it's always a challenge to wrangle 300-plus volunteers and tens of thousands of food items as one generation hands off organizational protocol to the next.

"We strive to stay consistent, but we've also evolved," says Jennifer Rich, CMI's executive director. "I think we've developed good cooperation between staff and volunteers to continue the festival for many years to come."

Established in 1733, Congregation Mickve Israel is as old as the city itself, and the food fest remains a vital link between the historic synagogue and Savannah's greater good.

"Our goal is to collaborate and be part of the community through food," says Rich, adding that feeding ourselves and others is a practice not limited to the Jewish community. "Food is the way we nurture."

As I remember my grandmother setting aside her aches and pains to indulge my childhood hankering, I feel the truth of those words in my heart.

But as I'm *fressing* over a plate of perfectly folded blintzes piled with fresh sour cream and strawberry jam on Sunday, I might just be a teeny bit relieved somebody else's *bubbe* made them.

Oct. 26, 2016

Would You Eat a Simba Sandwich?

Savannah was all about lions last week, and not just because Katy Perry kicked off her sexy Super Bowl halftime spectacle by riding in atop a ginormous feline robot.

There was another reason big cats were on everyone's lips, literally. Meat from the *Panthera leo* species was on the menu at a local restaurant during Restaurant Week, and it's caused what can only be referred to—*please forgive me*—a huge uproar.

The restaurant received so much negative feedback it took down its Facebook page, and legions of shocked citizens have vowed a boycott.

But while many have expressed dismay and disgust, others had no qualms ordering the appetizer, a slider made with farm-raised ground lion meat mixed with pork belly, topped with smoked gouda and served on a warm bun.

"Hey, the damn thing would eat me if it could," shrugged one delighted diner, who described the taste as akin to "really good Kobe beef."

Some reportedly ate it thinking it was a typo and they'd ordered loin burger. These are probably the same people shunned at the water cooler the next morning for discussing Katy Perry's loins.

Though a bit shaken from the vitriolic skewering he's received, the executive chef stood solid with his decision to serve lion, which he asserts is sourced from a farm in California and approved by the USDA.

"We wanted to do something different to draw in the culinarians and epicurious diners," he says of the special game menu, which also included crème brulée thickened with emu egg. "It was an amazing success."

Indeed, the chef and his kitchen staff plated over a thousand lion sliders, selling out the prix fixe dinners that also serve as a fundraiser and allowing the restaurant to make a sizeable donation to Second Harvest Food Bank.

Considering the backlash, would he serve it again?

"At this point, I would not put it out for the public, but I have had special requests for private lion dinners," he divulges.

Listen, I don't want to judge. I'm a gal with an adventurous palate and will pretty much eat anything, including giant snails, barbecued rattlesnake and a cherry pie recovered from a Whole Foods dumpster. (Look, I was young and poor and it had only been expired for one day.)

But lion? I don't know.

First, it's an apex predator, risky because carnivores carry parasites like trichinosis, those grody worms that spiral into your intestines. Then there's the undisputable majesty of lions, serving for millennia as icons of strength and courage. To eat them just seems...sinful.

Which is what makes it attractive, I suppose: It's a notch on the foodie belt, an assuagement of an epicurean itch. Yet even local gastronomic sage Tim Rutherford, who is kind of like our own Andrew Zimmern but a better cook, has his reservations.

"Doing what I do, I've eaten lots of stuff," sighs the longtime moderator of the Savannah Foodie newsletter, ticking off a gourmand list that includes armadillo, ostrich and alligator.

"Everyone has their own moral compass. Me, I wouldn't advocate eating lion any more that I would horse, even though horse has been regulated and on menus in Europe for decades. Most of us don't want to eat things that we have an iconic Disney image of."

Simba aside, let's examine this from a different standpoint. Apologies to the chef, who I honestly believe would not knowingly serve anything he didn't trust was of the highest possible quality, but it does not appear that the USDA inspects or regulates lion meat.

After many phone calls and a deep delve into the U.S. Food Safety Inspection Service website, I found out that the Federal Meat Inspection Act specifically regulates a dozen types of edible animal flesh. Rare ones like bison and yak fall under the Exotic Animal Inspection directive, for which inspections are voluntary and must be requested, for a fee.

I was not able to track down *anything at all* applying to the regulation of lion meat. One USDA public affairs specialist even asked me to forward my notes as her department "would be very interested in that information to consider whether investigation is appropriate."

Still, God bless America, lion meat is still legal to serve in all 50 states and has popped up in restaurants all over the country, from burgers in Mesa, Arizona to tacos in Tampa, Florida.

Each time is appears on a menu, the concerned folks at Big Cat Rescue flood the market with educational materials.

"Restaurants will tell you these lions are raised on a farm in California, but nobody knows where these farms actually are," cautions Susan Bass of BCR, which operates an animal sanctuary in Tampa and picked up on the Savannah dish through Google alerts.

Bass believes lions that end up on plates may come from "pay to pet" places like Miami's Jungle Island, where the public can hold cute cubs for a fee. Those babies eventually grow sharp teeth and claws, and those teenagers must be dispensed with somehow.

But again, this is America, and legislation is on the way: The Big Cats and Public Safety Protection Act was recently reintroduced to Congress and would forbid such direct contact between humans and big cats, putting those touchy-scratchy parks out of business. The act would also ban big cat breeding except at accredited zoos and educational facilities.

Most folks are surprised to learn that African lions are not considered "threatened" under the Endangered Species Act, but the U.S. Fish and Wildlife Service recently proposed to up their status, which would not only prevent the Hemingways from bringing home their African conquests but also outlaw the domestic sale of lion meat.

That'd be bad news for Anshu Paphak, who owns ExoticMeatMarkets.com and sells not only lion stew meat for $500 a pound through his website but also squab, frog legs and flamingo. To my utter shock, I was patched right through to him when I called.

Originally from India and a Hindu of the holy Brahmin caste, Anshu told me he forswore his vegetarian upbringing decades ago to become a merchant of the highest quality meat. In spite of some people's moral objections, demand for exotic flesh is booming, and he sees his business as an affirmation of life's bounty.

"What is ethical and what is unethical?" he asked. "Meat is meat. I am not violating any state or federal laws. I am an animal lover. I am not going to kill anything that is endangered. I am not doing this for publicity, not even for the money. I'm doing it as my passion."

He claims to be the mysterious lion farmer who sourced the Savannah sliders but remained vague about the farm's actual locale other than it is "near Las Vegas." He acknowledges that the processed meat isn't inspected but offers DNA testing to show that his lions are domestically raised and certainly aren't gamey old circus lions or cast-aside teenagers.

"I have invited the USDA here many times! I'm willing and ready to pay the fees so I can export all over the world!" he exclaimed, adding that "people buy from me because they trust me."

His other products—beaver hot dogs, anyone?—are processed at USDA-approved facilities, shown explicitly on his Facebook page. When it comes to his lions, Anshu promises they enjoy good lives up until the end.

"If you come to my farm, you would see how lovingly how I take care of them. I treat them as VIPs," he insisted, offering me an open invitation for a farm-to-table lion dinner anytime.

I declined, but as usual, I've ended up with more questions than answers.

Is it fair to vilify a chef for fulfilling the demand of his customers? If Anshu is for real about the self-governed practices of his happy lion farm, does that mean the meat is safe to eat? And just because we *can*, does that mean we *should*?

All I know is I'm cooking lentils tonight.

Feb. 11, 2015

True Nourishment

It's that of year when for some of us, food starts appearing out of nowhere.

Fruitcakes left on the doorstep. A pile of powder-dusted cookies in the breakroom. Fourteen kinds of cheese at the neighborhood open house, not including whatever is in those logs showered in chopped walnuts.

Yesterday I found myself running away from a nice lady in the hairnet handing out ham samples at Publix, only to be confronted by fudge at the dry cleaners. It's hard to imagine that anyone, anywhere, could possibly be hungry when you've got people practically sticking candy canes down your pants at the bank.

Yet as we scarf those empty calories, we must remember there are those among us for whom basic nourishment seems impossible. We may not know them personally. Maybe we do, and they're too proud to let us know it. But Rev. Carl Gilliard sees them every day.

"Things are so bad now for so many," the good reverend tells me on a recent visit to the Savannah Feed the Hungry Life Center, the facility he runs on Augusta Road just over the Garden City border.

"We've got so many new people coming in this month because of the changes made to the food stamps benefits, and they're every race and religion and color and age. We know here that hunger has no boundaries."

He's speaking from experience. The former car salesman and his wife, Lashawnda, started SFH three years ago after clawing back from hard times themselves with their four daughters.

"I lost my job, and then we lost our house, then our car. We literally had two pieces of bread and a piece of bologna at one point," he recounts. "I now call it the best experience of my life, but I don't want any family to have to go through that."

Undaunted, the Gilliards began contacting local produce distributors to solicit donations of extra fruits and vegetables. Their efforts quickly blossomed into an operation that hosts monthly sit-down dinners and free clinics as well as gives away hundreds of bags of groceries twice a week.

The softspoken pastor claims no superpowers. But with not a single penny of public funding, he has galvanized an impressively effective program of thousands of clients, hundreds of volunteers and over forty local business partnerships. And rather than work in a different orbit than Savannah's other service organizations, SFH often shares referrals with Second Harvest Food Bank and the Salvation Army.

"Everything seems to work together," Rev. Gilliard shrugs. "For all of us, the goal is to serve, and there is no shortage of people in need."

SFH is expecting 6000-7000 guests at their two free holiday dinners on Dec. 22 and 23 at the National Guard Armory, in Hinesville and Savannah respectively. Clothing, gift and toy giveaways will also bring comfort and smiles.

But one or two meals don't make the dent in people's hunger. It's the work that's done all year long to supplement the seniors as their power bills go up, the single parents, the working poor, the families living out of hidden tent cities on the west side of town.

When I showed up at SFH's cavernous warehouse last week, produce coordinator Mother Middleton was sorting cartons of fresh blackberries and beautiful bunches of beets while uniformed volunteers from Hunter Army Base's BOSS program lifted crates of ivory cauliflower, bags of crisp collard greens and bunches of grapes onto tables. Rows of brown paper bags stood neatly lined up on pallets with whole grain breads and carrot tops peeking out, looking every inch like they belonged in the trunk of an Audi stationwagon leaving the parking lot of Fresh Market.

While Mother assures me that such a cornucopia doesn't happen every single week, it's clear SFH is not just feeding the hungry—they're feeding them well, and with dignity. And teaching them how to cook, if necessary, offering free cooking classes through UGA Cooperative Extension.

"We want to give people a hand up, not a handout," explains Pastor Gilliard.

It's clear there are more than bodies being nourished here. Pastor Gilliard reiterates several times during the afternoon that he wants those who come to the Life Center experience a "good feeling" so their faith is restored that life is good, no matter what. It's an infectious vibe.

"People come here so worn down, so sad," says front desk volunteer Gloria Zipperer, a friendly redhead who first came through the doors as a client. "I know how hard it is to come here, so my first step is to give everyone a hug."

I get mine, and after so many days of too many sugary treats, my stomach finally feels settled.

Perhaps the sweetest part of the holiday season is being reminded how once we have enough to eat, how little it takes to fill each other up.

Dec 13, 2011

Honoring Brighter Day's Foodie Elders

Good lord, people, you'd think we'd never seen an organic potato before.

Whole Foods Market has been open for a couple of weeks now, and Savannah is still swooning as if the Messiah is in there singing karaoke and giving away free babies.

Not that I count myself apart from the entranced masses clutching canvas bags and ogling the artfully-piled pluots. As an avowed disciple of the gods of kale and nitrite-free turkey bacon, I, too, have already worshipped multiple times at this new megachurch of higher eating. I confess to skipping up and down the aisles like a hungry Hare Krishna, squealing with rapture at the rainbow of bulk quinoa and unpronounceable brands of kombucha.

And Holy Mother of Edamame, the salad bar.

It says a lot that the opening of a fancy grocery store is the most thrilling phenomenon to hit town since Hurricane David. First, clearly Savannah has been salivating for an upscale foodie experience that caters to the socially conscious palate. If only we lined up for better public schools like we do for housemade raspberry gelato!

Second, Whole Foods sets a high bar for creating instant community. At any hour of the day, all corners of Savannah are out representing in its customer base—one only need to see the mothers in Muslim headscarves milling along the pasta aisle with observant Jews to dispel the outdated notion that this city is merely black and white. And while there are haters who reject paying a few more pennies for pesticide-free produce, there are plenty of blue-collar folk planning meals amongst the housewives in expensive tennis outfits.

It's not just about who's buying but who's selling: An advance corporate team sussed out some of Savannah's finest artisan vendors: FORM's cheesecakes, Chocolat by Adam Turoni, Nourish Savannah's divine bath fizzies and local caffeine courtesy of PERC and Cup to Cup are among those taking their products to the next level.

"If there's anything local we can get, we do," avows associate team leader Emily Salzer, who relocated here from WF's Nashville store. "Every store is unique, and we do our best to reflect and respond to the local community."

Hello, did I mention there's locally-brewed beer on tap?

The philosophy extends to more than just food: Opening festivities included raising funds for the Savannah Tree Foundation and the West Broad Street YMCA as well as employing musical mainstays The Train Wrecks and City Hotel, who crooned away near the cheese display.

The store's design concept is also rooted in the Lowcountry, from the reclaimed shutters above the deli to the picnic tables built by Design for Ability. There's even a framed homage to Backus Cadillac, the pink concrete loaf of a building that sat upon this lot for over 50 years.

Maybe it's hard to swallow that a corporate giant is better at collating our local resources and packaging them up prettier than any of us ever could. Yet suddenly people who used to roll their eyes at the word "organic" are now knitting their brows over red snapper overfishing and fair-trade coffee beans. If shiny and fancy brings more people to the Altar of Sustainable Eating, that's a wonderful thing.

But it's important to remember *why* Whole Foods can bring the glamorous lifestyle of gluten-free macaroni and free trade chocolate to the mainstream: Because independent stores like Brighter Day Natural Foods have been touting it way before it was sexy.

In fact, when Janie and Peter Brodhead opened up Brighter Day on Forsyth Park in 1978, eating organic was downright revolutionary. Enlightening people about the ethical origins of their food was a neverending challenge, especially when the culinary choices weren't much more than sprinkling wheat germ on salad and carob cookies that tasted like baked lawn clippings.

Yet with patience and many delicious uses of tahini, the Brodheads have built a loyal and lovely conscious community from their historic building on the park. They know most of their customers by their first names, and Peter's vast knowledge of the medicinal properties of herbs and supplements is legendary— plenty of local doctors refer patients to him for advice on complementary treatments for cancer and digestive disorders.

I expected to see some long faces when I popped into Brighter Day last week in the midst of the Whole Foods fervor, but instead found the Brodheads and the rest of the bunch responding to their first competition in three-and-a-half decades with Buddha-like serenity and bootstrapping good cheer.

New construction buzzes near the produce, where a remodeled deli will give the culinary elves more space to create their magical nourishments (if you've never experienced a baked cheese sandwich with avocado, you're depriving yourself.)

Plus, the coolest thing ever is coming to the Bull Street side: A walk-up, bike-up, dog-friendly takeout window.

"Our goal has never been to be bigger, only to do things better," says Janie.

The Brodheads have found valuable support from the Independent Natural Foods Retailers Association, a national organization that validates the role of small health food stores as health food culture moves away from the fringe. Brighter Day's "boutique" status means being able to offer from

Hunter Cattle and Savannah River Farms, both highly evolved but not large enough to meet Whole Foods' distribution guidelines. Brighter Day has always been involved with local charities, raising over $10K last year for various non-profits.

"Staying independent also gives us freedom. We can be political," affirms Janie, referring to Peter's moving speech at the recent March Against Monsanto rally.

Though the coming of Whole Foods brought no small amount of handwringing, the Brodheads have faith in their passion for healthy, conscious living.

"It's kind of like the pretty girl whose dad works on Wall Street and rides in a limo to school just moved to town," admits Janie a bit ruefully. "But we're family. We're strong."

While the staff surely feels like kin, it also includes Janie and Peter's actual offspring: Andrew has been working the register for ages, and daughter Claire moved back to town from Asheville to apply some of the knowledge she learned working at organic farms up north. Oldest son and acupuncturist Ben recently moved back from the West Coast with his wife and kids to start a practice in Savannah.

"I think there's intrinsic value in the fact that we've been here for over a generation," muses Claire, who remembers toddling down the aisles.

I have to agree. Though I can literally walk from my desk to the front door of Whole Foods in less time it will take you to find a parking space (don't hate), I still make it to Brighter Day to shop and commune with these good people. And also for the revelation of Marilyn's tempeh salad.

Whole Foods is indeed a glorious promised land of victual bounty—and for many, a starting place to learn how and what we eat affects everything else. Perhaps it has brought you to the sacred ground of where food and community intersect.

True devotees will continue to make frequent pilgrimages to the place where it all began.

April 28, 2013

Local tradition, Sounds Fishy. Shad!

We take a break from our regularly scheduled outrage to bring you a story that started long before the current state of affairs.

Once a year for millennia, as the rivers that spill freshwater into the Atlantic Ocean along the eastern edge of the continent warm from south to north, massive schools of a certain herring-like fish have returned home.

The American shad spends most of its life in the open sea, snacking on plankton and circling the waterways from Florida to Nova

Scotia for four years as it reaches maturity. When it's time to spawn, both males and females make a mad detour towards the coast, following an internal GPS upstream of the exact river they themselves were hatched. Kind of a mind-blowing miracle, as the teenagers I know get lost on their way home from Wilmington Island.

This enduring rhythm is evidence of a clock that ticks further back than most can comprehend, and how shad continue to find their way in spite of dams, pollution and overfishing is another one of those natural mysteries that borders on the metaphysical. For those who appreciate the cycle of life and damn fine meal, shad season can be downright transcendental.

"The shad are running, the shad are running!" has been a ubiquitous spring cry since America's founding days, and its abundance during February and March in the Savannah, Ogeechee and Altamaha rivers have fed many a grateful generation around these parts, from the native people who occupied the bluffs to the settlers scraping out survival in General Oglethorpe's colony to current legions of Yeti cooler-wielding fisherfolk.

Low in mercury and other toxins and imbued with twice the amount of brain-nourishing Omega-3 fatty acids as wild salmon, shad has a Latin name, *Alosa sapidissima*, loosely translated as "super duper delish fish." I'd been told for years that females fat with roe make the best eating, though I've managed to miss Savannah's shad season in spite of chowing down aplenty on whiting, redfish, bluefish, and other local *fruits des mer* hooked by my own personal fisherman.

Frankly, I wouldn't have known what to do with one of these legendary specimens if he'd hooked one. I usually handle fish pretty well considering I was raised in Arizona, where the only seafood I encountered came from a can or on a bagel with cream cheese.

But shad can be intimidating, since it's notoriously difficult to filet, on account of all them bones.

"If you don't do it right, you'll be pickin' and spittin' all day long," advises Charlie Russo, Jr., the proprietor of Russo's Seafood, where his father, Charles, Sr. perfected a technique that has employees like Blanca Perez able to slice up a shad in five minutes flat.

"Daddy is the one who started doing it like this in 1946," he demonstrated last week, using his fingers to work over the rows of tiny bones of a fish that had been swimming upstream in the Altamaha less than a day before.

He gently pressed the peach-colored flesh with the tip of a long, curved blade. "See, you have to make three different cuts, and turn the knife upside down at the tail."

Though I hold no illusions of ever being capable of executing this complex feat myself, I watched closely as Charlie and Bianca whisked their way through a few at Russo's metal work stations across from Noelle Houston, who was deftly peeling a pile of plump wild Georgia shrimp, each almost as big as a banana. (True story, when I was a child growing up the desert I used to think all shrimp were the size of those tiny sea monkey things that floated in the sizzling rice soup at our neighborhood Chinese restaurant.)

Russo's has to be at least partly responsible for shad's popularity on Savannah dinner tables over the decades, making it easy to grab a nicely wrapped package from the refrigerated shelf for dinner instead of performing meticulous surgery. The famed family seafood market recently celebrated 70 years in business, a legacy left by the elder Russo, who passed away in 2008 at the age of 94, and carried on by his oldest son, whose demeanor isn't nearly as salty as you'd expect for someone who's spent his whole life cleaning fish and eating fish and just plain fishing.

Though he's cast a line from Chesapeake Bay to the Mediterranean, the seafood scion has always called Savannah's waters home.

"I moved away once, right after I graduated from Benedictine to work on a salmon boat in Alaska," recounts Charlie with a grin, blue eyes twinkling like the sea. "They were paying ten dollars an hour. That was a fortune in 1961!"

Upon his return from the Great North, the southern piscator took up the family mantle. He eventually married his high school sweetheart, Clara McDonough Russo, and the couple celebrated their 50th anniversary a few months before the beloved lady passed last March. Since then, he's been working as hard as he always has, finding solace in another shad season.

He makes quick work of the one in front of him, laying out the filets in neat, pink slices. He holds up the roe. Bright red and steaky, it looks more like a horse placenta than anything you'd want to put on a cracker.

But this "redneck caviar" is the culinary prize, the real reason the shad chase has been celebrated all these years. The *New York Times* published Elizabeth on 37th chef Elizabeth Terry's recipe back in 1987, and no mention of shad roe is worth a grain of salt without a bow to late, great chef and cookbook author Edna Lewis.

Charlie says Russo's couldn't keep the Atlanta Commerce Club stocked with it for fancy dinners back in the 90s. Yet these days you'd be hard pressed to find shad or its roe on any fine dining menu, even with many Savannah chefs' dedication to local produce and heritage-raised meats. Why the decline in popularity?

Charlie gives a shrug without a skip in the blade. "The younger generations aren't into it as much, I guess."

Apparently some palates prefer their fish all light and flaky, and shad has a reputation for being too strong. I say there's no such thing, but don't ask me, I was raised on canned sardines.

I do know enough to respect tradition. I prepared the filets and roe exactly as Charlie told me to: Dust both in salt and pepper, brush with lemon butter, and broil on a greased pan for 20 minutes, flipping the thick steak of roe halfway.

It tasted *sapidissima* to the max, as someone who has not studied Latin at all might say. The fish itself came out tender, with a robust flavor that reminded me of mackerel or herring. The roe was still weird-looking but tasty, and once I got over its appearance I enjoyed the texture—soft meat infused with tiny, crunchy eggs. I do believe I'll take redneck caviar over the Russian stuff any day.

According to Charlie, the shad should run for at least six more weeks, so there's plenty of time to pick up some filets. If you care to throw in a line yourself, be sure to check the regulations at Georgia Dept. of Natural Resources, and should you get lucky and want to take a stab at shad surgery, Charlie's brother, Capt. Vincent Russo, has a great tutorial on his YouTube channel.

Me, I'm content to leave the fishing to the fisherfolk. But that doesn't make me any less enamored of shad's yearly sojourn to our local waters or the ancient map that makes it possible, coded in all those tiny bones.

It makes a mind wander to the Great Mystery that binds us all, and just think: By the time the shad babies conceived this spring make their way back to their birthplace in four years, we'll be in a whole new cycle ourselves.

We can only hold faith that nature's revolutions will endure, eclipsing the rest in its long, slow clock.

Feb, 8, 2017

6 LET'S GO OUTSIDE! OR NOT

The beauty of natural world—whether wild or manicured—is a perk of living in Savannah, that is, when the humidity and bugs have receded back to Hades where they belong. But the days when the sun shines and the breeze blows make it all worth it. Love letters to the city's famous azaleas, aging oak tree canopy and even the inevitable showers of spring pollen paint a colorful picture of Savannah's unique outdoor gifts. But a meandering tour of the beleaguered Savannah River and a bout of hurricane brain also remind how fragile our environment truly is.

Eulogy For a Fallen Friend

Look, nobody lives forever.

Once you're past 80, I imagine the shadow of imminent demise is a constant creeping companion, following you into the grocery store and the doctor's office and even places no one else will, like the bathroom.

Even if you don't move an inch your whole life long, death will find you anyway, no matter how quietly you try to hide how weak you've become. Sure, you could live another 10, maybe even 20 years with the right care, but eventually, the last exhale will come. When that happens, I guess the best possible consolation is that you will be missed.

Dignity is paramount, and it's best to say goodbye to a tree while it's still standing.

More than 20 people and two dogs showed up there to bid a final farewell to such an old friend in Monterey Square last Tuesday afternoon, hunkered under umbrellas as the heavens poured down. You've got to admit, that's a pretty good turnout for a tree funeral.

Technically, the colossal magnolia wasn't dead yet. But it's only a matter of days before the city's saws come to fell this aging giant, which has been showing signs of advanced rot for months and is now leaning dangerously towards the Pulaski monument.

"Monterey Square will look very different from now on," mourned Karen Jenkins, director of the Savannah Tree Foundation. "Just think of how many millions of people this tree has shaded, how many animals it's sheltered in its life. It's soaked up rainwater and pumped out fresh oxygen."

This towering tree also pushed out white, dinner plate-sized blooms every summer, their heady redolence a cross between lemon pie and your grandma's perfume. July in Savannah will smell a little less sweet with the loss. (It also means a little less sticky yellow pollen to powder our windshields in the spring, but save that blasphemy until the poor thing is gone, will you?)

The tree's exact age won't be determined until the rings are counted on the shorn stump, but a good guess is somewhere between 80 and a hundred years old. I'm pretty sure attendee Dr. Joseph Rice hasn't celebrated quite that many birthdays, but he did admit to a long relationship with the giant magnolia of Monterey Square.

"I used to sit under this tree studying, and I thought it was big then," remembered Dr. Rice as the streetlights blinked on. "Then" was 1956, when he graduated from Armstrong College back when science and math were taught in what is now the United Way building. It must have been an excellent study hall, as Dr. Rice went on to practice internal medicine in Savannah for over 40 years.

My heels sinking into the mulch, I craned my neck back to take in the tippy-top of this glorious specimen, trying to picture a gaping space in the leaf canopy. I've always been a tree groupie of the highest order, escaping for hours as a kid to read in the nest-like branch of a neighbor's carob tree and falling deeply in love with the feather-fronded redwoods of Northern California.

As far as I'm concerned, the trees are what give Savannah its famously enchanting aura—without them, all we've got is pretty houses and a bunch of bald concrete. And as much as I dig the big live oaks, fluttery mimosas and lovely crape myrtles, the majestic magnolias are my favorite, probably because I don't have one in my yard to clean up after come leaf-dropping time.

Chatham County arborist Dennis Goldbaugh, who estimates he has witnessed the passing "of thousands and thousands of trees" but had never attended a tree funeral until this one, shares my affection. As we leaned against the soon-to-be deceased's coarse trunk, he told me that as a forestry student, he'd studied dendrology (that's the science of plant-naming for us layfolk), and the professor had cultivated in him a deep appreciation for the species.

"This guy was a tough-as-nails, old school forester. But when he introduced the *Magnolia grandiflora* to us, he got almost teary-eyed, saying there could be no more beautiful name for a symbol of the old South," recalled Goldbaugh. "I never had any trouble remembering that Latin name."

I have my own personal story about this particular Southern grande dame, though we only met in her sunset years. As a new teacher at Congregation Mickve Israel's Shalom School, I brought my kindergarteners out to the square one sunny morning several years ago to collect Spanish moss to make Baby Moses baskets.

"Look, it's so pretty!" I sang, entwining the grayish-green tendrils into a crown for one little girl's hair.

The boy who always complained that the graham crackers for snack were stale even though I just opened the package held out a few strands dubiously. "My mom says this has bugs in it."

"Well, your mother isn't here, is she? Everyone grab two more handfuls!"

We spent the rest of the class scratching each other's backs and painting clear nail polish on the itchy bumps. So I have the tree to thank for this most valuable lesson about Not Touching the Spanish Moss, as well as for many mornings sitting under its rustling shadow with my religious school charges, contemplating the beauty of Creation. Though now we use plastic grass when for the Moses in the reeds project.

Back at the tree memorial, Jenkins reminded that though the city will remove the trunk, stump and roots, it will be many years before another tree can be planted in this one's place.

As if on cue, the crowns of waxy green leaves shook in the breeze, spattering the brick walkway with loosened raindrops. We bowed our heads as she solemnly read the classic poem, "Trees" by Joyce Kilmer:

I think that I shall never see
A poem lovely as a tree.
A tree whose hungry mouth is prest
Against the earth's sweet flowing breast;
A tree that looks at God all day,
A tree that may in summer wear
A nest of robins in her hair;
Upon whose bosom snow has lain;
Who intimately lives with rain.
Poems are made by fools like me,
But only God can make a tree.

It so happens that a few weeks ago, the family and I visited the Joyce Kilmer Memorial Forest, a patch of untouched arboreal splendor tucked so far up into the nether regions of Western North Carolina that

Sasquatch could set up his own meth lab with no interference.

In 1936, the Veterans of Foreign Wars dedicated these 3800 acres of virgin growth hardwood forest to the young poet, killed at 31 by a sniper's bullet when his battalion crossed France in World War 1.

I've passed on my treehugging ways to my children, and we frolicked amongst 100-ft tall yellow poplars with trunks so wide all four of us couldn't reach all the way around. Some of these trees are more than 400 years old, and we nestled in the bosom of the roots, not wanting to leave its intimate embrace.

If they could talk, they might have told us a tale of a time when every tree that died caused a certain sadness in the forest, another one of Providence's soldiers fallen.

Each one a beauty, every single one precious.

Sept. 4, 2012

Ain't No Cure for the Summertime Blues

It's a certain sign of insanity to argue with the weather. Nevertheless, I'm gonna raise a fuss, gonna raise a holler.

Sure, lots of places in the Northern Hemisphere are hot as the eleventy-third circle of hell right now. Mephistopheles' melting pavement grounded planes in Phoenix earlier this month, and it's so damn sunny in Philadelphia that it's posing ongoing threats to the poor and elderly. Entire swathes of California and Portugal are *literally on fire.*

But I do believe summer in Savannah is its own kind of special wretchedness. As the heat index crawls into the triple digits like a drunk triathlete determined to cross the finish line, ol' Auntie Humidity is fixing to smother us in her fetid, batwing embrace. I mean, the trees are sweating, y'all. It might be a hallucination from exiting my air-conditioned cubicle too quickly, but I swear I just saw a squirrel shlepping a tiny bag of ice from the gas station.

Fortunately, there are plenty of cheap and easy ways to cool off our molten cores, such as a visit to the pristine Daffin Park Public Pool or a Pelican's Snoball bought with change scoured between the couch cushions.

But the extreme heat can take its toll on the soul. Depression rates this time of year rival those of winter, probably from all that Netflix bingeing in dark rooms. As we've already experienced, violent crime spikes during the summer months. There's also low-grade apathy brought on by the constant vexation of getting all dolled up to go out on the town, only to have one's eyebrows melt off on the way to the car.

'Tis the season of our discontent, my perspiry friends. And while there ain't no cure for the summertime blues, I humbly offer some coping skills:

Stop denying it. This isn't about the "there's no such thing as climate change" loonies; they're a lost cause who will suffocate sooner than the rest of us in their bad suits and long ties.

No, I'm talking about the bizarre, enduring romanticism about how the South is "sultraaay," as the middle school leading lady in a Tennessee Williams play might say. But no cat is stupid enough to hang out on a hot tin roof, so let's dispense with the myth that anything sexy is going on here.

Heretofore until fall, the only acceptable descriptors for the weather must involve the word "moist" or metaphors about your grandpa's wet socks. Or my most favorite, "like walking into an open mouth."

Also, anyone who uses the term "hot as balls" never wore a pair of Spanx to an oyster roast.

Succumb to the social awkwardness. We Savannahians are an affectionate lot, very smoochy. Kind of like Parisians, only instead of a series of slight brushes on the cheek, we use our entire bodies. Rather than duck the love and risk hurting someone's feelings, just accept the fact that you are going to be wiped in other people's sweat. It's why we drink.

On a related note, the heat makes the synapses extra soft when coupled with cocktails, so can we all just forgive each other for not remembering each other's names? I would propose that we all start wearing nametags, or maybe little blackboards on lanyards that could double as protest signs, but we'd never remember to wear them anyway.

Instead, let's just stick to saying "good to see ya," that ubiquitous and useful phrase employed by generations of Savannahians who know full well that it's impossible to recall every single person we meet in our friendly little city. This charming little shibboleth—coupled with a sudor-soaked shoulder squeeze—conveys, "I may or may not have made your acquaintance at another time but I was too toasted to remember, but hey, you're all right."

Let's talk about bugs, baby. Even if the temperature dips down into something tolerable, the pests of summer will ensure that we're perennially miserable. From the halo of gnats oscillating around our heads to terrorist roaches big enough to carry off a Styrofoam clamshell, "buggy" ought to be considered an official meteorological term by the National Weather Service. The only thing worse than being tortured by the screeching cicada cacophony is having one of these monstrous creatures buzz into your hair.

The mosquitos this year are downright dangerous with their Zika juice and West Nile nastiness, but I do welcome the beautiful swallowtails, iridescent dragonflies and other essential pollinators flitting about. (Speaking of which, Chatham County Mosquito Control still needs to work on notifying beekeeping residents of upcoming flyover sprays—I have heard multiple complaints this week that Wilmington Island folks were not contacted in spite of being on the call list, resulting in a bunch of dead hives. What a buzzkill.)

Personally, I prefer not to lather myself in DEET or other poison. Instead, I've been experimenting with making myself unpalatable to bugs from the inside out by ingesting large amounts of garlic, preferably in the form of hummus from Al-Salaam Deli and a lot of martinis with extra stuffed olives.

I can't tell if it's working on the bugs thus far, but it does have the side effect of repelling people, which means less sticky hugs from strangers.

Don't let the summertime badness get you down. Living in this place, in these times, is not for the faint of heart or weak of constitution. It's tempting to isolate ourselves with our screens in the safety of our air-conditioned boxes, but then we miss out on all that unique Savannah perspicacity—and perspiration—that gives us common ground.

It's hot outside, but that's where the good people gather, under the oaks, on the park benches, along the shore. So grab a fan and step into the maw of mid-summer: As local songtresses Natasha Drena and JJ Collins sang recently at the truly terrific Key Change Cabaret, "the sun is shining, come on get happy"—someone is surely waiting to take your hand.

Or at the very least, catch you up in a sweaty embrace and say "good to see ya."

July 26, 2017

The Hour of Flower Power is Upon Us

Spring has sprung forward and I'm waiting in my front yard. The air holds a vague promise of the months of warmth to come, but this morning it still stings cold, and I tuck my cheeks into the collar of my jacket.

It's common for me to stand vigil in front of my house so I can shake my fist at drivers peeling past at unacceptable speeds. But today, I'm not minding the street, only the line of dark green shrubs underneath the living room window.

These bushes, festooned with tightly-spiraled buds, are about to transform my yard into a magical wonderland of color. I'm determined to witness the exact moment these buds, sleeping like hundreds of tiny baby dolls, hear the clarion call sent silently through roots and stems that signals them to swivel open and show their faces to the world.

It happens every year in Savannah: One day everything is ho-hum green, and the next morning it's pinks and reds and purples and white in every yard, down every block, along every square—like heaven had a pep rally while we were sleeping and forgot to clean up the confetti.

I grew up in the concrete suburbs of Arizona, a place where stunning displays of color come not from foliage but from light dancing upon red clay cliffs and fuchsia sunsets fueled by city smog and dust kicked up off the desert floor.

Medieval castles of cumulus clouds are set ablaze on certain late afternoons, bathing the basins of land in apocalyptic orange. When I sang about "purple mountain majesties" in elementary school, I was quite sure Katherine Lee Bates, the lyricist who wrote "America the Beautiful," had the spikes of Superstition range in mind.

In my 20s, I wandered into the redwoods north of San Francisco and was bowled over by the vibrant greens of the rolling hills and varied browns of Muir Woods. For most of the year, the Bay Area's famous fog would not so much tiptoe in on little cat feet as it would drape a silvery blanket over the landscape, crisping the hues of the forests until it made my eyes hurt. Until I saw it juxtaposed against the loamy dark soil and feathery ferns, I'd never understood that gray was actually a color.

Yet none of this prepared me for the red and pink riot of spring in Savannah.

"Azaleashock" best describes the dizziness brought on by witnessing so many blossoms at once. Swoon-worthy clusters of cotton candy pink and seashell coral, tufts of grape purple and lipstick red to die for. In the morning light, the spectacle appears almost supernatural, especially when it's set off by the sheen of golden yellow pollen powdering everyone's windshield.

After transplanting from one coast to the other, I was deep in the throes of my first azalea stupor when we first walked up to a non-descript brick Midtown ranch with a "For Sale" sign. Our realtor didn't try to hide her impatience; she was already sure I'd reject this one as I had the hundred or so others we'd traipsed through in the last few months. She didn't bother to hang up her cell phone as she unlocked the front door to wave us in.

While my husband crossed the threshold onto hardwood floors and an open layout, I lagged behind in the yard, which was shimmering on all sides with pink and red and white flowers, not just with azaleas, but saucer-sized camellias and loppy-eared tulip magnolias.

Next door and across the street, more colors radiated in front of every house all the way down on the block. It was the remodeled kitchen with its granite countertops that clinched Mark's decision; my mind was already made up before I walked in the door.

By the time we moved in, the yard had receded back into an unremarkable greenness to sleep for another year, but I knew what the next spring held. We experiment with different mulch combinations and feed our shrubbery throughout the seasons, rewarded each spring with a few weeks of glorious blooms. During this time my Facebook page is filled with photos of close-ups and wide views, the antics and accomplishments of the children and the dog ignored until the last wilted angel drops.

Even after multiple seasons, my Azaleamania continues unabated. Judging from the online action on the subject of the South's azaleas, I know I'm in good company. When I cruise down the column of color on the main drag of Abercorn between Victory Drive and Derenne Avenue, I still stick my head out the window like a wind-hungry Labrador, lapping up the view.

So that's why you'll see my back if you drive through my neighborhood this week, even if you're peeling through far above the speed limit. That's me, sitting on the winter-fried grass in front of my shrubs like an anxious father on prom night.

Azalea season is almost here and it's only a few weeks long. I don't want to miss a single minute.

Mar. 17, 2011

A River Runs Through Us

Depending on where you're standing, we either live in a bucolic aquatic paradise or a post-apocalyptic industrial wasteland.

If you happen to be standing in a certain section of the Savannah River, you don't even need to move your feet to change your view: All you have to do is turn your head.

I experienced this dizzying paradox last week when I hitched a ride with Capt. Mike Neal, who spends his days ferrying folks around local watery nooks and crannies to ogle dolphins and see the sights. It made sense that I'd run into him at the recent Savannah Riverkeeper's Pick 'n' Pinch fundraiser over a mess of crawfish. I'd mentioned to him I'd never seen the back side of the port or its surrounding industry. Three days later, I was standing at a boat ramp in Port Wentworth, barely a mile upriver from the Port of Savannah.

I was wondering doubtfully just exactly how Capt. Neal's *Island Adventure* barge was going to possibly pass under the water-level Houlihan Bridge when suddenly the green metal scaffold swung around like a lazy susan, opening passages on either side. Tech nerds will appreciate that the Georgia Dept. of Transportation constructed this neat trick of engineering way back in 1922, and the historic passage to South Carolina remains only one of two swing-span bridges still operating in the state.

The boat chugged through and pulled up along the dock for me. At the captain's behest, I was crashing a private tour of newish Landings residents who had spent the chilly morning tooling around the pretty tributaries of the Little Back and Middle rivers. They welcomed me aboard with shivery hellos and a bag of pretzels, and soon we were chugging down the main channel.

The view got bipolar fast.

On our left, the Savannah Wildlife Refuge rolled by against a canvas of clouds. I watched a snowy egret alight on a patch of golden marsh, a thick green curtain of oaks and pines behind it.

Off to my right, something flickered in my peripheral vision. A split second later, I was goggling at a rusty collection of squat tanks and metal towers reflecting the sunlight. Before I could ask, the unmistakable stench of sulfur wafted into the boat, identifying this as the Weyerhaeuser plant, the first of two paper mills along this section of the river. Old-timers used to call the foul odor "the smell of money."

One of the Landings ladies, new enough to town to have thus far avoided those occasional early morning inhales that taste like a week-old hot dog, professed shock at the outright noxiousness.

"Oh, that's nothing!" Capt. Mike laughed. "It used to eat the paint off your car!"

True, air emissions and water effluent have drastically improved since Ralph Nader's Raiders came to town in the late 1960's to expose the hideous polluting practices of Union Camp—the other paper mill further downstream now known as International Paper. Their findings were chronicled in a 1970 book, *The Water Lords* (a fascinating read; go ask The Book Lady to track down a copy) in which author James M. Fallows used the term "aquatic slum" to describe the Savannah River of mid-20th century.

The book inspired radical environmental legislation that prohibited industry from using the river as a giant toilet, and International Paper has theoretically cleaned up its act. From the back, it still looks like an abandoned mental hospital.

Here in the 21st century, the factory also continues to gulp more freshwater out of the Floridan Aquifer than any other regional entity, leaving the City of Savannah and its denizens to draw the majority of its drinking water out of the increasingly salty Savannah River.

"And here we have the Kraft Plant, named one of the top ten polluters in the U.S.," announced Capt. Mike cheerfully as we passed the ominous black hills of Georgia Power's on-demand coal-burning facility. This behemoth was followed shortly by the sinister, singed cylinders of Dixie Sugar, where an explosion killed 14 workers and injured 42 in 2008.

I sighed and turned back to the left bank of the river to admire a cluster of live oaks on a high bluff. If I breathed through my mouth and squinted my eyes just so, it almost felt like we were cruising near uninhabited Wassaw Island. How can the Savannah River swallow more than five million pounds of toxic discharge a year and yet still be so breathtaking beautiful?

"It's always been a river of contrasts," ruefully explains Savannah Riverkeeper Tonya Bonitatibus of the 400-mile flow once known as the Westabou by the area's long-gone native inhabitants.

While the SRK has a small and growing presence in Savannah, the Riverkeepers' operations are based in Augusta, the midpoint between the river's headwaters in North Carolina and its downstream denouement, which is right here in River City.

Bonitatibus grew up fishing and boating on Lake Hartwell, where Georgia's Tugaloo River and South Carolina's Seneca River comingle to become the border between the two states.

"The first couple of hundred miles, the main use of the river is recreation, some of the most gorgeous places you've ever seen," she says. "Once you get into Augusta, though, it becomes an industrial workhorse."

It's a long river with 99 problems, but a lack of drainage ditches ain't one. There are 48 municipal and industrial outfalls into the river between Augusta and Savannah, spewing a soup of chemical, biological and nuclear wastes—treated, of course, but not anything you'd want to take a bath in. Many of those entities also suck water out of the river, including Plant Vogtle, which will consume around 86 million gallons *per day* when two new reactors come online (The project has been beset by multiple delays and a ballooning budget, and now that South Carolina has suspended its nuclear power efforts, it's anyone's guess what Georgia Power will do.)

It's a clear truth that the "assimilative capacity"—the river's ability to renew and clean itself—was sold out to industry many decades ago, as was its winding route. In the late 1950s, the U.S. Corps of Engineers straightened the river, cutting through its bends to ease shipping transport between Savannah and Augusta. It shortened the natural path of the river by 78 miles and destroyed countless habitats. Demand for water traffic between the two cities dried up by 1980, and the project is now lamented as another one of those expensive, short-sighted, inefficient, privately-lobbied, publically-paid-for infrastructure projects that seem to plague the Savannah River. (We'll get to another expensive, short-sighted, badly planned infrastructure project in a bit.)

"There's been a very orchestrated, conscious decision among the powers that be to turn the population away from the river," says Bonitatibus.

After years of mispronouncing her name (it's Bon-i-TAT-ti-bus), I finally had the chance to meet Tonya at the same SRK Pick 'n' Pinch at Hogan's Marina with Capt. Mike. It was a well-intentioned but woefully under-attended event, given the relevance of the river's health to our quality of life. More than a few folks lamented how much support the Ogeechee Riverkeeper garnered after the 2010 fishkill and the subsequent lawsuit against King America Finishing.

Not that they begrudge ORK's success in the least: Many folks belong to both organizations and cheer the victory that resulted in vigilant water testing and cooperation between the Ogeechee Riverkeeper and the textile plant's new owners, Milliken & Co. (Mark and I recently spent a gorgeous afternoon kayaking and fishing on the Ogeechee and can attest to its pristine glory. And yes, we ate the fat spotted bass he reeled in.)

But the question remains: Why doesn't the same enthusiasm for saving the Savannah blow up balloons around here?

"I think it's much easier for people to wrap their minds around the Ogeechee," muses Bonitatibus. "There's only the one industry, and people in Savannah know it more as a place where people fish and recreate. Whereas the Savannah, people here can't imagine it as anything *other* than industrial."

Definitely, most of us would rather skinny dip at the sewage plant than swim in the Savannah River. However, we all do plenty of recreating on Tybee Island, which we conveniently pretend is not at the mouth of the third most toxic river in the nation but some isolated beach on another planet. (This delusion is clearly helped along by copious amounts of beer.)

What might help the cause is breaking up the vigilance of the river into two sections: SRK plans to open a Savannah office to address the issues threatening the lower river, namely the Savannah Harbor Expansion Project (SHEP), the latest in the line of tax-payer-funded, Corps of Engineer-managed, privately-built projects that may just be the blade of marsh straw that collapses its ecological back.

I know. You're all "when is this woman gonna quit snarkering about the gawddang harbor deepening? It's happening! Let it go already!"

Well, I can't. I'm like the guy standing in front of the tanks in Tiananmen Square, only picture me floating in the way of one those post-Panamax ships wearing water wings and one of those stripey old-fashioned bathing suits.

Yes, SHEP is inevitable. But other parties have persistently pointed out the follies of the project—addressed in mitigative caveats that now make up more than half its total $703 million price tag. (Interestingly enough, part of the settlement in the lawsuit that SRK and the Southern Environmental Law Center filed against the Corps in 2012 includes funding to restore the original meanderings of the river that were mangled in the 1950s.)

The Georgia Ports Authority began shoveling in the outer harbor 2016 (see that giant crane from the beach, kids?) but the Big Dig cannot continue into the port until someone proves that the Hubba Bubblers designed to reoxgenate the depleted channel are going to work.

Oops, we're not supposed to call them "bubblers" anymore:

"Since the dissolved oxygen injection system, also known as Speece cones, does not create bubbles, referring to them as 'bubblers' is an error-in-fact and creates a false concept for readers," U.S. Corps of Engineers spokesperson Billy Birdwell gently chastised in an email.

The last thing I'm here to do is create false concepts; the facts kind of speak for themselves, no? The Corps own report shows how the harbor deepening ostensibly increases the economic viability of the port by putting the ecological sustainability of the river on life support. *[Note, 2017: With the advent of the Trump administration, federal money for SHEP has still not materialized.]*

Even without SHEP, the Savannah River might not survive the next decade anyway. Bonitatibus calls it "death by a thousand cuts":

Near Augusta, Georgia Power currently muscles more than 43 million gallons a day out of the river for nuclear Plant Vogtle, and the Georgia Assembly gave its blessing last week to double that amount for the two new reactors. A few miles away, the Savannah River Site leaks radioactive waste into the groundwater while the EPD examines its fingernails.

Down on our end, saltwater intrusion already creeps further upriver every year, evident in lines of ash-gray dead trees. Southern LNG recently received began construction to export liquid natural gas from Elba Island, which means twice as much LNG moving along the river. While a proposal to truck LNG through the city was roundly rejected in 2012, the company won't discount trying again in the future. Frack *that.*

I appreciate the necessity of industry, I promise. But I have to ask the question that must occur to anyone who loves where they live and work and can't bear to see it exploited; the Appalachian farmer whose fields are sludge because the mountain above was blown up for coal, the Masai warrior watching his ancestral lands usurped by Arab businessmen, the Peruvian tribesman forced out of the rainforest by loggers.

Why must profits exist only at the expense of the resources we're all entitled to share?

As if on cue, Capt. Mike brought us face-to-stern with the mythical monster of a post-Panamax ship. He explained that the big ships have already been calling on the port even without the harbor deepening, albeit lightly weighted.

Y'all, it was huge. Stacked 20 stories high with containers of every shade, it's hard to imagine what it would look like fully loaded. Even harder to predict what life on the river will be like once they're passing through every week.

"It's going to be 20 years before we know the real economic and environmental effects," said the captain, the brontosaurus necks of the port cranes on one side of him juxtaposed with the green bluffs of the wildlife refuge on the other.

The mood was thoughtful as we drifted under the double fans of the Talmadge Bridge, and the warehouses that were the site of last winter's tire fire gave way to the charms of River Street.

As the captain's barge steered a U-turn, I looked out towards the direction of the sea, trying to reconcile the foul tangle at my back with the beauty that lay just beyond.

I guess the reason why I can't quit hollerin' about saving this river is because it's so worth it: The dolphins leaping out of Lazaretto Creek at sunset. The shrimp boats hauling in the day's catch that still tastes marvelously (miraculously?) delicious. The serenity of the wildlife refuge, where ospreys soar above the tree line and the fragile tidal marsh supports an irreplaceable web of life.

Maybe it's not too late to make a U-turn on the fate of the Savannah River. It would mean a concerted effort to stand up to the wall of polluters along the banks, demand equitable use, and, while we're at it, insist on a fair cut to Savannah from every one of those giant ships that comes to call. It would mean the EPD doing its job, issuing permits and enforcing them.

But none of that will ever happen without the passion and persistence of those of us who live at the end of the line.

Dec. 14, 2014

The Zen of Pollen

It always sneaks up on me: One day, the evenings are chilly and dark; the next, sunlight floods the kitchen as we're clearing the dinner dishes.

Everything else seems to have gotten the memo. The daffodils have been bursting out their yellow trumpets for weeks. The azaleas are gleefully fulfilling their annual chromatic spectacle. Cardinals and bluebirds whistle and flirt from dawn 'til dusk.

To quote the mystical Bohemian scribe Rainer Maria Rilke, "it is spring again, and the earth is like a child that knows this poem by heart."

Unfortunately for us humans, Daylight Savings makes the turning of the season feel less like a gentle nudge by a beneficent Mother Nature than a sharp bludgeoning about the head by the Hound in *Game of Thrones*. Add in the shimmer of golden pollen coating our cars and nasal passages, and the epic majesty going on outside could be entirely obscured by spring cleaning and snot bubbles.

For me, the Spring Equinox also brings on an inner anxiety. Not only does it mark the unsympathetic march towards another sweaty southern summer, it's a reminder of life's inescapable ephemerality.

I don't need any more reminding, what with my children sprouting into full-grown people and another set of tires going bald. Frankly, I could use a nice coping shot of denial, but that only increases suffering. Or so I've heard.

"Let go of your attachments," counsel the Buddhist sages, making me clutch my daughter a little tighter. (I keep trying to sit on her head so she'll stop growing so fast, but she's a biter.) There are books full of the wisdom from these bodhisattvas, some ancient, some working for the enlightenment of all beings via their own YouTube channls.

"Make friends with impermanence," enjoin the wise ones, presumably inhaling deeply through their clear nostrils.

Please. No matter how much I'd like to party with impermanence or meditate on the noble truths, I remain hopelessly attached to people and my iPhone and the belief that I will be shopping in the juniors department forever.

Still, I sense that embracing non-attachment—or even just giving it an air kiss once in a while—is the path to a serene and fulfilled life. (Barring the always-imminent possibility of winning the lottery and buying my own Polynesian island.)

I had the opportunity to observe non-attachment in action a few weeks ago, when the monks of the Drepung Loseling Monastery came through Savannah to create a sacred Tibetan sand mandala. As part of their effort to bring their gentle teachings to the world, these serene robed ones tour from city to city, sprinkling colored sand into a circle of intricate symbols in a breathtaking combination of performance art and spiritual divination.

But anyone who saw these fellows doing their thing at the Jepson Center for the Arts a few years back may recall that things do not end well for the mandala.

This time, however, only a handful of people were there to watch its demise as the monks hovered above their artistic mastery. Gary and Greg Butch of Elizabeth's on 37th occasionally host these low-key rituals in their famed restaurant to help raise awareness and funds for the displaced Tibetan monks and their leader, His Holiness the Dalai Lama, a cause that the brothers have been quietly supporting for more than a decade. They were nominated for a Nobel Peace Prize in 2012 for their efforts, though they are quick to duck any recognition, standing unobtrusively in the back of the small room where the monks prepared the mandala's closing ceremony.

The air almost crackled as the seven monks filed in, clad in their signature saffron and maroon garments and identical pairs of plain brown oxford shoes. The mandala itself—the product of hours upon hours of work—sat on a square wooden table, its small piles of colored sand precisely carefully tapped out into lotus flowers, complex knots and the eight-spoked wheel representing the path of the Buddha.

Each mandala is created with a particular intention, this one meant to draw the universal compassion of the Green Tara, the Sanskrit goddess of salvation. (Green Tara also governs earthly cycles, so I think we can hold her responsible for the pollen.)

Donning enormous fringed yellow hats, a couple of monks lifted cymbals and drums, while others unfurled a pair of telescoping horns that looked like giant versions of the daffodils blooming in the front garden. One monk began to chant in a deep glottal tone that reverberated off the walls: *Om mani padme hum*. The others joined him in the mantra: *Om mani padme hum Om mani padme hum*, a sonorous symphony of meditative devotion.

Just when I thought I might levitate with the vibration, the chanting stopped. In the sudden silence, one of the monks smiled and bowed, walked over to the mandala and calmly shoved a knuckle into its perfect beauty. With a little broom, he methodically swept every last grain into a spiral-shaped pile, giving as much deliberation to the destruction of this labor of lovingkindness as to its creation.

It was at once humbling and liberating to witness, a visceral lesson that though our efforts at immortality are hopeless, they are inextricably part of the grand cycles of birth and death, growth and decline.

I hope to remember it the next time three days' worth of writing disappears into the void of my MacBook.

I left Elizabeth's with a tiny souvenir packet of the mixed-up mandala sand in my pocket, a little less attached to my own gerbil-wheel need to wring my hands over another season. Life will happen no matter what, and it'll be over before we know it. May as well smell the flowers than curse the darkness, or something like that.

I walked out into this unbelievably opulent spring, where—to quote Mr. Rilke again—everything was blooming most recklessly.

With an open palm, I wiped off my windshield, smiling at the yellow handprints I left on everything I touched.

March 20, 2013

The Crape Myrtle Murders

I'm a treehugger. Literally.

This endearing sobriquet is usually bestowed upon those who love nature in general and is often used derisively by those attempting to belittle environmentalists.

In my case, however, I do in fact make a regular practice of throwing my arms around trees. See, working on a computer all day can give a person a rather disconnected feeling, and nothing grounds me like touching something that has actual roots. After a long day at the office with my head in the glowbox, I find pressing my cheek against the tulip magnolia in my front yard quite relaxing and far less ruinous than tequila.

I often venture onto my neighbors' lawn to run my hand along the scratchy bark of their stunning dogwood tree when I'm walking the dog. This often creates anxiety for the dog, who seems aghast with pug-eyed confusion as to why I'm embracing a toilet.

I'm not shy about goosing any sexy arboreal specimen I see—there's a certain live oak on 61st Street with one helluva trunk.

I definitely find crape myrtles particularly compelling. (Garden geeks know that there's a controversy over whether it's "crape" or "crepe," referring the crinkly edges of the flowers. I'm going with the American Horticultural Society Encyclopedia's spelling.) With their papery, mottled limbs and kaleidoscopic blooms, the members of *Lagerstroemia indica* invite a leaf-lovin' gal to cuddle up and stay awhile.

My affection for them forces me to raise the alarm of the heinous crime currently being committed against crape myrtles across the South. Every year around pruning time, well-meaning landscapers and homeowners hack these branched beauties back to the knuckles, leaving gnarled knobs that are totally unsuitable for hugging.

This hideous mutilation is also known as "crape murder" and it must be stopped.

I bet you think I made up that term up for dramatic flair. Which is understandable. But crape murder is a real term, employed by professional arborists and Master Gardeners.

"It's awful," bemoans Master Gardener, former Savannah Tree Foundation President and crape murder expert Diane Houston. "Everywhere you go there are these ugly stubs all over the place. People think they're doing the right thing, but there's nothing right about it."

I called Patrick Grant of Certified Arborist Services to find out why people are so cruel to their crape myrtles. He sighed with resignation.

"People do it because it makes them flower like crazy, but they're doing so because the tree is reacting to a catastrophic wound," he explained. "It's a pruning technique called 'pollarding' but it's very difficult to do right."

Most people don't do it right, cutting below the previous year's gash and significantly shortening the tree's life. Grant points out that there are crape myrtles in Savannah over 150 years old, but one won't even live half that long if it's maintained with the skills of a drunk Edward Scissorhands.

Bill Haws, a Forestry Administrator for the City of Savannah, sees mutilated crape myrtles all over town that look like they've been pollarded by a toddler with a chainsaw.

"It some cases it's been done for decades, and those trees inevitably end up with pockets of decay," reports Haws. "It also makes the tree more prone to limb breakage with the storms we get."

To stimulate blooms without ruining tree structure, Haws recommends "deadheading" them—simply clipping out seed pods at the ends of branches. If you see a crape myrtle or any other variety of tree that needs attention on any of the 350 miles of public sidewalk lawns around the city, do not, I repeat, DO NOT take a machete into your own hands—call 311 so Haws and his team give it some appropriate TLC.

Houston thinks it's a combination of ignorance and peer pressure that's made this seasonal slaughter so widespread. Landscape professionals and property owners lop off limbs all over town and neighbors unwittingly follow suit, not understanding that while respectful pruning of crossing or dead limbs is warranted, full-on amputation is wholly unnecessary.

"Crape myrtles bloom on new wood, so they're going to bloom whether you cut them or not," pleads Houston. "We have a lot of educating to do."

She adds that some people murder their crape myrtles because they've grown too big for the space. Grant, Houston and Haws agree that in many cases, it's preferable just to cut the whole darn tree down and start over with a more appropriately-sized variety. There are dozens, from dwarves that only grow to two feet to mammoths soaring 30 feet into the sky.

So please, people, put down the saws. Call your landscape company. Demand an end to the senseless butchery of innocent trees.

That way, when you go out to your neighborhood crape myrtle for a quick squeeze, its arms might just be long enough to hug you back.

Feb, 28, 2012

Hurricane Watch: Should We Stay Or Should We Go?

A week ago, when Hurricane Matthew was still just a swirling blob over the Atlantic, some of you knew exactly what to do.

Those with clear means and ways took the cue from South Carolina to gas up and start packing. Others started securing their perimeters, coolly making a run for batteries, beer and extra toilet paper while nailing down the shutters.

The rest of us vacillated in a sine curve of indecision, trying to suss out the best situation for ourselves, given the unpredictability of this 500-mile wide monster. It lumbered slowly but evasively, like the injured roach you chase all over the kitchen that still manages to slip under the fridge.

Should we stay or should we go? we sang with a half-hearted shimmy, stoked to have a true punk reason to invoke The Clash but also seriously conflicted in our adulting.

If we go there will be trouble, the very least of which might include hotels we can't afford, valuables left behind and being stuck for 18 hours on the highway with a farting dog.

But if we stay there could be double, as in power outages, food shortages, mass destruction and possibly worse.

Some of us got caught in a roiling eddy of ADD and OCD as Matthew churned towards the Bahamas. We packed suitcases and filled up the bathtub. We cleaned out the Red & White of sardines and Gatorade, then fell asleep in the hallway while putting all the photo albums in plastic tubs. Conversations went in circles. Maybe they went something like this:

Spouse #1, glued to weather app: This is going to hit us hard. We should leave.

Spouse #2: OK. Where do we go?

Spouse #1: Oh, I'm not going anywhere.

Spouse #2: Uh, what.

Spouse #1: You take the kids. I need to protect the house and business.

Spouse #2: With what, a BB gun and a golf umbrella? No way, we're sticking together.

Spouse #1: Hurricanes don't really hit Savannah anyway.

Spouse #2: So we're staying?

Spouse #1: I didn't say that.

Spouse #2: I'll be over here, stress eating all the ice cream.

County and state officials seemed stymied as well, issuing partial evacuations for the islands but hedging a full out mandatory evacuation for the Georgia Coast, even as photos of heartbreaking devastation in Haiti emerged. We looked to the dataheads for assurance, especially the analysis of local Enki Research. We pored over the meteorological data and radar rainbows, trying to pinpoint ourselves in the Cone of Uncertainty.

Flummoxed by the thought of merging with several hundred thousand drivers who can't even handle coming off the Truman at rush hour, we remained in flux. The conditions worsened by the hour, devolving into a state of useless inebriation heretofore known as "Hurricane Brain."

Spouse #1: What do you want to do?

Spouse #2: I don't know. What do you want to do?

Spouse #1: We sound like the vultures from *The Jungle Book*. *[dancing around like a bird]* I dunno, whatchu wanna doo? I dunno, whatCHU—

Spouse #2: Your British accent is awful and I want to slap you.

**Blink at each other for ten seconds then repeat until a friend sends a photo of*

$5 hurricane cocktails at Cotton & Rye.

Spouse #2: I'll be over here, collecting tiny paper umbrellas.

The truth is, leaving home as disaster bears down is one of the hardest calls any of us will ever have to make. Even if all we really own is some nice paintings, garage sale dinner plates and a Rooms to Go couch, our houses are our nests and our refuge. Abandoning them to the elements—both natural and human—feels like giving up everything we cherish.

As Matthew buzzsawed Cuba and headed for Florida, plenty of seasoned storm watchers decided that Matthew might rattle the windows and down a few trees, but wouldn't be bad enough to bail. Others dug in for logistical and financial reasons, though transportation and provisions were ostensibly in place for my disabled neighbors, others with special needs and the homeless.

Some didn't have a choice. The brave men and women who serve as our firefighters, police, doctors, nurses, hospital administrators and government staff sent their families off to safety and squared up, enduring poor planning by upper management (most had to provide their own food) and the unnecessary shenanigans of assholes who just stuck around to party.

Finally, CEMA announced evacuation orders, which was our family's tipping point.

We got on the road without a clear destination, since every pet-friendly hotel, VRBO and Airbnb within a 200-mile radius was already booked. We pulled onto Highway 17, following South Carolina's official evacuation route via Augusta. It was shockingly empty, probably because our neighbors to the north had a day and half head start.

Spouse #1: Whelp. Any suggestions for this evacu-cation?

Kid #1: Can we go to Harry Potter World?

Kid #2: It apparated to Canada for the hurricane, stupid.

Spouse #2: Canada! Maybe Justin Trudeau will take us in. *[swoons]*

Sobered by the suffering in Haiti, Syria and that of the other 65 million refugees around the world fleeing bombs and starvation and torture, we couldn't even pretend to relate. I mean, no matter where we ended up, no one was going to spit on us and call us rapists and terrorists. Unless we got lost in the swamps with a Bernie sticker on the back of the Subaru.

We were unbelievably fortunate that friends Jay Winner and Nancy Wallace offered up their place in western North Carolina, where we gathered in a sports bar with other climate exiles from as far away as Florida. Tethered by digital clouds as Matthew's began to sweep water onto the Georgia coast, we spent Friday night and the wee hours of Saturday riveted by the Weather Channel and the drunken ribaldry of locals Jeremy Ribardy and Steve Todd from a Tybee Island parking garage.

The next day brought a stream of soft disaster porn, from downed pines knifing through roofs and broken grandmother oaks in Forsyth Park to docks swept away and flooded living rooms. Our buddy Tommy Holland's morning cruise down our block revealed that our house came through intact, though the neighbors three doors down now have a patio instead of a porch.

Some who dug in slept through the wind and rain; others were shaken and terrified. Though most avoided the worst of it, there was also news of terrible loss, including the tragic death of Isle of Hope's Jefferson Davis, a young father who'd stayed behind. Several denizens of the Presidents Street homeless camp are still missing.

As of this writing, the city is back open, though mostly without electricity. Some have rushed back, others are heeding the pleas of first responders and Georgia Power to stay the hell out of the way while they do their jobs.

The miracle of connectivity is showing us myriad stories of kindness and cooperation, but also revealing tension between the "stayers" and "goers," a disturbing and unnecessary rift for a community that must rebuild together. As I watched from afar as friends in town rushed to each other's aid and comfort, I will admit I felt a tiny bit envious of their shared experience of surviving the eye of the storm.

But looking at my spouse and the children and the dog sleeping safely on a borrowed couch, I have no regrets.

Oct. 12, 2016

7 ARTSY SMARTSY

Art and how to make a living at it has long been one of Savannah's most important objectives, evidenced by the pair of muses named "Art" and "Commerce" perched atop of City Hall. Starting in the 1970s, the Savannah College of Art and Design began preserving and transforming the city's aesthetic, launching the careers of legions of painters, sculptors, and multimedia artists, some of who even pay their rent with their work. In bigger cities, where there's art, there's prosperity, and a small-but-mighty public art movement continues the fight to color up the walls in the name of economic and cultural progress. While most artists still need to keep their day jobs around here, their work has found purchase in local iterations of the international phenomenon of Slideluck and the Moth's Unchained Bus tour—though it's clear that the city's muses haven't found a balance just yet.

Breakfast at Tiffani's

Like a lot of people in this eclectic little town, I'm an art groupie.

I worship at the paint-stained feet of Betsy Cain, Jerome Meadows, Katherine Sandoz, Matt Hebermehl, Adolfo Alvarado, Melinda Borysevicz, Tobia Makover, Troy Wandzel, Maggie Hayes and every other brilliant local who has hung work at Kobo Gallery or the walls of Gallery Espresso or just a random wall outside. I want to carry their canvases and clean up their messes and fill my house from floor to ceiling with their abstract marshscapes and ghostly portraits and urban swirls.

Oh yes, I heart Savannah artists. But Tiffani Taylor was my first.

One spring day in the early 2000s, when I was still just another tourist traipsing along Bull Street ogling the Spanish moss and the gold cornices on the Scottish Rite Temple, I found myself loitering in front of ShopSCAD. A huge canvas of red poppies hung in the window. The more I looked, the more I saw, bits of poetry and paper doll heads and gold drips and muddy smears. I fell in.

Forty-five minutes later I was still standing there. The only other time I had the experience of being so captivated by a painting that I wanted to live inside it was Magritte's *Son of Man*, but only because that apple looked so goddamned delicious.

When I moved to Savannah and landed a job as the editor of the now-defunct *skirt!* magazine, Tiffani was the first person I sought out to interview. The valedictorian of the 2002 SCAD graduating class then painted in a tiny bedroom, struggling to pay bills with mural commissions as collectors and curators were starting to take notice of her layered floral landscapes. We talked about her impoverished childhood in rural Utah, where she learned how to find acceptance and love in what was blooming in the fields and forests.

"Nature is my cathedral," she told me back then, showing me a handful of dirt that she would later rub into a future canvas.

Candlewax, coffee grounds, old sheet music and even food stamps peeked out from beneath the delicate flowers and gold-flecked sparrows (yeah, Tiffani was putting a bird on it before it was a thing.) Hers is an alchemy that combines femininity and grit, bridging the relationship between authenticity and happiness. Also, her work is just so, so pretty.

The feature I wrote was one of her first pieces of press, and there have been many dozens—hundreds!—since. Her artwork now hangs in private collections around the world.

I remained obsessed with those red poppies, decoupaging the refrigerator with cutouts photos of Tiffani's paintings until The Best Husband in the Whole World bought me a real one for my 40th birthday.

Nowadays, Tiffani's lovely countenance and philanthropic efforts (she donates paintings to women's charities and started a SCAD Scholarship Fund in 2009 to help other struggling students) have also attracted attention, as has her gentle support of young artists, taking interns under her wing and encouraging their visions.

"In the Renaissance, artists were nurtured and valued, and I think that's starting to happen again now," she told me recently. "The myth of the starving artist needs to die."

Inspired by Impressionist Claude Monet, who said "It's not everything to paint; you have to sell and live," Tiffani has also cultivated another elusive muse: Business acumen.

In 2012, she opened the Tiffani Taylor Gallery at the north end of Whitaker Street, a gloriously sunny and strategically shrewd spot to showcase her work. Longtime patrons visit after lunch at their favorite downtown restaurant. Tourists often wander in on their way to The Lady & Sons and leave with a small painting or a piece of hand-painted pottery.

Sometimes, when it's not enough to drink my tea next to the single poppy painting in my kitchen, I like to go over and sip in the glow of an entire wall of them. Tiffani and curator Arlene Kidd (who also happens to be her mama) don't seem to mind, even if I drop a few crumbs from my fig kolache from the Coffee Fox.

Her poppies have undeniable broad appeal, and Tiffani has been courted over recent years by companies who wanted to market her designs for bed, bath and beyond. But she has fought the temptation to turn a quick buck, instead protecting her copyrights like baby birds, waiting until she could put up the money herself.

The gallery's first anniversary coincides with the launch of the Tiffani Taylor Lifestyle Collection, an affordable array of pillows, pendants, coffee mugs, iPhone cases, purses, scarves and other charms that make it possible for everyone to own a piece of her art, even groupies of humble means.

"I am my own investor, and I'm so proud of that," Tiffani tells me as we set our poppy mugs down onto a pair of her bird coasters. "I needed to keep the integrity of it all, to preserve the drips and splatters and every word."

The line is available exclusively at the gallery and online, though there are whispers of big things in the works for Tiffani Taylor. For now, however, her motto is "infinite possibilities," a phrase that appears in her artwork as well in conversation.

"Anything can happen," she shrugs with a smile when I suggest that her poppies might become as iconic as Van Gogh's *Starry Night.*

Did you know Van Gogh used to eat his own paint? Lead-based, which explains why he was so batscat crazy. He also died a pauper. The lesson there for artists and those who love them is don't snack on Cerulean blue, and don't be afraid to succeed.

Or as Tiffani puts it: "Art and business shouldn't be a dichotomy."

April 2, 2013

The Gospel of the "Muralcle" on 34th Street

In the beginning, there was a bare brick wall.

Then, the Voice of Creation—speaking through a bunch of local folk who like to paint stuff—said, "Let there be art!"

So the local painter folk sought blessings from the Powers That Be and made art on the wall where there once had been nothing.

Soon a majestic abstract marshscape swept across the concrete bricks, followed by a meadow of portraits blooming with a colorful cross section of city denizens.

Later, a gorgeous sea goddess rose from the cinderblock to preside over the empty lot at Habersham and 34th Streets in hues of teal and purple.The artists—along with the neighbors and the bureaucrats—saw that it was GOOD.

Sadly, as of last Thursday, it is GONE.

Baptized "The Muralcle at 34th Street" in February 2012 when it became the first legal public art mural in the history of the City of Savannah, the wall was sacrificed to the bulldozers of progress as the long-vacant edifice it adorned was demolished.

Locally-owned Enright Properties acquired the foreclosed-upon property from the bank last year, and the half-acre lot will soon house a mix of apartments and retail space on what for a couple of years served as sacred ground.

No amount of supplication could amount to a divine intervention. In a few deafening cracks, the beloved kaleidoscopic vista was leveled in a cloud of dust and asbestos.

"We would have liked to save the mural, but the building itself just isn't salvageable," contractor Joe Duckworth lamented apologetically as the Caterpillar's mighty claw tore through Adolfo Alvarado's oceanic deity to reveal a garage of rotted wood. "It just couldn't be helped."

For those who worship at public art's grand altar, the demolition felt like desecration. A small but devoted crowd came to the vacant lot to bear witness to the mural's crumble, many of whom had been there for the first swathes of paint. Some had sat in the summer sun for a chance to be immortalized within the latex layers.

Like pilgrims at Lourdes, we were somber but serene, hauling off the best bits of concrete as if handling holy relics.

"I brought my students out here just a few weeks ago to teach them about abstraction and design," mourned SCAD professor Heather Szatmary as she schlepped pieces of Katherine Sandoz's Turtle Island landscape. "They're going to be heartbroken."

Something of an artistic zealot myself, I waited solemnly for the piece of concrete to fall on which Troy Wandel painted my likeness in back in June 2012, hoping to lay it to rest in my garden among the precious plaques of my children's handprints.

When the brick threatened to dissolve under the claw's rough scrape, Richard Marlowe of Groundworks Unlimited stepped off the 'dozer to kindly chisel it away by hand. I think he recognized my righteous fealty, good man.

I might have broken out the hairshirt if the reluctant priest of this particular parish hadn't reminded everyone that there was really no need to be so damn fanatical.

Even as he conceived it back in 2011, artist/activist Matt Hebermehl had known that the wall might have to come down. The property's neglect was what made it prime art space in the first place, and the eventual transfer of ownership would mean its inevitable declension.

"This was the test case," shrugged Hebermehl as he maneuvered a wheelbarrow piled with blocks to the edge of the lot. "It was the petri dish where we found out what was possible. But a lot has happened since."

Preach, brother: In the two and a half years since he and SeeSAW cohort James "Dr. Z" Zdaniewski put on suits and ties and convinced City Hall to adopt a mural policy under the MPC's Site and Monument Commission, Savannah has seen several notable public art projects. Walls in Midtown, on MLK Blvd. and at the West Broad Y have hosted color and concept. SeeSAW's "Before I Die" crowdsourced blackboards weren't without controversy, but it is our city's mural that now graces Candy Chang's hardcover book out of dozens of others that participated in the project.

We can also be consoled that another mural might be resurrected from the rubble like Lazarus from the crypt. Enright Properties' Jeremy Graves has enthusiastically endorsed the idea of public art on the new complex, ideally on the side of the corner café planned for the site.

"I'd love to incorporate another mural once the project is finished," said Graves on the phone last week. "There's going to be a whole wall of masonry that would be perfect."

It's difficult to predict how new development will shape a neighborhood, and we can only pray that the Powers that Be give the same thoughtful consideration to high-density housing as they do to mural proposals.

Which reminds me: There are often spots available on the Site and Monument Commission, along with a whole host of other city board openings, including the MPC. If you have the spiritual strength to face the devil in the details of the city's future, go apply.

In the meantime, the faithful must remember that just because the mural is gone doesn't mean the miracle wasn't real.

The gospel of public art is now a sanctioned reality in Savannah—an egalitarian way to create conversations that can become the foundation of a community that values art and artists. Every wall is a chance for communion, but there's no need to express one's creative piety with blasphemous scrawls. We can venerate the Muralcle at 34th as a sacrificial lamb that makes way for a new testament.

"It just means we need to make more," grinned another ever-upbeat evangelist of the cause, Art Rise Savannah's's Clinton Edminster, as he carried off another brick.

I can't think of a better benediction.
Oct. 22, 2014

Feelin' Slidelucky? Well, are ya punk?

I have this recurring fantasy that one day all of the fascinating, creative, marvelous Savannahians I meet on this job will be at the same dinner party.

The artists and the activists will hobnob with the literati and the laugh riots, the din of so much spectacular conversation mingling with background tunes from local troubadours.

Everyone will bring something delicious to share, and after we've stuffed ourselves silly, we'll all settle in to look at some slides of cool art, possibly made by the same person who brought the wasabi artichoke dip. Suggested attire will be your favorite pair of comfy pants, and afterwards people will fake-argue over who gets to do the dishes.

I'd invite y'all over to my house, but my old yellow Formica table only seats eight. Plus, crowds make the guinea pig nervous.

But, guess what? We're in luck! More specifically, Slideluck:

The world's sexiest community potluck returns to Savannah this Thursday, ready to showcase local art and your homemade casseroles.

Pairing a crowdsourced meal with a carefully-curated selection of 2-3 minute slideshows, these non-profit events were first conceived in a Seattle living room in 2000. Slidelucks are now hosted in more than 85 cities around the world, and until recently were known as the Slideluck Potshow (still illegal in Georgia, but there's always next election cycle.)

The official goal of Slideluck is to "strengthen community through food and art." (As if there's a better way!)

Its secret mission, however, is to season Savannah's aesthetic cravings without spoiling anyone's appetite.

"We want to demystify the art experience," explains co-organizer Summer Teal Simpson. "This isn't a snooty gallery. People can look at art with their friends and not feel like they're supposed to say something about it. They can just like it, or not."

Apparently we like our art demystified around here, because the first Slideluck practically blasted the roof off the American Legion Post 135 ballroom back in January 2013. Summer and another of Savannah's most delightful and unpretentious arts patrons, Francis Allen, sifted through almost a hundred submissions and about as many types of pasta salad for the homegrown production.

They also had to turn away folks at the door, causing Slideluck Global to sit up and take notice. The international non-profit has been courting the Hostess City for another event ever since, but anyone who has checked the Sav Happs app lately knows we keep our dance cards pretty full.

"Savannah had such a strong showing, but it was such a huge undertaking," sighs Summer, who has volunteered fountains of blood, sweat and tears for tons of other excellent cultural happenings from the Stopover Festival to Fashion Night. Now with a steady gig at Focus Lab, she's had to pare down her extracurriculars but remains Slideluck's beneficent ringleader. "I've let almost everything else go, but this was my favorite thing I ever did."

Francis has his own Roots Up Gallery to run with his lovely Leslie Lovell, so Slideluck II has enlisted the aid of some of Savannah's other big brains, couched in its most fabulous shoes:

Socially Yours proprietor and Pintrest dominatrix Autumn Van Gunten has taken on production duties (the centerpieces are baby terrariums, *shut up*). Gallerist Jeanne Svendson returns with her essential aesthetic guidance, all while finalizing the last details of her wedding—just a tiny affair of a few hundred that takes place two days after Slideluck, no big deal.

Bree Halverson of Orange PR rounds out this formidable cadre of feminine superpower, sprinkling a gentle rain of publicity upon the fertile ground of Savannah's eager communitarians. While new to the creative coven, she's attended Slidelucks in other cities and expects we've got the recipe down.

"In New York, you're desperate to find community," muses Bree, a recovering Brooklynite. "In Savannah, it's here—it's just about finding a big enough space."

My point exactly! The Legion ballroom can hold 300 before the fire marshal starts grousing, so the popular Savannah practice of showing up an hour late for dinner might get you relegated to the foyer.

If potlucks strike the fear of marshmallow-flecked Jell-O in your belly, don't worry: Dept. 7 East's Meta Adler and Michele Jemison are bringing trays of their dreamy pimento cheese tea sandwiches, and there will be a fancy Savannah Bee Co. cheese and honey board. Save room for something ridiculously delicious for dessert from Natasha Gaskill's A-Squad Bake Shop. Other notable noshes will come from Flirt with Dessert, 22 Square and the Sentient Bean.

Foodie coordinator Shabnam Gideon admonishes y'all to arrive early, label your dish and serving utensil and take it all home with you at the end of the night—or you may find someone stirring their cocktail with your ladle when the Legion bar finally opens again after a fire toasted it earlier this year.

The supper serenade comes courtesy of the cool cats of Missionary Blues, and other local support comes from Blick Art Materials and the audio/visual aces at Kaufman & Heinz, whose gargantuan screens will ensure that this slideshow will be nothing like sitting through 150 fuzzy shots of my parents' 1979 trip to Greece.

As a reward for our tremendous togetherness, Slideluck Global is sending down 26 cases of beer from Brooklyn Brewery for this 21+ event. Hello, free beer? Not even part of my original fantasy, but sometimes you don't even know what you want until it shows up.

But the finest fare of the evening will be the art, served up sans pomposity. I can't wait to loosen my belt for the paintings, photographs, sculptures, jewelry and mixed media fashioned by local and Savannah-connected artists, some whom we know well and some we've yet to meet.

So pass the salt and excuse my elbows on the table: At Slideluck, there's no such thing as a stranger.

Nov. 14, 2014

Collaboration and Public Art: A Cautionary Tale

Maybe you glimpsed their festooned glory on your Instagram feed, or perhaps you got to gawk at them in person as they toured the town on the back of a flatbed truck. The Yarn Children of Collaboration bombarded the streets and social media last week, and hopefully, Savannah will never be the same.

First conceived to help fulfill the mission of the A-Town Get Down Festival, the splashy mobile sculptures were assembled by the kids of the Loop It Up Savannah art program at the West Broad YMCA—a fine, fun example of how the sum of many creative efforts can add up to a single piece of art. The back story, however, has more layers than a Kardashian wedding cake.

A few months ago, artist and A-Town art coordinator Jose Ray approached Loop It Up director Molly Lieberman and myself about a yarnbomb for the event. A "yarnbomb" is what happens when knitters get nutty and cover an everyday structure—a mailbox, a stop sign, the neighbor's dog—with fibers, instantly transforming the mundane into art, or at least something a little less ordinary. I got awfully excited, 'cause doing stuff that will make people laugh, stare and/or point is kinda my hobby. (A group of us yarnbombed Green Truck Pub in December, and the dashboard of my minivan is kind of a situation.)

A yarnbomb also serves to bring together makers and viewers in unexpected ways, making it a perfect opportunity to thread together A-Town, its connections with SCAD, the local art community and the families of the West Broad Y, as well as honor A-Town's inspiration, Alex Townsend, a vibrant young soul who died in a car accident in February 2010.

Several brainstorming sessions ensued. Our intrepid triad realized this project would need to travel, and building a mobile structure from scratch would require time and power tools, both in short supply. I went to ask sculptor Jerome Meadows if he had any suitable spare items lying around his studio behind Indigo Sky Community Gallery.

Always down for any kind of artistic mischief, Jerome showed me a massive propeller blade reclaimed from an industrial site. Too unwieldly.

He put his hand on a block of granite. Oy, too heavy.

He thought a minute and disappeared into the back of his cavernous work space, then toddled out a three-and-a-half foot human form made of twisted chicken wire and stuffed with wads of paper. He introduced it as one of three armatures used for a public art project ages ago, and we were welcome to them.

"They're perfect," I exclaimed, clasping my hands at the trio of magical creatures.

There was definitely something spellbinding about the Children, even basic and faceless. As we loaded them gently into the minivan, taking care to avoid any sharp pokes, I briefly wondered if they needed carseats.

The Loop It Up kids spent many afternoons weaving ribbons and yarn on cardboard looms to dress them, giving the girl form a purse and naming her "Diva." Purled squares made by the elders of the Hudson Hill Golden Age Center appeared on arms and legs.

As they became bedecked in every color and fiber imaginable, including swaths of donated violet fabric called "Savannah Plaid," the Children became softer and more alive, as if they might dance right off their foundations. We found ourselves patting their heads and cooing to them, and they enchanted everyone who walked past, their vibrant fringes giving off the effect of three friendly shamans.

Diva and the boys looked wildly regal as Jose, *Connect Savannah* intern Sinjin Hilaski and I strapped them to a flatbed truck for a tour of the city, with a plan to snap photos for a social media blitz and introduce our charges to the age-old Savannah pastime of "see and be seen."

Jose drove us through Frazier Homes, the public housing community where many of the Y kids live, past City Hall and around the squares. We cruised Broughton, checked out the Telfair, and stopped for coffee at the Sentient Bean.

The Children seemed to take in the uproar they caused everywhere we went with a wise, quiet humor. They didn't complain at all as they jostled on our shoulders as we carried them to the Forsyth Fountain and crowded into the elevator at Drayton Tower.

Frankly, they were much better behaved than a lot of children I know. Come to think of it, most adults, too.

But whose children are they, anyway?

Because of Jerome's low-key modesty, I didn't pick up on the marvelous relevance of the chickenwire children until I did a bit of research on the actual sculptures they spawned. It turns out our colorful little beings served as the molds for the bronze figures in Yamacraw Square, the $300K public art project that brought Jerome—a master of public art known all over the world for his curated community gathering spaces—to Savannah from Washington, D.C. in the first place.

Back in 1992, Leadership Savannah voted to do something that could connect Savannah's bustling tourist district with the public housing site Yamacraw Village. The site of Gen. Oglethorpe's first meeting with Chief Tomochich, the shady blocks were a working class neighborhood of Jewish folks for the first part of the 20th century, and for the last half giving way to mostly black, mostly poor folks, its historic significance obscured by a dangerous reputation. It's just steps away from downtown's busiest hotels and restaurants, yet it might as well be miles.

Meadows' vision was to transform the patch of land across the street from the historic First Bryan Baptist Church into a space that was at once enjoyable and educational. Paths lead into the courtyard through the apartments from Bay Street, past a series of walls designated for historic lore and stone benches meant for communing. The centerpiece is a fountain upon which three beautifully-rendered bronze figures—the solid counterparts to our yarn children—dance and play, showing their joy to the world.

"It's the only spot where Savannah's African-American, Native American and mainstream histories collide," he explained when I finally figured out that our yarn children were, in a way, reincarnating his original idea of collating different niches of our larger community.

Due to bureaucractic clustercussery and ballooning budgets, the Yamacraw Square Public Art Park wasn't dedicated until 2007—almost 15 years after its conception. Corners had to be cut on construction, and the intended bronze plaques were replaced with cheaper tintypes. Vandals defaced these almost immediately, and in spite of many dedicated community volunteers, Yamacraw Square didn't exactly "take" as a unifying gathering place.

These days, the bronze children dance in an empty fountain, broken glass at their foundations. The city still cuts the grass and empties the trashcans, but maintenance isn't the same as upkeep, and there's no public money to fix the park.

"This is a complicated case," sighs MPC Urban Planning Director Ellen Harris, who oversees the Site and Monument Commission. "The city says the Housing Authority is responsible for it, the Housing Authority says the city is responsible. It's been a stalemate for years."

Harris has received a $100K budget proposal to restore the park, but not a strategy on how those funds would be raised.

"Even if the city maintains them, monuments are generally paid for with private money," she explains, adding that newer projects, such as the WWII Memorial on River Street, are required to have an escrow account from which restoration funds can be drawn in perpetuity.

Though nearby residents were engaged in the original design process and a committee of progressive citizens helped raise the cash, the momentum has dissipated. Project leaders already spent a decade and half collating the original capital, which included $70K of SPLOST money, and no one can blame them for feeling a little burned out. Still, the idea that Yamacraw Square should be treated differently than any other city property doesn't sit right.

"If something happened in Pulaski Square, somebody would be there to do something about it," points out Earline Davis, Executive Director of the Housing Authority of Savannah. "Why are some public spaces treated like stepchildren? They're all a part of the system."

Davis gives a rueful laugh when it's suggested that her agency put up the cash to fix the art park.

"Believe me, if the money was there, we'd do it," she says. "There is value in art, and if you don't have access to it, you can't be expected to grow and know about the world."

But with 12,500 residents in eight public housing neighborhoods to oversee, Davis' priorities are just keeping the lights on. That may change as HUD public housing projects transition into Section 8 properties, giving local agencies ownership over the apartment buildings. In the meantime, Yamacraw Square remains neglected by the city at large.

"If you don't maintain the relationships, it doesn't really work," says Davis. "It was well-intentioned, but they didn't give it enough long term thought."

It would be easy to view the plight of Yamacraw Square with the same lens through which many view Savannah, that the effort has been made and there isn't anything left to be done. That the chasms between the haves and have nots, between our black and white citizens, between those deemed deserving of public art and those who should just be grateful to have a place to live at all are just too large to bridge, even if the physical distance isn't so far at all.

But collaboration makes strange bedfellows. Molly has had tremendous participation in the Loop It Up program, and both the Yarn Children and their forgotten bronze counterparts have already brought together people of all ages and colors. The marvelous coincidence that allowed us to bring these figures out of their neighborhood onto to the streets serves to remind that life in Savannah is far more vibrant and complex than simple dichotomies. But it takes a willingness to ask the same questions and visit the same issues over and over again, keeping faith that patience and passion will yield progress—even if it takes decades.

I visited Yamacraw Square on several occasions, with and without the Yarn Children. The first few times, the park was clean but desolate, the surrounding buildings dotted with boarded up windows, a line of drying laundry nearby the only evidence of human presence.

The scene summed up the story I'd been told about this neighborhood, but something kept calling me back. Intern Sinjin and I popped over again one late afternoon last week, just as the schoolbuses were pulling up. Soon the square and street were flooded with uniform-clad tots bouncing balls and whipping past on scooters.

We struck up a conversation with Talethia Dortch, who lives next to the park, and she assured us that even its derelict state, it still gets used for barbecues on summer evenings and occasionally, a wedding.

"It would be nice to have the fountain working again," she said amiably, keeping an eye on her 8 year-old daughter, Marinsaja, as she pushed a toy baby carriage along the sidewalk. "The kids would really like that."

Talethia is working towards her nursing certification at Savannah Tech, and she and Marinsaja often enjoy Forsyth Park and Savannah's other public spaces. She grew up in Yamacraw Village and moved back a few years ago, and she's well aware of the simple version of her neighborhood's story.

She points out that the economy has directed the shift in public housing discussed by Davis and that there are plenty of white families moving in, though she assures she's not talking about race when she says, "Nothing is ever just black and white if you look at it closely."

As for Savannah's enduring perceived chasms, she is cheerfully optimistic.

"People will get over these things if we have more places to connect," she says.

No one need be blamed for the plight of Yamacraw Square and its bronze statues; that just isn't productive. But next time you're downtown, maybe you'll walk across Fahm Street for a visit—because our favorite past time of seeing and being seen is the first step to communion, cooperation and collaboration.

As for the Yarn Children, they have not only been seen but absolutely adored, their effect reaching far beyond their original conception. At the A-Town Get Down Festival, people cooed over the installation and were fascinated when their deeper significance was revealed.

Circling his babies in the pavilion of the Charles H. Morris Center, Jerome was so delighted with their decorated condition he seemed almost giddy. He confessed that though he often purges his studio of finished projects, some mysterious element had influenced him to keep these three forms all these years.

"I always thought they might have some kind of afterlife," he laughed, shaking his head as he touched the hem of Diva's dress.

The Yarn Children have yet to find a permanent home, and are, in fact, currently lording over my desk at like a trio of wacky silent Buddhas. I find their presence both comforting and unnerving, as if they really could step off into the world on their own.

Now that they have seen and been seen all around the city, from the banks of the river to 12 stories up, who knows what they could inspire next?

Feb. 26, 2014

Unchain My Heart

I may be hopelessly biased, but I'm pretty sure the world runs on stories.

As much as food and water, stories are essential. Even when humans run out of fossil fuels and the last can of kidney beans is eaten, the last few folks will be crowded over a trash can fire surrounded by the crumbling ruins of Western civilization, telling tales of what came before and what might happen next.

When a good story is told—and by good, I mean anything that absorbs you so completely that not only do you forget to check your phone but you sort of forget where you are—something happens between its teller and its listeners, a mysterious weaving of images and ideas and inspiration that wasn't there before. A kind of energetic nourishment is transmitted back and forth, altering everyone's reality.

In the hands of the professional storytellers of the Unchained Tour, your contact high might last for days. Saturday night brought the last stop of a ten-day sojourn that led a cantankerous blue bus full of raconteurs through a heart-shaped loop around the South, stopping at independent bookstores to spread the Gospel of the Good Story.

Judging from the string of sold-out shows in places where more guns are sold at Wal-Mart than books, it's evident that there are plenty of hidden factions that worship at the altar of plain old-fashioned yarnspinning.

Conceived by author and founder of the New York storytelling phenomenon The Moth, George Dawes Green—who proudly assumes the mantle of "high priest of this bizarre religion"—Unchained has become a required pilgrimage for the devoted.

Back home for the tour's finale, Green and his band of merry minstrels were greeted with all the fanfare of its outlandish megachurch, with a three-hour daytime jubilee featuring local music, E. Shaver Booksellers and hand-pressed bookmarks by the Soda Shop, followed by fire twirling and hulahooping as the night crept in. By the time almost 400 disciples had crammed themselves into the Knights of Columbus ballroom, the mood was positively zealous.

A true believer myself, I shimmied up to the second row and plopped into a single open seat, a view so close I could practically read the small print on the cut-out heart streamers dangling from the ceiling, made from the pages of donated books. No healthy tomes were harmed in the project, promised Megan Luther, who led a team of volunteers in their construction.

And then I was swept away.

The show began with hymn-like, haunting cowgirl blues from Rachel Kate (formerly of The Shaniqua Brown) and quirky accordion riffs from multi-instrumentalist Joel T. Hamilton. Then Brooklyn-based Dawn Fraser lit up the stage with a story about her Trinidadian roots and her twin brother, who is challenged with Down's Syndrome but not hampered. She was followed by Savannah native and New York theater legend Edgar Oliver, who recounted in his wonderfully peculiar grandmother voice his unlikely rise to military greatness at Benedictine Military School.

After intermission, Green popped up to give a sermon, sporting a velvet waistcoat and massive head bandage as a result from a fall earlier in the evening (from excitement? Exhaustion? Epiphany? He couldn't decide.)

"If you want true bliss, then the books you read need to be real books," he intoned to the audience, evoking a chorus of hallelujahs, hosannas and amens.

The revival reached full fever as he anointed Joni Saxon-Giusti, also known as The Book Lady, as a patron saint, and hailed Unchained's producer, business manager and all-around badass Samita "TCB" Wolfe as "nothing but soul."

Emcee Peter Aguero grabbed the mic for his unapologetically raunchy narrative of sex, blood and bong hits that had strangers squeezing each other's knees with laughter in the crowded rows. Then the air crackled as Aguero introduced the last raconteur, one of the messiahs of modern storytelling: Best-selling author of *American Gods, Coraline* and dozens of other books, the award-winning, ridiculously cool novelist Neil Gaiman.

"He's just a guy who's done some stuff," Aguero warned in his New Jerseysian growl, obviously wary of what happens when you travel with a Big Author to Small Places. "So RELAX."

Gaiman appeared in his signature black, and the room went quiet, reverential even. As a fan of his books—fiction that marries the fantasy of superheroes and ghosts and parallel worlds with the weirdness of humanity—I was surprised, then mesmerized as he told a subdued, stark tale of his own loneliness and redemption that involved an elephant, a dog and a woman. It was a valuable wisdom: The most powerful stories are the ones that are true and simple and happen to you.

Then the tour was officially over, and the crowd bounced out, buoyed by the stories and a sense that all of us were now connected having shared the experience.

I stuck around for the after party, hoping to score the interview I had scheduled with Gaiman that his publicist canceled before the tour began. But artist/DJ/Unchained bus driver Jose Ray started spinning the vinyl, and I got distracted by the Knights' cheap bar and a bunch of Savannah people I really like.

By the time Gaiman showed up a few hours later, having finally escaped the line of fans that followed him down Liberty Street, I was really in no condition to take notes on anything.

But now I have my own story about how I almost met the Big Author and may have stepped on his toe while dancing to the Pointer Sisters by the light of a single desk lamp.

I'll let your know more if you buy me a drink. If I may witness, the glory is in the telling.

Sept. 22, 2012

Adventures in Museumland

Entertaining children is not my strong suit. Where I come from, children entertained themselves or they were sent outside to the golf course with the coyotes. If you were very good, you got to play Atari for 30 minutes after dinner. The rest of the time you either read a book or fed bugs to the cat and that was that.

Yet somehow I ended up with five young people in my care last Wednesday morning, all of them looking expectantly at me as if I was supposed to do something fascinating, such as pull gold coins out of my ears or morph into a unicorn.

It was a daunting audience: Three eight year-old girls who can shatter glass with the combined power of their shrieking and two moping preteen boys whose only source of solace is the knowledge that they will one day be old enough to drive themselves to the mall.

As a pack, they can ravage a person of her hearing and the delusion you were ever cool. I almost panicked, since the last two weeks before school starts is when they're at their most feral.

Then I remembered: The Savannah Children's Museum opened the doors to one of its exhibits this summer. I was saved!

"A museum? Uggggggh. I don't want stand around and LOOK at

things," hollered Liberty.

"Yeah, we wanna TOUCH stuff," demanded Charlotte.

"And not have people telling us to be quiet," glowered Ella pointedly. "Like you do when we're playing Rock Band."

I winced. "Well. What if I told you this was a place where not only could you touch everything, you can be as loud as you want?"

The girls squealed, causing the windows to tremble in their frames.

Abraham and Luke rolled their eyes so hard they fell backwards. "Is there wi-fi?"

"No, but there may be a trip to Hot Topic in your future if you cooperate."

With everyone on board, we headed downtown to Tricentennial Park, where the Coastal Heritage Society oversees a veritable compound of historical delights, including the epic Georgia State Railroad Museum (trainheads still call it the Roundhouse) and the Savannah History Museum. (CHS also has Old Fort Jackson under its umbrella and recently acquired the Pin Point Heritage Center.)

Upon arrival, the children stood gap-mouthed, looking up at the ancient towering smokestack used by the Central of Georgia Railroad. Even the boys dropped their jaded veneer for a minute to ogle the steam engines.

As we traipsed to the west end of the property to the site of the museum's Exploration Station, there was a moment of solemnity as we read on the markers that the Revolutionary War was fought right under our feet.

"That's kind of the crazy twist that sets this apart from other children's museums," said CHS Marketing Director Patricia "Kiki" Knight. "You actually get play in ruins. You get to touch history."

This sounded fantastic to the girls, who ran past the gates and immediately began sticking their hands in the nearest exhibit, a rushing watertray that serves as muddy mess disguised an archaeology dig.

Then everyone scampered over to a rack of giant blue building blocks that the girls used to build up giant towers and then knock them down. Like forty times.

The boys built their own cave and plotted their takeover of the world.

We wandered over to a table of drums and shakers and other instruments to fulfill their noise-making promises. Still thinking I had a chance to impress this group, I grabbed a mallet.

"Look, a cowbell! More cowbell!" I cried. I pounded out a beat, reveling in my own hilarity.

Abraham eyeballed me with disgust. "It's not a cowbell, Mom, it's a gogo bell. From West Africa. Duh."

To underscore my musical idiocy, he and Luke began picking out the strains of Gotye's "Somebody That I Used to Know" on the mammoth xylophone. I reminded him that he once tried to eat a Native American shaker pod at Kindermusik.

Situated on an acre of soft green grass, the Exploration Station drops down inside the reinforced brick arches of an old CofGA carpentry building, where international children's museum designer Lee Skolnick has created world of wonder: A wooden maze to get lost then found. A cooling mist shower embedded into an old chimney. A cozy reading hideaway tucked under the brick arches sponsored by Live Oak Public Libraries.

"No Harry Potter," sniffed Abraham, yet then settled into the pillows anyway to reread a few childhood favorites.

The girls took a breather in the no-spaz zone of the tranquil Frogtown Garden, lush with marigolds, basil, eggplant, peppers and lavender. Giant checkerboards lend a certain Alice in Wonderland vibe, and the color scheme is a blend of natural hues—as opposed to your typical kid-themed, primary-colored sensory overload. Kiki relayed that parents of special needs kids are particularly appreciative of this element, though any parent would approve of a spot that marries nature and play.

"I bring my son here once or twice a week," Christopher Berinato tells me as his toddler, Max, stacks giant blocks. "He has fun every time, and I also like being here. That's pretty important."

The outdoor Exploration Station is only the first phase of what the Children's Museum will become: When it's finished, the $17 million project will certainly be a big bright feather in Savannah's tourism cap, offering 40,000 square feet of hands-on "edutainment" for the juice box-and-Goldfish set, including an indoor ship to climb aboard.

After several hours, lunch beckoned and I seemed to remember a promise involving the mall, so I went to round up my posse. The girls seemed to have shrieked themselves out and were reading quietly. I found the boys at the Whimsical Wardrobe area, trying on hats.

Luke swung around wearing an elephant nose and holding up a pair of drum mallets.

"I give this place two drums up! Badabump!"

"Nice. Time to go, guys," I called.

"What? Already?" groused Abraham, sporting a chef's hat and giant sunglasses. "But we just got here!"

Kids. You just can't win.

Aug. 12, 2012

Saving Nina

The cheerful rebels of the world love to say how it's easier to get forgiveness than permission. But those people have clearly never waded into Savannah's public art debate.

Around these parts, if you want to add an exciting design or a pop of color to the exterior of any property—public or private—that can be seen from the street, there are signatures to secure and a bureaucratic process to follow. Should you skip the red tape, you can expect a visit, or at least a strongly-worded certified letter, from the heavies at Code Enforcement, who will ask you to remove your creation or they will be happy to do it for you.

That's not necessarily a bad thing, since the same such ordinances are what obligate slumlords to clean up crappy tags from untalented vandals and keep your nutbag neighbor from fingerpainting a swastika on his garage.

But submitting stacks of paperwork and attending long meetings in the middle of the day can also suck all the juice out of a legit creative vision—if you were even aware of the requirements in the first place.

In late 2015, when large portraits of prominent African American cultural figures painted by beloved local folk artist Scott "Panhandle Slim" Stanton began popping up in areas of town where many fear to tread, no one thought to ask for permission.

"We didn't know any of the rules when we started," avows Elder Erika Hardnett of Agape Empowerment Ministries, one of the driving forces behind the Walls of Hope project. "We just wanted to bring something positive to the community."

Over the past year and half, more than 30 colorful likenesses of and encouraging quotes from historic influencers like James Baldwin, Bob Marley, Shirley Chisholm and India Arie have found their way to the façades of shuttered businesses on Waters Avenue, the sides of convenience stores on Montgomery Street, and increasingly, into the wealthier, whiter neighborhoods in between.

Most have welcomed the Walls of Hope to their blocks, heralding Panhandle Slim's pieces as a soulful salve for a city wracked by poverty and violence. The great masked rabblerouser Banksy once said, "art should comfort the disturbed and disturb the comfortable," and we've got far more of the former than the latter around here.

But Walls of Hope's artful sedition eventually caught the attention of the Metropolitan Planning Commission and the City, which sent out letters to property owners last summer giving them the choice of pursuing a permit or removing the portraits. Some took them down to avoid authoritarian conflict, though all it takes is a cruise around town to see that plenty have ignored the edict.

Homeowner Paul Suszynski filed a petition to keep the portrait of musician and Civil Rights activist Nina Simone affixed to the side of his 1886 clapboard house on Habersham near Hall Street, and it hit the agenda last week for the MPC's Historic District Board of Review monthly meeting.

Paul stuck around for the first couple of hours as the board debated the aesthetic value of rounded roof lines and metal pilasters, but eventually had to go back to work. (His petition was #27 on a list of over 50 items, and HDBR members approved the design of at least three new hotels over the course of the afternoon.)

Those of us remaining zoned out during the zoning discussions but perked up when Historic Preservation and Urban Planning Director Ellen Harris presented the petition to save Nina's portrait. She explained that while she and her staff were not opposed to the concept of a mural in the neighborhood, because the artwork was submitted "after the fact" and wasn't "visually compatible" with the surrounding architecture, staff recommended that board deny approval of the petition.

"This was a difficult review and a difficult decision to make," she said to the room.

Fellow public art policy nerds know that's not just lip service. Ellen has been a huge advocate of public art in Savannah but also has a job to do. In addition to her vast preservation expertise, she was a major player in crafting the mural policy adopted by the city in 2012.

While cumbersome and unspontaneous, the mural policy is still the only avenue by which artists can go big without the City dispatching buckets of beige paint. However, Nina isn't technically a mural—she's painted on a piece of reclaimed piece of wood that "can come down as easily as it went up," clarified the artist himself as he took to the podium to address the board.

Panhandle Slim also recounted the significance of Nina Simone and the quote taken from her heart-wrenching lament, "Sunday in Savannah," which she sang to tearful crowds in the days after Martin Luther King, Jr. was assassinated.

"This message is important to American history, to Georgia, it's important to Savannah," he implored to the board.

While some of the board members nodded in agreement, others weren't having it.

"This isn't the first piece of art of yours that has come before this group. There is no way you're ignorant of how this process works," admonished Chairman Stephen Merriman, Jr. of the artist's civilly-disobedient tendency to leave works of art around the city for anyone to claim.

Neighbor Tim Coy spoke against leaving Nina where she was, complaining of arbitrary code enforcements and citing how the city made him comply with an exact type of clasps for the shutters on his carriage house renovation. Also he just doesn't like it.

"When my wife and I first saw it, we thought it was graffiti," he said. "We have to look at it every day and we don't find it inspirational at all."

Historic Savannah Foundation Executive Director Daniel Carey weighed in against letting Nina stay. "It's not about the aesthetics, it's whether it is visually compatible with the guidelines and does it work with the surroundings."

The ensuing deliberation volleyed between the social worth and the architectural inconsistencies of the mural/not mural. Of the board members, Dwayne Stephens called the piece "disruptive" in a good way, and Kellie Fletcher posited that Nina and her quote represented Savannah history and culture, declaring "that's what we're here to preserve."

Scott Cook and Becky Lynch agreed that while they are in favor of more public art, they didn't feel that this piece belonged on this particular block.

Keith Howington and Debra Caldwell proposed a time limit for the public portrait, which the HDBR isn't qualified to impose and would have to be steered back through City Council.

"I see it every day, and it makes me feel good," Mic Madon said simply. "It makes me smile."

In the end (which wasn't even the end of a verrrrry long meeting, bless the board for volunteering their time), the lack of permission found forgiveness: The petition squeaked by with a 4-3 vote; Chairman Merriman abstained.

So Nina Simone will see at least a few more Sundays in Savannah, at least until Historic Site and Monument Commission convenes on August 3, since approval from both boards is required. [Note: The HSMC vote tied 3-3, which effectively denied the petition, and the mural was removed the next day.]

If it seems like I'm walking the fence here, it's because I am. On one side, I adore Panhandle Slim's work, and I'm all about delightful disruption and bold color in public places. But I also appreciate the work that went into the mural ordinance and how its guidelines are intended to inspire more expression for and *from* Savannah, if only there were more artists willing to commit to the process. And I'm quite happy it keeps Nutbag Joe's artistic endeavors indoors.

Still, I can't help but think of another quote from Ms. Nina herself: "There's no excuse for the young people not knowing who the heroes and heroines are or were."

The Walls of Hope project and its artist have shouldered the responsibility of reflecting great women and men back to those who may not know them otherwise. Surely that kind of benevolent sedition deserves absolution?

Jul. 19, 2017 [Update, November 2017]: The vote didn't pass, and neither did an appeal to the HSMC. The mural was removed a few weeks after this column was published and remains languishing in Panhandle Slim's backyard.

8 CREATURES AND CRITTERS

Life is wild in Savannah, y'all, and I'm not just talking about the packs of crazy bridesmaids loping through City Market. You never have to travel far to have an up close-and-personal experience with the non-human population, which includes handsome cougars, matriarchal owls and lost squirrels. Come explore Savannah's slightly feral edge, along with a couple of shaggy dog stories that reflect our loving rescue community.

Please Don't (Breast)feed the Squirrels

There it goes again, that skreeky garbled chatter. Two squirrels are noising it up in the water oak in my front yard, bickering over who left the top of the acorn open, or whatever it is squirrels argue over.

From the ground it sounds like Charlie Brown's teacher and her friends downed too many Red Bulls. Since I already have two human children nattering at me, I throw a pinecone into the canopy and watch them scatter.

Usually, I go gaga over Savannah wildlife—I almost crashed my bike yesterday following a massive hawk through Daffin Park—yet I tend towards the apathetic about squirrels. My spirit droops every time I see one of them flattened in the street, but there's no denying they look like big-eyed, bushy-tailed rats. (Rats do not count as wildlife—there's the whole bubonic plague thing, plus the fetid little jerks snarfed all the peppers in our garden this summer.)

Squirrels fall into the same nebulous category of urban wildlife as pigeons: Cute critters or disease-ridden pests? A wholly unscientific inquiry conducted on Facebook last week revealed that it can go either way, depending on how many of them are breeding in the insulation in your attic.

There's also another role these beguiling rodents can play that many of us haven't considered, since we are soft and spoiled and like our meat already skinned: Apparently, squirrels make pretty good eatin'.

I wasn't aware that Georgia's official squirrel hunting season opened up a month ago, but Dept. of Natural Resources regional supervisor David Mixon assured me that it's a venerated fall pastime across the state.

"It used to be more popular, and in certain areas it still is," says the Brunswick-based regional supervisor. "It's a good way to introduce young people into sport hunting."

To legally hunt squirrels, you must first obtain a license, use a registered firearm and observe the maximum daily limit of 12 dead 'uns. Before y'all go around shooting up the neighborhood, please note that discharging a gun anywhere in the city limits will bring a SWAT team down upon you and get you permanently disinvited to block parties. If I need to tell you that hunting squirrels in parks and other public property is a no-no, then you may need a short vacation somewhere with straightjackets.

These are the legalities for small game, but Mixon told me that the game warden isn't going to cause you any issues if you off a squirrel with a BB gun or air rifle in your backyard for eating the birdseed. Though I'm not sure I'll want to come over for a BBQ anytime soon. Then again, I'll eat pretty much anything as long as someone else cooks.

Speaking of which: According to Mixon, squirrel does not, as the old adage goes, taste like chicken, but rather has a taste all its own. His recipe? "I wrap it in bacon and bake it. It turns out great."

Our family has been watching episodes of *Man, Woman, Wild* on Netflix lately so it's heartening to know there's a plentiful food source should our minivan break down on the Truman Parkway and we must survive off the land while waiting for AAA, and I'm pretty sure Mark can start a fire with a Styrofoam cup and marsh gas.

Please know that I am not advocating the death of any squirrels here; I am simply providing information. I personally have nothing against squirrels and think fondly back to when my son would only wear a white shirt to Forsyth Park so his furry friend Rico—distinguishable by a notched right ear—could recognize him.

Many of you adore squirrels and find their ubiquitous chatter delightful. You may have even, so help me, touched one. But there is a line.

A few weeks ago, my daughter and I were sitting in front of Brighter Day enjoying some tempeh salad when a couple and their son came out of the store and sat down. The mother was cuddling a tiny squirrel while the father smushed what looked like peanut butter into an eyedropper. We watched with eyebrow-raised interest as the mom, wearing a strapless maxidress, made a nest of paper towels on the ample shelf of her bosom and nestled the animal into her cleavage.

My daughter looked at me in horror. A baby anything is pretty darn cute, but this was getting weird.

Over the next ten minutes, several people stopped to coo over the mother's breasts, sharing their squirrel rescue stories while we tried to finish our lunch. A lady came out with her groceries and squealed.

"Oh, wonderful! Have you raised squirrels before?" The family admitted they hadn't. The lady commenced an informative lesson for the new squirrel parents, explaining that the most important thing was to keep it hydrated. She relayed that the last squirrel she raised after it fell onto her porch seemed to really enjoy breastmilk.

At this, kombucha sputtered out my nose and I could no longer mind my own business. "Excuse me, ma'am, but did you just say you BREASTFED A BABY SQUIRREL?"

All of them looked at me. The woman sniffed as the other squirrel mother shifted her chest nest around to protect it from such rudeness.

"Well, no. I pumped it first."

My daughter exploded into a hacking cough designed to cover up an acute case of the giggles. The woman turned back to her squirrel-raising protégés and continued her lecture on imprinting, pouring a slosh of her $4 coconut water into their eyedropper.

My daughter's coughlaughing was getting convulsive, so we tossed our recycling and got on our bikes. Now that I cannot shake the image of the lady breastfeeding a baby squirrel, I may never be able to hunt a squirrel—no matter how dire the circumstances.

Even though someone just told me that Hilton Head has squirrels the size of small dogs.

Sept. 18, 2012

Owl Ya Like Me Now?

Forget your Buzzfeed quizzes and futzing with Instagram filters: There's a new timesuck in town, and it's broadcasting from the marsh next door.

The Landings Bird Cam went live recently with a 24/7 feed of a female great horned owl brooding on a pair of eggs, and frankly, I haven't gotten a whole lot of work done since. Emails go unanswered and the laundry pile overfloweth as I click "refresh" throughout the day and night to watch this magnificent creature.

What is the owl doing now? is my first thought of the morning and every two minutes hence.

What about NOW? as I arrange my phone on the pillow before bed.

Are you looking at porn? my husband asks hopefully.

Not so much, but what could be sexier than real, live wildlife voyeurism?!

It doesn't help that the quality of the video feed is so damn fine. Every striation of her banded feathers shows up in the sunlight, the outline of her heart-shaped face clear as a pen stroke, the imperial tufts on her head ruffling gently in the wind. At night, infrared keeps each twig of the nest crisp and clear.

Basically, it's a neverending peep show for bird nerds.

We have the folks at Skidaway Audubon to thank for this alluring distraction. The local environmental nonprofit raised $15K to have international extreme video expert Tim Sears install two Sony SNC-WR630 cameras 85 feet atop the loblolly pine last summer with the intention of watching the aerie's original inhabitants.

A couple of bald eagles had raised several seasons of eaglets in the five-foot wide lair, but only one of the pair returned for a short visit this fall, perhaps due to a tragic aviary drama of which we'll never know the details.

It didn't take long for a duo of horny owls to set up a squat, and the camera—a lightning storm took down the inventory down to one—found its stringine starlet. (Great horned owls usually co-opt the construction of other species, often adding to the décor with shreds of bark or their own feathers.)

Our rapturous raptoress laid her first egg on New Year's Day and the other a few days later. According to Skidaway Audubon's partners at the Cornell Lab of Ornithology, owl eggs take between 30-37 days to incubate, which could put the first shell crack as soon as this weekend.

Until then, it's a subtle type of action. Our owl mama rotates her head 180 degrees one way, then the other, a golden-eyed sentinel of all that passes by her perch. Once a day or so, she gently turns over the eggs with her compact beak, making sure the warmth is evenly distributed. She usually gives a couple of hoots at sunrise, but mostly the soundtrack consists of the peeps and caws of other birds and the occasional lawnmower.

Our feathered friend leaves the nest briefly at dawn and again at dusk. The Auduboners believe these are rendezvous with her mate, who hasn't been seen since the eggs arrived and may be bringing her delicious dead things to eat in another tree if he is any type of gentleman.

We all know owls are nocturnal, but like most mothers, this one seems to be perpetually half-awake and slightly annoyed. Sometimes she looks straight into the camera and I swear, she can see me. That's ridiculous, of course. But a girl can fantasize, cain't she?

"Actually, we're discouraging people from anthropomorphizing the owl," said Skidaway Audubon member Jim Siler. "Sure, it would be good for publicity. But when biologists deal with wild creatures, they don't give them names."

Bummer. However, I am not a biologist, so we've been placing bets on either "Owleanor" and "Beyonceowl" around the office.

I was worried that my constant lurking made me some kind of secret owl pervert, and Siler kindly volunteered to show me the nest in person last week. I enlisted my colleague, the equally owl-obsessed Anna Chandler, to accompany me.

"Maybe we can find a food pellet and dissect it!" grinned Anna, wringing her hands gleefully as we rolled past the Landings main gate into the serene paradise of Savannah's toniest neighborhood.

We picked up Jim at his house and parked along the marsh. He led us past a small pond prickling with tadpoles, and we tiptoed through a backyard of manicured azaleas to the edge of the golf course. We could see the underside of the nest in the bald branches, and Jim explained that the tree is already half-dead from a pine bark beetle infestation. Anna tromped off into the bushes to look for the neatly packaged remains of our owl's last meal.

A retired computer consultant and a Georgia Master Naturalist, Jim has lived in the Landings for 20 years, enjoying the combination of amenities and access to nature. He admits he's given up his golf membership for now, preferring to help Skidaway Audubon with its various projects, including relocating clutches of diamondback terrapin turtle eggs that come up from the marsh to nest in the golf course sandtraps.

It's generous of these Landings birdlovers to share their window that allows the rest of us up-close owl observation and appreciation, and I thanked Jim as Anna examined a small skull of an indeterminate species.

Ms. Owl Herself was only a mere 85 feet above us, but we didn't even catch a glimpse of her. Yet it was just so lovely to be outdoors instead of staring into a monitor, and I inhaled deeply. I had fallen into a brief meditative stupor when Anna sidled up next to me.

"I have a pocketful of bones," she whispered, wagging her eyebrows behind her horn-rimmed glasses.

Poor Jim nodded wanly at Anna's carcass collection; he already seemed traumatized by his ride in the Absurdivan, which is short a hubcap and has a menagerie of plastic animals glued to the dashboard, including several owls. We were thinking of ourselves as owl superfans, but I think we might have come off as a little creepy.

Back at my computer watching the owl half-sleeping in her own browser window, I thought about what it means when our most intimate interactions with wildlife happen on a screen. As I learned that afternoon, being near an animal doesn't necessarily afford the details we can marvel at via webcam. It is undeniably a wonderful use of technology, one that educates and helps protect habitats. But does it really increase our connection with the natural world? Or is that just a convenient delusion as we spy on it from the comfort of our desk chairs?

More uncomfortably, does peeping on wild animals somehow diminish their very wildness, the way the internet makes it so easy to remove the humanity from sex and violence? Our society is already so detached from nature, and I'm not sure it helps to put it in the same streaming format as *Real Housewives of Atlanta.*

Maybe Jim is right; giving our owl a name only reduces her authentic magnificence. Though nothing short of the Apocalypse is gonna keep me from watching those owl babies being born.

Still, I can't help but feel like a creep—especially since Owleanor just looked right into the camera and turned her back.

Jan. 28, 2015

Everyone Loves a Shaggy Dog Story

Just so there are no unnecessary tears, I'm going to tell you straight up that this tale does not end with a dead dog. It started out on a busy stretch of Victory Drive on a foggy morning last week. I was driving to work, tea in hand, listening to Georgia Public Broadcasting's weather forecast delivered in those soothing tones that encourage serenity, even when a hurricane is approaching.

All was bliss until I spotted something in the turnspot between the median. In the splinter of a second that it took to whoosh by, I could see the thing was not a pile of Spanish moss with feet but a dog, wearing a frayed purple collar and enjoying the remains of a fast food container mashed into the asphalt, oblivious to the four lanes of giant metal boxes hurtling past.

In the next tiny crumb of time, I circumnavigated the moral dilemma: Should I stop? I should stop. But I'm late for work! Someone else will stop. Face it, lady, today, you are the someone. But what if it has fleas? Shut up and try to save the damn dog!

So I pulled my minivan into the median, punched the hazard light button and reached back to gently open the sliding door with a plan to lure the dog in with the rest of my bagel. Instead, it looked up at me with frightened eyes and ran right into oncoming traffic.

I couldn't look. I heard the brakes screech and a sickening thud, followed by yelping. I sat frozen. Not even public radio was going to make this better.

When I finally peeled myself off the steering wheel, I was relieved not to see a mangled pile of fur in the road. A gold Honda had pulled over and a woman in a suit jumped out.

"I saw it run through this yard," she called to me as I gave a small wave to the two worried-looking girls peering out from the backseat. The front bumper of her car hung down, cracked.

Shaken, she introduced herself as Shonese Clark, on her way to work as the admissions coordinator for Hospice Savannah. "Everything happened so fast, I'm just so sorry," she said, wringing her hands.

I told her I felt responsible for startling the dog into her bumper, and together we poked around the azalea bushes, neither of us sure if we should call 911 or Animal Control or stand in the street and cry.

We were close to doing all three when we were joined by a couple of employees from the nearby Savannah Mission Bible Training Center, who had already called police and told us they'd seen the dog roaming the neighborhood for months. They said the owners had never made much of an effort to contain the dog, even after receiving polite requests to keep their canine out of other people's flowerbeds.

"I'm sorry to say that it was only a matter of time before it got hit," lamented Justin Sellers, one of the center's directors, his chin jutting towards the wall of westbound traffic. He and his colleagues had called Animal Control several times before about the house.

"I'm an animal lover," he said. "It's hard not be judgmental."

He pointed out the carriage house on the lane where the dog lived. Shonese and I were walking over, heavy-footed, when one of the city's community service specialists drove up. The officer assured us that Shonese was in no way liable for hitting the dog. In fact, the dog's owners could be held responsible for the damage. Shonese attested that she didn't give a fig about the car, she just wanted to know that the dog wasn't suffering.

But it was getting late. After one more pass along the fence line, she relented that she had to get her kids to school.

Not ten seconds after she left, a green sedan pulled up to the maybe-dead dog's house. The officer and I went back over to bear the bad news, only to be told by a tired-looking man that the brown dog definitely belonged to the people who lived in the main house.

We walked up to a cluttered porch with a broken door. The woman in pajamas who came out was not friendly.

"Morning, ma'am, I just wanted to let you know your dog was hit—"

"What do you need with my dog?"

"No, no, I'm trying to tell your dog was in the road—"

"And I am telling you, my dog is in the backyard." She put her hands on her hips menacingly. This was not going well.

The officer commanded quietly that since we were all here, the woman could just show us her dog so we might all get on with our day. You've never seen such a sneer. I think I actually ducked.

We walked around the side and she opened the flimsy side gate. After some nudging with a slippered foot, out crept the brown dog with the stringy purple collar, with those same frightened eyes.

It had a quarter-sized scrape above its eye, but it was alive. The scary woman was triumphant, then confused when it dawned on her that the dog had indeed escaped, been hit and returned. But not contrite.

I was relieved my attempted random act of kindness had not ended in roadkill. But I was deeply disturbed by the woman's indifference for the welfare of her dog and her neighbors.

In my own fight with apathy over saving the dog, I had encountered an even more insidious, glazed-eye dispassion, the kind that makes it seem like the world might unravel into a barbarous hell any minute. Whether it's the Penn State cover-up, the defrauding of retirement accounts, the polluting of the Ogeechee River or the sad life of that sorry pooch, it's more evident than ever that all evil needs to flourish is for good people to do nothing.

The woman's jeers that I ought to mind my own business about her dog only laid out the truth clearly: Making it our business to care about each other's pets, kids, elderly neighbors and each other is the basis of a civil society.

I called Shonese at work to tell her she had not in fact killed a dog, which made her very happy. The officer departed, promising the owner a visit from Animal Control very soon.

I drove off, for the moment consoled that for every jerk I meet like the undead dog's owner, there are at least a few Shoneses and Justins who care deeply about what happens to the beings around them, who will speak up when they see abuse of a pet or a child. So perhaps the scales keep tipping to the positive.

Then again, maybe if I had minded my own business and not stopped at all, the dog never would have been hit in the first place. Life is forever flummoxing.

Nov. 19, 2011

Who's the Cougar Now?

How do I know it's been too long since I took my kids to visit Oatland Island Wildlife Center? Because when I told them we were going to meet the new cougar in town, my 14-year-old son looked alarmed and asked, "She doesn't like men with braces, does she?"

You may conclude that I've let him watch too many episodes of *Scandal* on Netflix. You might be right. In any case, I arched a righteous eyebrow and apprised him that while Shanti the Cougar may indeed sound like a Chardonnay-swilling dipsomaniac with a wardrobe of Lululemon yoga pants, he was sorely mistaken. I also grounded him from live-streaming for the next month.

This all had to be explained to his little sister, who, thankfully, had no idea what the 21st definition of a cougar was. Until now.

"So then what's an older man called who goes after younger women?" she wondered next, flattening her tube of yogurt with a slurp.

My son considered this, ostensibly reviewing the melodrama of Shonda Rimes' White House in the cobwebs of his already summer-stunted mind. He replied, "A creep."

"That's it, no TV until November," I yelled, dispelling any trace of the Zen I thought was supposed to come with my new yoga pants. "Get your shoes on, *now*."

As we turned onto Oatland Island's shady drive, I realized it had been at least a year since we'd last visited, though my hard drive overfloweth with past images of my two sassymouths scampering across the wooden walkways and screeching at the barn owls. Thankfully, this pristine maritime forest remains a respite for humans as well as more than fifty animal species.

Oatland Island is a veritable hundred-acre wood of Winnie-the-Pooh wonderment, even if the center's beloved old black bear passed on to the Big Honeypot in the Sky back in 2008.

No one knows its charms better than Friends of Oatland (FOO) chair Kim Carver, born and raised on Wilmington Island and a habitual visitor since she was "knee high to a grasshopper." The senior cabinet finisher at Gulfstream has been a dedicated volunteer here for years, and now that her son's in college, she's ramped up her passion even more.

"There's just no place like it," said Kim as we shpritzed on bug spray to stave off the inevitable clouds of gnats. "This is a real treasure in Savannah."

She took us through in the center's main building and sunny atrium, home to a couple of rat snakes and a sleepy pair of possums named Aster and Tulip. A recent art installation of a mighty oak tree made entirely of naturally-dyed wool hangs from the ceiling, brimming with a diverse ecosystem of crocheted species (We can thank the Fiber Guild of the Savannah for this exceptional yarnbomb of the highest order.)

Kim explained that Oatland's stately brick edifice, first built as a retirement home for railway workers in the 1920s and served as the sterile laboratory where the U.S. Public Health Service once studied sexually transmitted diseases, has evolved quite a bit.

"What's syphilis?" whispered my daughter as she eyed a baby alligator.

"It's like leprosy," informed her brother. "Your nose falls off."

He's watched enough cable to know full well which body parts fall off, but I guess he felt he was protecting his sister's innocence.

While the facility itself is owned by the Savannah-Chatham County Public School System to host educational programs, it's the non-profit FOO that raises the funds to maintain the visitor's center and support the care of the resident critters, mostly through donations and gift shop sales of adorable stuffed creatures (the kind manufactured Chinese factory workers, not by taxidermists.)

Kim told us how FOO helped with the acquisition of Shanti, the 2-year-old male *Puma concolor* that's been sending animal lovers of all ages into a tizzy since his society debut at the end of May.

"Our next goal is to bring back some bears," she promised as we skipped through the saw palmettos and demonstrated to our old owl pal Wahoohoo that we could still screech with the best of 'em.

When we came to the new Cougar Crossing, we ran into facilities manager Kevin Morley, who has been building animal dream homes at Oatland for 20 years, including the wonderful wolf enclosure that allows folks to get up close and personal with the predatory pack. The master craftsman envisioned a similar interactive habitat for the new cougar and his panther roommate, Comanche, the soporific 16-year-old who's been around long enough to grow his own Spanish moss. (Comanche passed away in 2016.)

"We had to renovate the fence anyway, and I thought 'Let's do something on ground level so people can see how magnificent the animal really is," shrugged Morley, deflecting our applause for his cantilevered wooden shelter with its fine finishes and a tier of massive windows.

If you've ever read *The Dangerous Lives of Altar Boys* by Savannah-born novelist Chris Fuhrman in which a main character tries to break into Oatland Island and meets a violently cougarlicious end, you will also appreciate the reinforced locks on the gates.

And suddenly there was Shanti himself, pacing back and forth like he was waiting for someone to buy him a cocktail. Kim had warned me that he likes to play peek-a-boo, but I still gasped when he brought his broad face up to mine, ducked around the corner and pounced at the glass.

"I think he likes you, Mom," tittered my daughter.

When it comes to catcalls from strange men, I'm usually prone to flipping a middle finger in response. But this big handsome feline fella, I gotta admit, I was flattered. That tawny coat! Those hazel eyes! Those teeth!

I gawked as Shanti strutted over to a shady grove, plopped down and crossed his paws. I swear on my best kale plant that he winked at me.

"Let's come back next week and see him again," I gushed.

My son rolled his eyes in disgust. "*Gawwwd*, Mom. Who's the cougar now?"

He's right; I'm way too old to be admiring the muscles of an adolescent male, even if he does have four paws. Plus, interspecies crushes never really work out.

Instead, I channeled my concupiscence back at the gift shop, where I laid out a very reasonable $45 for a year-long FOO family membership. I also ordered an engraved board to be placed on one of the wooden walkways at the wolf enclosure for Mark as a Father's Day gift to remind us of the happy scampering childhoods, even after the kids' feet grow bigger than ours.

And I'll be back to Oatland Island sooner than later, 'cause you're never too old for a perfectly innocent game of peek-a-boo.

June 4, 2014

Of Course It's Safe to Go Back in the Water...for Now

When the great American poet Henry Wadsworth Longfellow wrote "my soul is full of longing for the secret of the sea, and the heart of the great ocean sends a thrilling pulse through me," I'm pretty sure he wasn't talking about the murky waters of coastal Georgia.

When *I'm* bobbing in the waves and a secret of the sea brushes up against my legs, I don't experience so much of a "thrilling pulse" as I do a spasmodic dose of adrenaline that sends me back onto the sand shrieking like a Ritalin-addled seagull.

Don't get me wrong; I love our beaches and the robust tides and the dolphins dancing after the shrimp boats at sunset. But even when I'm standing safely on my paddleboard or on a boat, I have a healthy fear of Mother Ocean and its creatures, born out of deep respect and the understanding that from its depths, or perhaps the next sandbar, something large, gilled and hungry thinks I would make a delicious snack.

I know, just another victim of a 70s childhood that employed the *JAWS* trilogy instead of a babysitter. But guess what? I've never even watched *JAWS*! Just the trailer had me bathing in the bathroom sink for a year! And *Shark Week* on the Discovery Channel? The whole reason we don't have cable.

Still, as the wife of a fisherman and a sometimes-denizen of Tybee Island, I've learned to enjoy splashing in the water a few minutes at a time, frequently anesthetized by a few beers. This summer, however, I've found myself panicking—er, packing an extra six-pack: Last week marked the seventh shark attack off the coast of North Carolina this year, and there have been three more disturbingly closer off just a couple of sand dollar skips over the border from us in South Carolina.

But even as the Outer Banks becomes a boogie board buffet, the statistics encourage everyone to remain calm. In spite of the alarming uptick in shark-to-human tastings up north, none of Tybee's numerous black tips, tiger sharks or the formidable great white Mary Lee, who sometimes pays a visit near our shores, have made any menu pairings yet. The experts remind us that there have been no more fatalities than usual in 2015 and we're all still twenty times as likely to be killed by a cow than a shark. (Anyone floating on a raft in the middle of a cow pasture probably deserves it.)

In fact, the marine animals we ought to dread most around here are not eight-to-twelve foot bloodthirsty predators with multiple rows of serrated teeth, but something much smaller. Microscopic, actually.

Tiny enterococci bacteria gave Tybee beachgoers trillions of icky reasons to stay out of the water recently: This June, the Coastal Health District issued an advisory that the insidious organisms had exceeded the recommended levels set by the EPA, indicating the presence of human and animal fecal matter. Fortunately, this round of miniscule menaces dissipated quickly, and the advisory was lifted the next day. But while we were stranded on shore with our plastic shovels and melting ice, I weighed what felt like one of those sadistic *Fear Factor* conundrums: Would you rather swim with sharks or poop?

Enterococci won't take off a limb (that's the flesh-eating *Vibrio vulnificus*, another saltwater pathogen found more often off the Gulf Coast) but the bacteria can cause severe gastrointestinal illness, the kind of debilitating diarrhea that might make you wish you could trade in a toe to make it stop.

They're as ubiquitous as the sharp-toothed threats hanging out in the surf zone, and like the sharks, there's not much anyone can do to avoid them except stay out of the water.

"All warm-blooded animals have enterococci in their intestinal tracts," gently reminds Elizabeth Cheney, Beach Water Monitoring Coordinator for the Dept. of Natural Resources. "Elevated levels can be caused by marine wildlife, or it could be as simple as someone didn't pick up after their dog or left a dirty diaper on the beach."

Cheney explained that Georgia DNR tests the water at five different points around Tybee every week all year long under the BEACH Act passed in 2000, along with hundreds more points on the coast. Fecal coliform advisories happen rarely (the last one was July 2014) and mostly occur on the Savannah River end of the island.

The recent spike occurred in the section called the Strand between 11th Street and the pier, and none of the surrounding areas showed more than the usual amount of poopy particles, which rules out leaky sewage pipes as a cause. Federal standards dictate that the public must be informed of anything above 104 enterococci per 100ml of ocean; the June sample registered at 108, "well within statistical variations." Raw sewage would have sent the count into the billions.

"In this last instance, the samplings from the mid-point of the beach and on the south end had very low levels. The Strand wasn't much above the threshold, but it triggered the advisory," says Cheney, adding that an advisory merely means the presence of bacteria; it doesn't shut the beach down or give explanations.

The BEACH Act only provides funding to DNR to scoop the scat tests, not analyze the source. That's the job of the state Environmental Protection Division. (By the way, I talked excrement with no less than four government agencies for this column and didn't snicker once, which is more than I can say for the people with whom I share my dinner table.)

The EPD confirmed that the numbers weren't high enough to be caused by flushing toilets, and neither were they high enough to warrant an investigation. Temporary peaks like the one a few weeks ago are usually written off to heavy rains or someone's *Caddyshack* moment.

"A sample of 300 is when we start looking at surrounding facilities to make sure there weren't any upsets, like line breaks or station overflows," clarifies Alice Vick, program manager for the EPD's Coastal District office.

Tybee mayor Jason Buelterman also personally checked with the island's sewage treatment plant and found nothing amiss.

"In all likelihood, it is caused by birds," says Buelterman, an avid surfer who has faced ocean beasts big and small. "There is nothing we can really do other than educate the public about the issue."

Even a series of low-number advisories can set off alarms, and Vick says her department uses "an abundance of caution" when it comes to fecal coliform critters.

"If we see a consistent problem, we're going to investigate," she promises. "We want clean water. We swim out there too!"

For now, all sources indicate that it's perfectly safe to go back in the water.

But if the microbes come back or any fins pop up, I'm gonna need a bigger cooler.

July 8, 2015

Yet Another Shaggy Dog Story

"You need another dog like a *loch in kop*," sniffed my mother, invoking the Yiddish term for a "hole in the head."

She was right. The first dog already gave me enough *tsuris* (my people's word for "troubles") with her insulin shots and tendency to plunge blindly off stairs and walkways. Plus, the family zoo was full up with the several menopausal chickens, a sullen ball python and a chatty guinea pig.

But last winter when friend Paul Rockwell pulled a tiny black puppy out his backpack that he'd found behind a trashcan behind the Sentient Bean and plopped it into my palm, our menagerie expanded because, puppy breath. One Love Animal Rescue facilitated the adoption, and Dumpster Dog celebrated his legitimacy by eating the corners of every rug in the house.

We named him Ogeechee after one of our most beloved local bodies of water, and though his markings and mismatched eyes suggested Rottweiler and Husky genes, he quickly morphed into a Suessian mutant with a long body, short legs and no swimming talent whatsoever.

"Oy," my mother sighed when I held up a destroyed bathmat over Facetime.

Geech indeed proved to be more *tsuris* than the rest of the animals combined. He dug up the daffodil bulbs and tried to bury one of the chickens alive. He has ingested shoes, clothing, homework assignments, phone chargers, empty yogurt containers, snotty tissues and the stuffing out of his own fancy bed.

We've had success in curtailing his habit of stealing dirty socks, but he has maintained a propensity for "tasting" new people with his teeth.

He caused his most disturbing crisis last week when he leapt out the front door to greet me after work. As I was juggling groceries and my giant purse, Geech ran into the street to taste one of the neighbors—right in front of an oncoming car.

There was a sickening thunk and a squeal of brakes and a piercing shrill that I realized was my own scream. In the pulse that followed, I forced open my eyes, expecting carnage. Instead, I saw Geech running on his stumpy legs at full speed across the neighbor's yards, his whorled back end disappearing towards five o'clock traffic on Abercorn.

Our son took off barefoot after him, shouting. Dear neighbors Eileen and Wes Sessoms hopped on their bikes and combed the blocks. Family and friends soon joined the hunt.

Not being fleet of foot or calm of nerves, I did what I could: I sat down in the front yard and posted a hysterical missive to the 3200+ members of the Lost and Found Pets Savannnah Facebook page. Hopes were not high. Even if he survived the bumper bonk in his adrenalized state, Geech would probably try to taste anyone who came near him, making him difficult to rescue. And though he had a tagged collar and a microchip in his head, it was hard to imagine anyone from Animal Control chasing him down, with their five overworked officers trying to cover the entire county.

Also, Geech had been last seen a half mile away bolting west across Bull Street, that invisible but definitive line that divides urban Savannah, into east and west, middle class and impoverished, and for the most part, white and black.

My husband, Mark, and another first-responder friend, David Eichelbaum, kept up the search until almost midnight, calling Geech's name through the blighted neighborhoods and overgrown lanes, peeking under sagging porches for a pair of mismatched glowing eyes.

Despite the fact that they were two middle-aged white dudes creeping around, folks here in these neighborhoods expressed nothing but kindness and concern. One gent even called later to say that he hadn't seen our missing mongrel but had found some puppies if we were interested.

Would we do the same for these neighbors if they came calling for their lost dogs over our back fences? Though bouyed by the human compassion he encountered, Mark returned bereft for our pet and despondent over the poverty and poorly maintained streets that exist just a dog walk away.

None of us ate or slept much that night. I obsessed over the thousands of people who had shared Geech's photo. A few total strangers even commented that they had gone out and looked for him. Even if Geech was gone forever, it was heartening to see such sympathy in the midst of the political drama and arguments over gun rights amidst actual gun fights.

We may not like each other sometimes, but we sure will rally behind a sweet furry face. One helpful share came from Carol Williamson, who runs Speaking Loudly & Often for Animals, a page dedicated to educating Savannahians about animal protection legislation and monitoring its enforcement.

Currently creating momentum for a ban on puppy mill pets sold at local flea markets, Carol also works with a state initiative to combat dog fighting rings and helped officers with the huge bust on Quacco Road in 2010. She has met with Savannah-Chatham Metro Police Chief Jack Lumpkin to discuss the proven connection between crimes against animals with those against property and humanity.

"Even if you don't have empathy for animals, you have to recognize that the same people who do horrible things to dogs are capable of committing other serious crimes," explains Carol, who adds that tips on animal abuse have exposed child abuse situations and led to drug-related arrests. "The way we treat animals and the way we treat other people—it's all connected."

The chief agrees whole-heartedly and has asked Carol to share information with his officers in the many-pronged effort to get the city's crime under control. Carol collaborates with dozens of other local animal advocates who tout their own specific causes, from rescue work to feral cats to carriage horses. She also alerted me to a memo from the Dept. of

Agriculture announcing that it would begin enforcing a 1999 directive to limit rescue groups from "pulling" animals from government shelters, a devastating turn for those who work to save thousands of animals a year from being euthanized.

Fortunately, a Change.org petition against the directive collected over 29,ooo signatures in just a few days, and the DOA quickly changed its tune. "The beauty of Facebook networking is that it gives us an arena to gather voices," says the passionate retiree.

It can also yield humble miracles: At around nine in the morning after Geech's disappearance, photographer Catarina Teixeira, a complete stranger, messaged me that she might've glimpsed a black dog running through Ardsley Park, several blocks away from our house. We had already accepted the worst, and I doubted that Geech would have double-backed across the railroad tracks after a night in unfamiliar territory. But we set out anyway, hollering his name.

"Is that him?" asked a couple walking twin terriers, pointing to a familiar swirled tushy trotting down a lane.

A few minutes later, Geech was wriggling in our laps, unharmed save a tender spot where his back met the bumper. As we rejoiced and succumbed to whole-body tongue baths, I thought hard about what Carol had said about the connection between animal welfare and Savannah's systemic problems. If attention to the fate of smaller creatures can help tackle crime and poverty, then the cooperation and caring brought out by one doofus dog might also serve as a barometer of our collective character.

In any case, we're so grateful to all who helped bring Geech home. Even if he is currently expressing *his* gratitude by tasting the cord to my laptop.

May our love for our pets help us extend our empathy to all of our neighbors, even the ones we have to cross uncomfortable lines to get to know.

Oct. 14, 2015

9 FIELD TRIPS

There's no place like home, but once in a while, a girl's gotta get out of town for a little perspective—or maybe to show up for court in another town. I've never needed to go far to have an exotic adventure, especially when pristine undeveloped islands and one of the Atlantic's Ocean's busiest live bottom reefs are just a boat ride away. But whether I'm taking a road trip to see Taylor Swift in Tampa or a transcontinental flight to Paris, Savannah somehow always manages to stay on my mind.

Counting Sea Stars and Other Science: A Landlubber's Expedition to Gray's Reef

I know this is practically sacrilege around these parts, but I am not a boat person.

Whether it's my desert roots or that I've watched *Titanic* and *Jaws* enough times to consider them cautionary gospel, the ocean scares the—well, everything out of me. Sure, I can dig *putt-putt-putting* through the marshes and out to our lovely barrier islands, but once land is out of sight, I turn a shade of moss green and empty all bodily systems with impressive force.

If I had had to come across the Atlantic with my ancestors from Europe, I'd still be making *rugelach* in the *shtetl.* I mean, I once slept in a life jacket on a Disney cruise.

But I'm never one to turn down adventure, so when Michelle Riley of Gray's Reef National Marine Sanctuary invited me on a local media expedition 40 miles off the Savannah coast, I accepted. Then I promptly purchased all the seasickness remedies money can buy, including a double pack of Bonine and a nifty pair of terrycloth acupressure Sea Bands that made me look like 70s-era Jimmy Connor.

Capt. Todd Recicar assured me that the R/V *Joe Ferguson* had just come off a year's worth of maintenance and was in tip-top shape, but I'd seen this episode of *Gilligan's Island* before. I showed up to the Gray's Reef office on Skidaway Island prepared for shipwreck in my very boaty husband's sun-protective fishing shirt and a pair of his swim trunks stuffed with flares.

But first we had to set sail on our fateful trip. Or in this case, motor up: "R/V" stands for "research vessel," and this 41-foot catamaran was designed specifically to ferry scientists, educators, divers and curiosity seekers out to the 22-square mile live bottom reef to study its remarkable abundance of critters, including sea stars, sponges, turtles, assorted fish, and **gulp** sharks.

After a quick reminder not to climb up front and pull a DiCaprio, Capt. Todd piloted us past the last buoy of the Wilmington River and with it, the last vestige of cell service. Soon the thin green strip of spartina grass was left behind, nothing but open ocean all around.

"Isn't this fabulous?" asked WSAV's relentlessly upbeat Renee LaSalle as she sunned her cute self on the back of the boat, which I know is called the stern from *Moby Dick*, which used to be required reading for every 11th grader before Common Core.

I whimpered and stuffed my cheeks with stomach-settling candied ginger from local business Verdant Kitchen, keeping my eyes fixed on the horizon. Michelle kindly kept me distracted by explaining that Gray's Reef was discovered in 1961 by UGA marine biologist Milton "Sam" Gray and designated a protected marine sanctuary in 1981 by President Jimmy Carter, one of 13 off the U.S. coast. The site is managed by the National Oceanic and Atmospheric Administration (NOAA), itself within the Dept. of Commerce, which seems weird at first but makes total sense as the coastal economy is directly related to commercial fishing, tourism, and other industries dependent on a healthy ocean.

An hour and a half later of blessedly calm waters, Michelle announced we'd almost arrived. All I could see was more ocean, because, duh, all the action was underwater. In fact, you'd never know unless you had the right coordinates that one of the busiest and most diverse live bottoms in the world was 60 feet below the hull. (Basically, I learned every seafaring term I know from Herman Melville.)

A speck in the distance soon revealed itself as the NOAA Ship *Nancy Foster*, a 187-foot rust-streaked Goliath equipped with wet and dry laboratories, diving vessels, oxygen tanks and a slew of data collection and analytical tools to gauge what kind of creatures are out there and how many there are.

It also accommodates a full-time uniformed crew and revolving teams of meticulous researchers who sleep aboard the ship for two weeks at a time in roomy berths and dine in a well-appointed mess hall that serves ridiculously good barbecue chicken and roasted vegetables (hello, three kinds of sriracha.)

We climbed aboard just as the scientists had finished their morning dive, eager to discuss their work. Chief scientist Kim Roberson oversees operations and takes the plunge twice a day to count specimens, collect invertebrate samples and observe conditions in the protected research area that comprises a third of the overall sanctuary and is closed to fishing and other recreational diving.

"We'll use this data to look at changes over time in a place that sees little to no human activity, and we do as much as we can in the time that we have in the oxygen tanks," she explains, adding with a grin, "Since I haven't grown gills...yet."

Her conservation biology colleague Peter Auster has been diving to Gray's Reef every summer for nine years for the abundance of fat yellow jack, Spanish mackerel, sea bass, grouper and other species that congregate around the reef's rocky ledges. (Unlike a coral reef, Gray's was formed when invertebrates began collecting on the sandstone outcroppings around 18,000 years ago, forming a living carpet of complex ecosystem.)

Peter, a gray ponytailed gent who runs the Mystic Aquarium in Connecticut, has been studying how predators interact with prey, which in addition to being the main plot of many horror movies has also revealed that multiple species will work together to hunt smaller baitfish by driving schools towards the bottom.

"That's not something that's been detailed before in the southeast," remarked Peter, pointing to his computer streaming the feed from one of two cameras temporarily mounted on the ocean floor. "The diversity here allows us to understand that web of behavior and document the invisible relationships of how fish communities function."

The diver-scientists know where to look thanks to Italian biologist Fabio Campanella, who spends the majority of his time above board "mowing the lawn"—what the other scientists call his technique of combing sections of the reef with sonar to monitor densities of fish in particular areas. Other projects going on simultaneously on the Nancy Foster are Dr. Danny Gleason's audit of sponges and sea squirts for Georgia Southern and sea star counts by Valdosta State's Tim Henkel.

The data collected at Gray's Reef reveals tons about individual species and their relationships with the vast marine world around them, providing policy makers valuable information.

Of course, the decision makers don't necessarily make the choices that suit everybody. Seismic testing for oil exploration off the Georgia coast is back on the table in spite of the risk it poses to the North Atlantic right whale, which calves at Gray's Reef in the winter season. Overfishing remains a challenge for species like red snapper and flounder, and federal agencies continue to juggle commercial demands with imposed catch limits. Pollution caused by agricultural fertilizers and pesticide runoff, oil spills and plain old garbage threaten marine life and the balance of the ocean itself.

Regarding policy the researchers remain deferentially apolitical, other than to maintain that good science will triumph if people will listen.

"This belongs to all of us," Peter reminds as a leatherback sea turtle swims majestically into the frame of the monitor. "The challenge is to inspire a sense of stewardship by bringing the big picture back to the public."

Other than through the wonderful Gray's Reef Film Festival hosted in Savannah every winter, opportunities for landlubbers to glean how vital this unique underwater paradise is to Georgia and the nation can be as elusive as those North Atlantic right whales (Captain Ahab could relate.)

Fortunately, we can see its wonders on the big screen this summer at Gray's Reef Tuesdays at the Tybee Post Theater, a captivating weekly film series focusing on the Georgia Coast. Budding engineers can also compete in the underwater robotics contest at the Skidaway complex, and a few lucky teachers get to experience this "living classroom" each year as the finale of the Rivers to Reefs program, imparting their hands-on knowledge of the connections between our watersheds and the sea to their students.

In fact, we passed the *R/V Savannah* carrying a load of Georgia schoolteachers out for their turn on the *Nancy Foster* as we made our way back to the mainland. The chop had picked up a bit, but with Capt. Todd's deft navigation and my giant bag of ginger chews I was comfortable enough to take a ten-minute sweat nap below in the cushiony hold.

I may have kissed a pile of pine needles upon my return to solid ground, but I did so with a much deeper appreciation of what goes on beneath the surface and beyond the horizon. I'm thinking I just might grow some sea legs yet.

But I don't think anyone is ever going to call me Ishmael.

June 28, 2017

Fast and Furious in Darien

Maybe I was lulled into a Supremes stupor by the oldies radio station, but I didn't notice the speedometer creeping up.

Maybe I was just tired, cruising home from the Jacksonville airport from a trip to Phoenix on a Sunday night with two mewling children. Mark insists it was because I was squawking at him for leaving his glasses in the hotel room in Miami.

It could've been because I was driving his Honda, and I'm not used to piloting anything other than my beleaguered minivan that shakes like an angry drunk with the DT's when I push it past 65 mph.

Whatever the reason, I momentarily placed a little too much pedal to the metal. It was at the wrong place—the notorious stretch of I95 near mile marker 46—where it's always the wrong time. While the illegal speed traps of southeast Georgia supposedly disappeared in the '70s, these are still the 24/7 hunting grounds of the Darien Police Department, and anyone skating even one mile on the superfluous side of the 70 mph speed limit is prey.

Blue flashing lights descended upon us like steroidal aliens. The cop, unimpressed by my Diana Ross impersonation, shined a flashlight in my face and said he clocked me at 90 mph, which I found hard to believe since I had glanced down to see 75 during the chorus of "Stop! In the Name of Love."

But he stuck his face in mine and growled "Do you think lasers LIE, ma'am?" Officer Meanie didn't even tip his hat when he handed me the ticket with the guilt trip that a mother should know better. I groused, of course. But as a mostly responsible grown-up, I understood it was my civic duty to pay the fine. I was speeding after all, if only for a minute.

When I discovered the cost of getting caught in McIntosh County equals more than a week's pay and would tack three insurance-bloating points on my license, I decided to keep my court date in order to throw myself upon the mercy of the judge.

Here's an account of my trip to Darien court last Thursday:

• **7:30 a.m.:** I leave Savannah in the Absurdivan, eliminating any possibility of speeding anywhere. In the last mile of I-95 before Darien, I pass four police cars pulled on the side of the highway, each paired with a victim. I send a silent fist pump of solidarity to the poor suckers.

• **8:30 a.m.:** I arrive in Darien, founded in 1736 by a clan of Scots who sailed up the Altamaha River and now serves as the McIntosh county seat with a population of 1,700. Driving past shuttered restaurants, a dessicated car dealership and empty storefronts, one can understand why the town's focus on giving out speeding tickets might be an attractive revenue generator.

• **9:00 a.m.:** The tiny courtroom is packed. Purses and cell phones are forbidden, cutting us off from the outside world. A pack of prosecutors in blue blazers mutter with their heads together, fanning themselves with manila folders. I half expect Atticus Finch to roll in. No sign of the judge.

• **9:18 a.m.:** Deprived of Facebook, I chat up the young Marine in uniform next to me, who received her speeding ticket on Veteran's Day. We agree this is a travesty to God and country. She tells me she was supposed to have been deployed to Afghanistan today but got a reprieve until spring. For now, she'll remain at the Marine Corps Air Station in

Beaufort, S.C., and fix helicopters. And stay out of Georgia.

• **9:48 a.m.:** A couple of clerks have clopped in wearing stunningly high heels, but the judge's seat remains empty. People are clicking their feet, biting their nails, drumming their fingers and basically exploding into a storm of tics without their phones. I chew on the irony of how very slow things appear to run in the Speeding Capital of South Georgia. The collective redolence of other people's perfumes, hair gel and coffee breath approaches dizzying levels.

• **10:21 a.m.:** A murmur ripples through the room: "Here comes the judge!" His Honor hobbles into the room, an esteemed but clearly ancient arbiter of the law. The first case called is a DUI, and the judge stares for so long at the paperwork I assume he fell asleep.

• **10:42 a.m.:** Still on the first case. The judge keeps asking the prosecutor to repeat himself. I practice my yogic breathing and imagine all the clever social media updates I could be posting right now.

• **11:07 a.m.:** Things continue to move glacially. My Marine friend is called to the bench and leaves smiling, so perhaps justice prevailed. The woman on the other side of me keeps up a running commentary while dabbing at her runny nose. "Take the probation," she hisses to a stringy-haired man charged with possession of marijuana who can't pay the $1,000 fine. I resist pinching her. I notice that no matter what gender or age, everyone adopts the same obsequious head-bobbing tic when in front of a judge.

• **12:15 p.m.:** The judge announces we'll take an hour-long break for lunch. Everyone files out, pawing at their phones madly. I wander two blocks towards the water and find a delightful vision: A wildly painted bungalow housing The Purple Pickle, an "eclectic eatery" full of colorful local art and servers who call me "honey." I settle into a pink-cushioned booth and console myself with a giant slice of chocolate cake before I must return to the sad, stuffy world of the courtroom.

• **1:15 p.m.:** Court resumes right on time, though it seems more than half the defendants have disappeared. As each case is called, it becomes evident that though the judge may be old, he is not lenient. It occurs to me that I may have driven to Darien for no other reason than to enjoy some truly stellar chocolate cake.

• **1:48 p.m.:** Finally, I'm shaken out of a sugar coma by the sound of my own name. I approach the bench with my best groveling face and a cheery "Yes, sir!" Within 30 seconds we ascertain that I am guilty of speeding, but I that I am very, very sorry. Since it's my first offense, Judge Methuseleh will knock off the insurance points but I still get to pay the full fine plus court costs: $408. I bob my head like a serf that's been bestowed a year's worth of gruel.

The morals of this story: No. 1: don't speed, especially near Darien.

No: 2: Should you end up in court there, be sure to bring a book and stop by the Purple Pickle for some cake.

And, third, most importantly: Even with the ticket fine, a day of work lost and the gallons of gas burned, it was still cheaper to fly out of JAX than Savannah.

Jan. 20, 2013

A Flannery Pilgrimage to Andalusia Farm

The road to Milledgeville was probably paved with the best of intentions, but barreling down Hwy 441 in an ancient Mercedes during a nasty rainstorm brought out every hellish pothole.

We had already crossed half the state, and with 60 miles left to go, the last leg of this day trip appeared to be leading to perdition. I mean, if the priest in the backseat is nervous, you know it's a doozy.

"Do you think we ought to pull over and wait it out for a bit?" murmured Bishop Kevin Boland in his lilting Irish accent.

I peered over the steering wheel into the steel wool of the sky, pulsing with thin, blue lines of lightning. Sheets of water slapped the windshield. Next to me, writer Beverley Willett gripped the handle above the passenger seat.

"I think we can make it," I said, as Old Gold's chassis hit another puddle.

We were scheduled to arrive at 11 a.m. sharp at Andalusia Farm to meet up with our fellow board members of the Flannery O'Connor Childhood Home, and what can I say, I inherited my *bubbe*'s peeve for punctuality. Besides, Beverly is also a former attorney, and with the head of the Catholic Diocese of Savannah in the car, I figured Satan couldn't wait to get far behind us.

Frankly, a brimstone sinkhole could've opened up and I would've sailed around it, I was so thrilled to finally make the pilgrimage to Andalusia, the adult home of Flannery O'Connor. I've been on the board of the Childhood Home on Lafayette Square for a couple of years now, contributing what I can to its mission of preserving and promoting the house museum where Southern culture's gimlet-eyed scribe spent her formative years.

Last fall, when Meredith Gray, the board's unofficial spirit booster, suggested a group retreat to the 544-acre dairy farm where our own "pigeon-toed child with a receding chin and a you-leave-me-alone-or-I'll-bite-you complex" wrote many of her famously dark stories, I volunteered to chauffeur, not knowing I'd be piloting through the devil's weather. The storm must've been impressed with us because it receded right at the outskirts of town, and we crunched up the long driveway only a few minutes late, wiping our feet carefully before entering the white two-story house.

On the yawning front porch, we joined Meredith, board member emeritus Francis Allen, architect Mark Taylor—who rents the Childhood Home's garden apartment, lucky duck—and Helen Turnage, the board's sole member from Augusta and a distant cousin of the O'Connor family.

The Savannah-Flannery contingency was greeted by Elizabeth Wylie, Executive Director of the Flannery O'Connor-Andalusia Foundation, which isn't a foundation at all but a non-profit struggling to stay afloat. Elizabeth filled us in on the challenges and charms of our sister site, from fundraising woes and family entanglements to its melon-hued bedroom-cum-gallery space and the annual October bluegrass festival on the gorgeous grounds.

"We're using contemporary art to activate these historic spaces and keep them alive," she explained, describing the diversity and internationality of Flannery fans who come to pay homage to their literary heroine.

A good four miles outside Milledgeville proper, Andalusia was only reachable "by bus or buzzard" back in 1959 when O'Connor moved in with her mother, thinking it would be a temporary arrangement. Instead, she found herself hostage to her deteriorating health, writing in the bottom floor bedroom and tending to her flock of ungrateful peafowl. ("Over the years their attitude toward me has not grown more generous," she lamented in a 1961 essay.)

Though she had a social life in Milledgeville and hosted guests with the martini set displayed on top of the Hotpoint fridge bought with her windfall selling the TV rights for "The Life You Save May Be Your Own," her isolation from the New York literary scene she longed to be a part of still feels palpable in the tidy, tiny kitchen.

We'll never know if the serene view of the pond from her window inspired her, but I think it's safe to presume the barn out back sure did, its tall ladder and hayloft looking mighty similar to the description of the one where that good-fer-nuthin' bible salesman stole Hulga's fake leg in "Good Country People." The recalcitrant peacock in the pen out back also seemed to channel her wearied presence, refusing to show off his plumage.

But it's the bedroom that really got me. Cordoned off by rope and seemingly untouched since she died in 1964 at the age of 39 from lupus, the corner space brings FOC's life here into full relief all at once: The typewriter, grotesque in its size and irrelevance, sits on her "large ugly brown desk" facing away from the crucifix on the paint-peeling wall. The stack of Bibles next to the bed, the bedspread stitched by her mother's hands. The hated crutches leaning against the wardrobe.

This is the homey hermitage where Southern lit's grande dame wrote and prayed, the space still electric with demons wrestled and art created. It was once a place of solitude, now it is a shrine.

The room's stark vulnerability reminded me of what a tragedy it is to have lost Flannery O'Connor so early. What light would her voice have cast upon the South and beyond if she'd been around for the last fifty years? How would her writing have changed? What would she have said of today's hypocrisies, society's ugliness spilled over?

I really have no idea, I'm hardly a scholar of O'Connor. I read "A Good Man Is Hard to Find" my freshman year of college and was very disappointed that it contained no hot sex scenes at all. *Wise Blood* isn't exactly light reading, either. I do keep *The Complete Stories* on my night stand, flipping through it willy nilly, reading certain ones again and again ("A Temple of the Holy Ghost" is my favorite.) But my experience is that a diet too rich in O'Connor can have serious misanthropic side effects.

Yet I've become a dedicated Flannery freak since living in Savannah, first through the annual birthday parade gathering that is both ridiculous and reverent, then through the marvelous, varied group of people who steward The Childhood Home, where someone begins every board meeting by reading a selection from the collection of her profoundly personal thoughts, *A Prayer Journal*.

While her literary contributions are legendary, what continues to resonate for me is her devotion—to her craft, to her truth, to her faith.

"It will be a life struggle with no consummation," she laments on the loneliness of the writer's life. "...I want to be the best artist it is possible to be, under God."

Some see paradox in the brutality of Flannery O'Connor's stories and her Catholic fealty; I can only imagine the inner turmoil that came before the words and the spiritual sacrifices offered at the tiny writing altar in her high-ceilinged room. I do believe it takes great faith to make art, and it has long been a suspicion of mine that the deeply devout of this world—the Tibetan monks chanting deep within the mountains, the cloistered nuns thumbing their rosaries, the everyday saints who pray purely and without judgment—are what have been holding it all up all along.

After our visit to Andalusia and a delicious lunch at downtown Milledgeville's Metropolis Café, we walked over to Memory Hill Cemetery, where Mary Flannery O'Connor is buried with her parents. The sun shone as Bishop Boland said a prayer over her gravestone, then Beverly and I continued on to the Sacred Heart Church where the conflicted writer came to town to worship, a plaque bearing her name in the sanctuary. Here I also felt the presence of her monumental faith in the face of poor health and dreams fizzled, the kind that transcends religion to become grace.

Before we headed on to Augusta where Helen would host us for the night, Bishop Boland presented me with my own copy of *A Prayer Journal* from Andalusia's gift shop, a thank you for the ride, bumpy as it was.

I'll never know if it was his prayers in the backseat that got us there safely, but who I am to doubt?

May 30, 2017

Lessons from a Schizo Holiday Adventure

Last year, as I was stumbling around the first days of January with wrapping paper still stuck to my head and digging Chanukah candle wax out of the carpet with a butter knife, I made a promise.

"Enough with this orgy of gluttony," I announced to the dog, who had been following me closely ever since I dropped a gingerbread cookie on the floor the week before.

"Next year, this family isn't going to overbuy, overeat or overindulge. We are going to have an experience of What's Really Important."

By Important, I am talking about meaningful family time. Since our Christmas plans usually only involve Chinese food and a lot of napping, this year I made a reservation for a cabin in the woods, far from the madding crowds and traffic, where we could be a Family Who Means Things.

"Time spent in nature is the ultimate indulgence," I announced to the children, who were furious that I foiled their plan to spend the entire day playing Wii. However, they were quickly consoled by the fact that they would finally be able to toast marshmallows, an activity I had to nix after finding them huddled over the lit menorahs with toothpicks.

At the cabin, we would be exposed to the important lessons of Entertaining Ourselves Without Electricity and Realizing How Little We Need to Be Happy. We would also be exposed to an under-appreciated study of How Lucky We Are to Have Toilets At Home.

The cabins are in a rustic spot, a hippie stopover place known as Hostel in the Forest. By Hippies, I mean a certain breed of kind and lovely human beings who reuse and recycle practically everything and who may not bathe on a regular basis. I find their gentle presence calming, just the fine influence we needed to counteract the evil toxicity and materialism of the Real World.

I looked forward to a few days blissfully discussing the Deep and Authentic Connection Between All Things while the kids absorbed the patchouli-scented wisdom.

My husband, who responds to "Namaste" with "Gezuhndheit," had a different scheme in mind. Rather than try to escape the insanity of the season, he figured we might as well to surrender to it, and that there was no better place to be subsumed by the flashing frenzy than in the nexus of capitalistic fun, Disney World.

I told him the whole point was not to overbuy, overeat or overindulge, activities that are the fundamental activities at Disney World.

"Come on," he reasoned. "What kid wouldn't remember going to Disney on Christmas?"

You might think I met this suggestion with rabid eye-rolling opposition. After all, it was the exact antithesis of the ascetic experience I thought would induce Unhampered Family Togetherness. But I understood that he had saved all year to provide this big blowout for us, and he was probably right: The kids would certainly enjoy poking sticks into tree trunks, but it couldn't beat getting dizzy on Space Mountain and dancing to animatronic Tiki birds.

Also, I secretly adore the Magic Kingdom, because no matter how manufactured the brand of fun that Disney produces is, there is no doubt they do it right. And the drunk guy waving his foot on the bridge on Pirates of the Caribbean always cracks me up.

In the end, we compromised. We spent a day and night scampering through the woods, throwing different types of tree bark into the campfire and singing with the Hippies. Then, as we were tucking into our lunch of lentils and home-baked bread, we announced that we were leaving this earthy happy place for the Happiest Place on Earth. The kids, who were already beaming with the healthy hyperness that comes from fresh air and organic vegetables, went into turbo drive.

The Hippies were very gracious and non-judgmental about our plan B of materialistic gluttony, which is how you can tell they were real hippies and not the fake kind, who pretend to be All Good but are actually just Assholes with Dreadlocks.

We arrived at the Land of the Mouse at dawn, our hair still redolent with campfire smoke and patchouli. As we crossed the gates, I fretted that juxtaposing a total nature immersion with a over-the-top rides, robots and junk food extravaganza was a terrible idea. But it was too late to back out. My daughter squeezed my hand and shimmied with excitement, and we were off into the swirly, colorful world of rollercoasters and Mickey Mouse.

Though it wasn't as serene or cheap as the first part of the trip, it was still an experience full of Teaching Moments. We quickly became experts in Learning to Abstain from Funnel Cake Before Spinning Teacups and How to Fast Pass Your Way to the Short Line. And because we were together, laughing and enjoying it all together, it met my requirements of What's Really Important.

As the park became more crowded (who knew Christmas was one of Disney World's busiest days of the year?!) we escaped to Tom Sawyer Island, a tree-filled refuge in the middle of a manmade lake. Here, the kids seemed relieved to be able to run around freely instead of being boxed in line or tracked around in small carts.

The polar opposites of this holiday adventure began to blur. Forested with rustic cabins and real dirt, the island so resembled actual woods that one of us Who Shall Remain Nameless took a nature pee behind some bushes. I relaxed on a bench overlooking a grassy bank and realized that the peace of mind I sought from the Real World might just be managed anywhere.

I think the Hippies would have approved.

Jan. 3, 2013

Lost and Found on Ossabaw Island

I was definitely lost by the time I saw the little brown pig. The laminated map had shown a single loop trail, so simple that I'd left it on the coffee table of the Clubhouse so my hands would be free.

I'd set off into the wilderness of Ossabaw Island at a brisk pace, rolling the bottoms of my boots silently along the pine needles so I wouldn't scare off the wildlife. I'd been rewarded almost immediately when a pileated woodpecker as big as a chicken swooped down from the moss canopy and landed on the trunk of a loblolly pine about ten feet away. It twitched its red mohawk and began to hammer out a frantic rhythm as I slid by.

The quiet settled again like a cloak, the branches of the live oaks reaching up and out in their slow motion dance with the sky. Then the Old Cabbage Garden road had split, and I'd picked what seemed like the most traveled direction, Robert Frost be damned. The tamped grass trail had diverged again, and now I'd been traipsing in the forest for hours, second guessing not only my scouting skills but my decision to come to the Ossabaw Island Writer's Retreat at all.

Who do you think you are, leaving civilization for five days to fiddle with a novel? asked the sneering voice in my head, the same one that criticizes my housekeeping and wonders nastily whether skinny jeans belong on anyone over 40. *You're a newspaper woman. Stick to what you know.*

In my college creative writing workshops, I would sit at the back doodling on photocopies of my terrible short stories while my peers picked over the plot flaws. I never gave a thought to MFA graduate school, dogged by the feeling that I didn't belong in a classroom discussing craft and character development. All I wanted was to be on the road like Jack Kerouac, scribbling out observations and adventures on a single scroll of toilet paper.

Moleskine notebooks and a laptop proved more durable, but that's mostly what I've done, churning out true stories and contentious commentary for the last couple of decades. But lately my heart has tugged with a book to call my own, even if it means actually having to learn how to write one.

I figured this barely inhabited island would be a good place to concentrate. I did a little dance when my sample chapters passed the retreat's application process. But after my first workshop, I realized my plot had all the sense of a whiskey drunk and that my main character was an irredeemable asshole.

To process the practical wisdom I'd received from my instructors Lenore Hart and David Poyer (bestselling novelists both), I'd decided to take a walk in the woods. Now I was not only adrift in my fictional world, I was completely disoriented in the real one.

You are one sorry specimen, said the sneer.

As cold and nervous as Little Red Riding Hood without her cape, I was about to turn around again when I came upon the small brown pig nosing around under a yaupon holly tree, its cloven hooves planted delicately in the loamy ground.

With its beady-eyed stare, it seemed to mark me as an imposter. I froze.

My mind went to Sandy West, the brave heroine who saved Ossabaw island and its wild things. At 102, she still lives in her family mansion on the marsh, part of the deal struck when she sold the island to the state in the 1970s.

Understandably reclusive these days, she remains a fierce character in the nail-biting drama about the preservation of one of Georgia's last wild places. What will happen in the chapters after she passes is anyone's guess.

Sandy West would never be scared of a pig, scoffed the voice. *She could probably still outrun it.*

Truth be told, it wasn't that I was afraid of being gored by a wild hog or swallowed up by an alligator or even being chased by the ghost of a bloodthirsty Creek Indian.

My biggest fear was that I would be *that* visitor to Ossabaw, the one who leaves the Clubhouse without a map or a phone at four o'clock in the afternoon and gets everyone all worried when she doesn't come back by dark and then Ossabaw Island Foundation's fix-it guy Mark Frissell has to drive around in the green pick-up with the bad transmission until he finds the idiot guest crying next to a magnolia tree, chewing on a piece of bark.

I imagined myself humiliated in front of my writing peers, ostracized from the dinner conversation about the specificities of emdashes and semi-colons. Worse, I might be deemed unworthy of Ossabaw's magic, banished forever by Sandy herself.

Then I remembered a conversation that morning with Armstrong State University creative writing professor Dr. Tony Morris, who's organized this retreat for five years.

"This island has a certain kindness, a generosity," he had counseled as two of Ossabaw's resident donkeys ambled over to the Clubhouse porch for extra apples. "There's something here you can trust."

A poet of precision and integrity, Tony is not one to throw around careless metaphors. If he spoke of the island's benevolence as real, it must be.

So I took a small scout step forward. And cracked a stick.

The pig scuttled back through the saw palmettos with the confidence of a creature that knew exactly where it was going. I hoped it wasn't to round up its bigger friends and mount an attack on the pale, two-legged animal walking around in circles.

After the pig disappeared, I wandered for another hour before finally stepping onto the well-worn track of the island's main road. The Clubhouse was still miles away, and my literary notions far from fruition.

You'd better just keep walking, grumbled the voice.

I arrived just in time for dinner, ready to get back to work.

Later that night, while I was nursing my blisters on the back porch with a cup of tea, a pair of headlights would cut the darkness and a cotton tuft of white hair leaned out the passenger side of the cranky green pick-up.

I squinted disbelievingly over the railing. "Is that Miz West?"

"It sure is," came a good-natured holler.

Hopping down the stairs to meet the island's elusive icon, I saw Sandy in the passenger seat and longtime Ossabaw friend and artist Betsy Cain at the wheel.

"We're going out to the field at Middle Place to gaze at the stars," Betsy offered, as if it was perfectly normal to be driving around late at night in the inky black wilderness with a centenarian.

The other writers came outside to pay their respects, and though hard of hearing, Sandy asked us all what we were working on and whether the island was treating us right. Before Betsy drove off, Sandy caught my hand in a surprisingly strong grip, her nails painted coral.

"I'm so glad y'all are here," she rasped with a laugh.

"So am I," I smiled back, meaning it with all my heart.

March 3, 2015

A Swiftie-Tilting Planet in Tampa

Haters gonna hate hate hate, but as it turns out, I totally heart Taylor Swift. TBH, I wasn't sure that was true until recently.

I've always *appreciated* TSwift, but, like, from a grown-up's perspective in that she writes her own songs and is a savvy businessperson and doesn't flash her hooha all over Instagram. You've gotta have mad respect for anyone who takes on Apple, and she handled the whole Kanye thing with grace. And every woman makes a mistake like John Mayer, so I don't judge.

She's also styled herself as a role model for universal equality and radical self-acceptance, which is tricky to pull off for a heteronormative white girl with legs like a supermodel giraffe. So, as a mother and a feminist, I *approved* of Taylor Swift, but I did not quite *adore* her.

I'm a grown-up. I have Important and Serious Things to ponder, like voter turnout and the world falling apart and stuff. It's not like I'd ever sing along to Taylor Swift's bubblegum jams, and if I did, it's only because my 11 year-old daughter programmed all the preset buttons in my car to the same Top 40 station and it took me three weeks to change them back because the freakin' buttons are so tiny and I couldn't find my reading glasses. I don't even know how these TS lyrics got all up in here; I must've tapped into someone else's James Dean daydream.

For sure, I did not mewl like an espresso-addled Muppet when our BFFs Kim Spencer and daughter Anna Brooke surprised us with VIP tickets to T. Swift's sold-out, super-special-Halloween-last-stop-on-her-U.S.-tour in Tampa, FL.

Of course I did not paw through the cool TS swag that came with the tickets like it was lost treasure. I definitely did not spend hours coordinating matching cat costumes for the show (FYI, rhinestone kitty ear tiaras are cheaper when purchased in bulk) or spend $18 on a tube of MAC Ruby Woo to make sure we had that red lip classic thing that we like.

OK, maybe I'm just a pretty little liar. Maybe I was so thrilled to see Taylor Swift live and in person that I secretly choreographed a "Bad Blood" routine to perform in our row H seats.

Then I started to panic. My inner grown-up realized that we would not be enjoying Taylor's musical stylings in an intimate nightclub with a few hundred well-behaved music appreciators, but at Tampa's Raymond James Stadium with 55,000 other people, most of whom would be tweenage girls with the capacity to shatter glass with their collective squealing.

Us grown-ups, we don't like crowds so much. Personally, I start wheezing when there are too many people in the grocery store and I can't get to the Muenster cheese. The last concert I remember attending with that many screaming fans, Def Leppard's drummer still had two arms.

Kim reminded me that most of the shrieking Swifties would be under 12 years old, and if chaos broke out, I could probably scale the walls faster than they could.

"Quit acting like such a boring adult," she commanded, flourishing a stack of temporary flash tattoos.

Giggles overruled my handwringing as our glitzed-up girl squad skipped towards the massive arena, flanked by thousands festooned with feathers and sequins and Swiffer napkins (best Halloween costume ever, *der*).

My anxiety was easily tempered by cute boy opening acts Shawn Mendes and Vance Joy and had dissolved almost completely once Taylor herself rose up out of the stage surrounded by cute boy backup dancers, her flawless face magnified by a thousand in the Jumbotron, every enhanced eyelash visible.

I was totes magotes caught up in the sick beats when La Tay announced, "I named my new album *1989*, after the year I was born!"

I gagged. "That's the year I graduated from high school!"

Kim rolled her eyes. "Oh yeah? That's the year I graduated *college*."

Not to be outdone in this grown-ass-woman pissing contest, I raised the bar. "Well, my *car* is five years older than she is."

My BFF patted my shoulder. "Congratulations? Now shut up and dance."

From there it was all uphill: Taylor belted out her frothy hits, strutting down the moveable runway in a dazzling variety of costumes (the matching booties, OMG!) Rubber LED bracelets handed out at the door and controlled by unseen forces lit up the night in synchronized syncopation.

Between tunes, Miz T chatted to the crowd with her intimate teenage folksiness, though come to think of it, she didn't say "like" once.

The record-grossing *1989* tour has become renowned for its cameos of other famous folks, and TS saved the best for last with Alessia Cara and Idina Menzel, the latter playing *Frozen*'s regal Elsa to Taylor's goofy Olaf. I didn't see Pope Francis on tour, but I'm betting any stop on his circuit couldn't rival the ecstatic reverie of 55,000 Swifties scream-singing "Let It Go."

And let go we did—of my own middle age ruminations, of Kim's worries about the autism families she champions with the Thinking Moms' Revolution, of how the hell we were going to get of out here without being trampled by ten thousand pairs of kitten heels.

Even the grizzly-bearded dad in front of us swayed to the music as he put an arm around his disabled daughter, who was wearing a turquoise tutu and a large pair of hearing aids. Her name was Stefanie, and they had driven all the way from Indiana so she could see Taylor for her 21st birthday.

"She's been on the liver-kidney transplant list for a year," Stefanie's mother explained with a shrug. "She's not expected to live much longer."

But Stefanie was just shaking it off, a sparkle in her eyes as her younger sister signed the lyrics to her with bouncing hands. It was the same glimmer I saw on our daughters' faces, blessedly healthy but facing a world of grown-up challenges nonetheless.

Taylor Swift may be an exceptionally brainy, blue-eyed, billionaire Barbie, but she's also a young woman kicking ass as she champions kindness and generosity. We need more examples of that, please.

To her fans, this was more than a show, but an education in the pinnacles of possibility, of artistic excellence, and how to behave oneself in a crowd. (Nothing but politeness afterwards as 55,000 people competed for the same 150 Ubers.)

So thanks to my BFF, who gifted me with a fabulous spectacle that was more than an escape from real life but a much-needed reminder that it's OK not to be such a lame adult all the time.

And thanks, T-Swizzle, for schooling me in another most important life lesson: No matter how old you think you are, if you know the words, there's no shame in singing along.

Nov. 11, 2015

A Savannahian in Paris

When you arrive in Paris fresh off the red eye, do not—I repeat, do NOT—give in to the temptation to take a nap.

Even if your head is full of fizz from the Champagne served by red-lipsticked flight attendants (Air France keeps it so classy in coach!) and the six-hour time change has tangled up your circadian rhythms into a dissonant jangle, you must. Not. Sleep.

"Otherwise, you'll waste three days on jet lag," warned NYU Paris student Jordan Veitinger, home for the summer working at the 5 Spot, where we dined the night before our departure. "Just throw down your bags, get a coffee and go."

Jordan's advice proved most valuable. It was 10 a.m. when we arrived in the Marais district, a culturally-rich neighborhood of cobblestoned streets dating back to the 1200's where Victor Hugo penned *Les Misérables*. Bleary-eyed, we schlepped our giant American suitcases up narrow spiral stairs to the 17th-century apartment I booked online, a sunny roost that looked out onto a shared courtyard blooming with red geraniums, pink hollyhocks and a neighbor who liked to exercise in his underpants.

Two tiny loft spaces meant each kid had their own "room"—a rarity on our travel budget—though they were more impressed with the apartment's fancy Nespresso machine than the fact that Jim Morrison died in the building next door.

The crisp white duvets beckoned, but we headed back through the cerulean blue iron gates to explore the architectural feast that lay within walking distance of our *domicile temporaraire* on Rue de Beautreillis, aided by several tiny cups of espresso each. And we thought Notre-Dame's buttresses were flying!

We whirled through many of the city's iconic checkpoints on that very afternoon with my parents, seasoned Parisian visitors who rented their own place in the Marais for the entire month, part of their sagacious plan to spend their children's inheritance while they're still around to enjoy it with us.

My indefatigable mother led us past the historic administrative offices of the Hotel de Ville, draped in rainbow flags to express solidarity for the Orlando tragedy, to Île de la Cité, where the famous cathedral rises into the sky in all its Gothic gargoylian glory. From the gardens, we walked to the sunken Holocaust Memorial, still cordoned off from recent flooding as the Seine lapped its famous banks.

We crossed over the Pont au Double to Shakespeare and Co., the English book purveyor, and later sipped melted chocolate at Angelina's, overloading our senses until the olfactorily-challenged members of the family staged a small revolt after too much time in a cheese shop.

A word on multi-generational travel: It can be hard to herd everyone at the same pace, especially when the spry septuagenarians forge forth and the teenagers trail behind with their faces in their phones. Plus, there's always that one person who always gets distracted by shoe stores. (How will I know what's chic if I don't browse?!) We found that assigning one person at a time as "Le Chef" in charge of routes and maps can prevent meltdowns, except for that time I took the lead and marched everyone into traffic on the Champs Elysées.

By the end of that first day, we were all punch drunk (some of us regular drunk from a bottle of rosé with dinner), and we fell into bed exhausted but fully adjusted to Parisian time.

We all know that wherever you go, there you are, so of course I packed my Savannah-colored glasses, the ones with the civic-centric lenses. I was particularly interested how Paris handles being what journalist and recent Savannah guest Elizabeth Becker cites in her best-selling *Overbooked* as "one of the best examples of tourism in the world."

Obviously, Paris dwarfs our little Southern American hamlet in size and scope, its habitation documented from prehistoric times, its politics and history and art fused in layers so complex and deep that my public school education never even began to touch them. (Though my high school French did serve me quite well, *merci beaucoup*. And as far as deep layers go, I did get creepily close to the artfully-arranged skulls and bones in the Catacombs, the ancient limestone quarries deep below the metro trains and plumbing where six million bodies were re-interred in the 1700s after existing cemeteries started, er, overflowing.)

Paris has a lot to handle in any season with more than 32 million visitors a year, but this summer was particularly tricky. Last November's terrorist attacks means armed soldiers regularly stroll through public spaces, though I never saw anyone stopped or frisked. The famous public transportation system ran on time and boasted classically-trained busking musicians, and most subway cars and buses were standing room only at all hours. More upsettingly, some cafés ran out of croissants by 9am.

Peak tourist season was still a month off, but the streets were already full of international brigades of rowdy soccer fans in town for the 2016 Euro Cup. I went against every hooligan-fearing instinct in my neurotic brain to follow the *futbol*-mad members of the family to a match at the 80,000-seat Stade de France, where the super-tight security and intelligent funneling of bodies allowed me to relax and enjoy watching Iceland steal the ball and beat Austria in the last two seconds. I haven't seen that many grown men cry at once since group therapy in the '90s.

And the museums! We eschewed the long lines at the Louvre and the Musee D'Orsay for the Picasso Museum and the small (by Paris standards) Musée Marmottan Monet, home to "Impression, Soleil Levant," the painting that launched the Impressionist movement. Our minds were completely blown by the Musée de la Chasse and de la Nature, dedicated to the region's nature vs. man lore and fancifully combining hunting artifacts, contemporary art and taxidermy. We may have missed the Mona Lisa, but we thought it better to digest smaller rooms rather than spend seven hours wandering huge halls with thousands of other cranky tourists. (In case you weren't aware, teenagers hate museums. All museums. Even the ones with a stuffed giraffe poking its neck through the floor.)

One of the points of *Overbooked* is that cities with the most successful tourism strategies plan for the people who live there, and any added infrastructure is built to be accessible to all. Paris' public bike system is clearly a hit with the locals, who cruise from one *arrondissement* to another on the sturdy frames all day long, silk scarves streaming behind them and front baskets overflowing with fresh baguettes.

Abandoning the grandparents and kids to each other one afternoon, Mark and I rented a pair of bikes at one of the kiosks *pas de problème* and rode to the Eiffel Tower along a well-marked bike route. Though apparently bus drivers also like to use this lane, too, which gave me occasion to use the filthy French I've been saving up all these years.

That isn't to say that Parisians don't have their issues, and they aren't afraid to march about them. A 20,000-person demonstration against President Hollande's labor reforms at the Place de Bastille near next to our metro stop closed down the streets for hours as *gerdarmerie* in full riot gear directed traffic. Several more protests cropped up during the week, and the French Robocops gave them a wide but impenetrable berth when we tried to look on.

But even with a recent garbage strike, there was still way less litter on the streets of Paris than the gauntlet of discarded fast-food bags along Abercorn. And the only shots fired were by feet at goalposts.

The less demonstrative locals appeared to take it all in stride as they lounged in the cafés in those pretty cane chairs, smoking hand rolled cigarettes and rolling their eyes over Brexit. These are the people who perfected the art of *blasé*, although I noticed with great consternation that the chic-est among them paired their tailored frocks with Adidas sneakers.

But underneath the jaded façade, I found that Parisians are a generous lot, eager to share their pride of place as well as food and drink. (Kind of like Southerners, though I don't see that kiss-on-both-cheeks thing happening around here.)

My brother had the good fortune to marry a gorgeous French woman a few years ago, and we spent an afternoon just beyond *la peripherie* of the city in her mother's glorious garden with our extended family and friends, savoring *saucisson* and more rosé. (Savannah's Best Sommelier Jason Restivo promised me back in May that the whole world is drinking pink wine right now, and he was right!)

Yet even on another continent, my own city was never far from my mind. Surrounded by centuries stacked around a city bustling with people working and living, I couldn't help but see shades of Savannah everywhere:

Sitting in the grass of the Place de Vosges, the oldest planned square in Paris bordered by fabulous homes built for the friends of Henri IV. Peeking through wrought iron gates to glimpse secret *jardins* or hanging laundry. Looking out onto the steeples and skyscrapers from the roof of the ultra-modern Centre de Pompidou and sensing that past, present and possibility somehow can exist at once. Even Le Marais translates as "the marsh."

My provincial perspective was surely boosted by the sight of actual other Savannahians: One magical evening, just after the nightly sparklefest at Le Tour Eiffel, we ran into Byrd Cooki Co. president Geoff Repella with partner Warren Bimblick and daughter Grace, a recent Savannah Arts Academy graduate. Later in the trip, we took the fast train to Provence, where the SCAD family welcomed us to its *magnifique* Lacoste campus, housed in a mountainside medieval village with its own chateaux and rosé vintage, the bee flag flying above the lavender fields.

So maybe our French connection isn't so far-fetched. When it comes to a blueprint for a wondrous destination that gets it right, we'll always have Paris.

Still, it was nice to get back to the real marsh, where ordering ice in your wine isn't such a *faux pas*. I guess it's true that there's no place like home—or your own bed.

July 13, 2016

10 JUNK DRAWER

Everybody has that drawer in the kitchen. This is where extremely useful yet totally unrelated items find a place—mismatched shoelaces next to extra flea medication for the dog, an assortment of screws of all sizes arranged willy-nilly around a ball of rubberbands. For those of us who are hopelessly housekeeping-challenged, this may describe all the drawers. This random collection features salient topics near and dear to my heart that didn't quite fit anywhere else, including a meditation on being temporarily phoneless, a eulogy for the beloved art vehicle known as the Absurdivan and being wrapped in the loving arms of Savannah's diverse and amazing Beloved Community.

Savannah Struck in Ardsley Park

I have a habit of getting around town, mostly because I'm nosy and always wear good walking shoes.

Yet no matter how many parties I invite myself to or dark lanes I get lost in, I still get bowled over by this city's stunning beauty and sheer architectural awesomeness. Roof cornices give me goosebumps, and I have been known to wax poetic about triple-crown molding.

If you come across me standing with my mouth hanging open and my to-go cup spilling its contents on the concrete, I am probably not catatonic. I am simply "Savannah struck," a condition that is unfailingly provoked by entering a private home with Corinthian columns. Its main symptoms are speechlessness and nervous shuffling, brought on by being too intimidated to set one's cocktail down on any of the furniture.

Such was my state as I stood in the grand foyer of Daniel DePlanche and Jim Martin's glorious Ardsley Park manse. A pair of erudite gents who know their Beaux Arts sculpture from their Art Deco sconces,

Daniel and Jim had generously offered up their historic Washington Avenue home for a fete to honor two of the local LGBTQ community's most fabulous, Mark Hill and Clinton Edminster.

The benevolent hosts opened their sumptuous home for full access, allowing guests to amble around the azalea-fringed brick courtyard and through the second-floor bedrooms bedecked in vintage wallpaper. Fortunately, I had actually received an invitation and didn't need to explain my presence as I mooned over the smoke-blue velvet window treatments.

I had a small conniption in the master suite, which includes a bidet and a crystal chandelier over the bathtub. ("A true *salle de bain*," noted SCAD architecture professor Ryan Madson with a sage nod.) Momentarily hypnotized by a pair of stained glass Tiffany lamps, I almost spilled my G&T on the bedspread but caught myself in time to convene without incident around the majestic spiral staircase to hear from the evening's honorees.

Known for his tireless activism and soft-spoken charms, Mark Hill is passing on the reigns of Savannah Pride after 16 years of nurturing the event and its organizing body from just a few volunteers into a family festival attended by thousands. He's also served on the Chatham County Health Commission and is a regular at the Georgia Assembly, reminding legislators of the power of the gay voting bloc in his charming West Virginia drawl. (You hear that as your pen hovers on that ridiculous "religious freedom" bill, Gov. Deal?)

Dressed in rainbow seersucker, Mark stood on the glossy bottom stair of the living room to address the crowd about the evolution of the city's gay identity and the work still yet to be done.

"We are part of a living, thriving Savannah," he said, admonishing guests to get involved, if not with LGBTQ issues then with another local organization that moves the city forward. "We have learned to take care of ourselves. Now we have to take care of each other."

Our dear Clinton Edminster manages to find his way into this column on a regular basis, with his colorful contributions as executive director of Art Rise, owner of Starlandia Creative Supply and all-around *bon vivant*, though it is his gleeful status as an out-and-proud gay man in his 20s that earned him adulation at this particular event.

"When we found out Mark was stepping down as director of Pride, we thought it needed to be recognized, and Clinton is part of the generation coming up. We wanted to bridge that legacy," explained Mark Krueger, another Pride founder who has lived here since 1980, when the climate towards queer folk wasn't always so friendly.

Krueger reminded that in spite of its abundance of turrets and cornices, Savannah hasn't always been a fairy tale for LGBT acceptance. While it has long been an under-the-radar enclave, it surely owes its current openness and growing reputation as a gay-friendly destination to those who founded the First City Network, Georgia's oldest LGBTQ advocacy organization.

Many of those quiet revolutionaries were present at Saturday's fête, and the rest of the guest list sparkled as brightly as the gold brocade curtain tassels along with the rest of the city's moving, shaking gay community and its many allies (at least those who were free and still ambulatory on this extended St. Patrick's weekend). Kevin Clark of Georgia Equality poured drinks behind the bar, and urban farmer George Wilson offered gardening tips in the kitchen. In the living room, the amazing Anitra Opera Diva performed a dreamy aria followed by a transcendental cover of the Talking Heads' "Psycho Killer." Anitra's always resplendent companion, tour guide Nicodemus Hammill, looked straight out of a steampunk fantasy in his light coat and top hat.

Sometimes-mermaid Dame Darcy and her doll, Isabelle, rapped along with 80s MTV favorite "I Know What Boys Like" on the stairs as networking guru Scott West chatted with Clerk of Superior Court Tammie Mosley near the grand piano.

I admired the antique dining table with Russell Kueker, formerly of Stopover and now launching his own real estate design service firm and exchanged cheek kisses with real estate agent and activist Pam Miller next to the elegant china cabinet. Busy bee entrepreneurs Yusak Bernhard and Jeff Manley took time away from their third TailsSpin location on Whitemarsh Island to stop by to pay their respects, and the marvelously-mustachioed Jeffrey Downey and Donald Lubowicki of Circa 1875 Gastropub managed to escape the downtown madness to raise a toast in the parlor.

By the end of the evening, I was so overwhelmed that I allowed myself to rest for a moment on one of the angel white satin upholstered chairs (after first balancing my cup on an end table with a coaster, of course.) I thought it was the columns in the hallway that finally brought me down, but in the end it was the social architecture that made me swoon.

I realized I must be a different kind of Savannah struck, a joyful stupor brought on by witnessing just how much love, creativity, compassion and hard work can fit into a single house, even one as big as a palace.

Which reminds me: Daniel and Jim's place is for sale, listed for just under a million with Keller Williams' Ron Melander. A word to the next tenants: If you invite me to the housewarming party, I promise not to faint on the divan.

Mar. 23, 2016

Phoneless in Savannah

It all escalated rather quickly. I wasn't even in a bad mood, just trying to wrangle the family to make a rare appearance at synagogue after a packed season of Saturday soccer games.

We had exactly seven minutes to drive downtown and park, which sounds dangerous and impossible from midtown but totally doable if you catch the light at Victory and Abercorn. But my phone kept dinging with texts and the dog started yapping and then my son was stalking around the front yard in his underwear muttering that he couldn't find his pants and the dam just broke. Suddenly I was screaming "I'm pretty sure your pants are NOT in the goddamn azaleas" loud enough for the people on the next block to hear and performing a dramatic interpretive anger dance that culminated in the throwing of what I call my little church purse at the car with a rather impressive *thunk*.

Lipstick and a driver's license do not make a sound like that. A clonk of that particular heft is reserved only for a flat rectangular object of a certain weight. An object just upgraded a few weeks ago, for which I had not yet bought a protective case.

When I picked up the little church purse off the yellowing fall grass, I unzipped it to reveal the screen of my new iPhone as dark and shattered as the dreams of a graceless rhinoceros hoping to join the roller derby.

My rage instantly dissipated into tail-tucked shame. I apologized to all who had witnessed my hysterical diva act. I guess I hadn't noticed the stress levels ratcheting up, what with hosting the holiday feast and the whole work/life balance wobbly plate-spinning act, not to mention the introduction of an alien-developed "new math" in my fourth grader's class that appears to have done away with actual numbers in favor of conceptual essays. At least I could find comfort in the fact that my marbles had exploded on my own lawn and that no one appears to have posted it on YouTube.

It was only after I got glass shards in my finger from pathetically begging an impassive SIRI to text my husband that we would not be seeing each other in the pews that I realized I had done more than embarrassed myself: I had effectively cut myself off from the rest of the world. A trusted friend advised that I not air the dirty laundry of my adult-sized temper tantrum here in this column, but for the sake of exploring the foibles of humanity, I am always willing to sacrifice my own dignity.

Surveys conducted on and offline reveal that I'm not the only person who has ever turned their smartphone into a blunt projectile. And when it comes to dependence on our little rectangular boxes, I think we can agree that I'm in fine company. Our phones are so much more than pocket-sized computers that allow us instant email access and flattering filters for our profile pictures. They're our security blankets and loyal BFFs, providing us an escape when we feel uncomfortable at a party and fostering the illusion that we are working when we are actually shopping for sweaters on ModCloth.

They are emblems of style, a carefully chosen accessory to reflect our allegiance to one operating system or another. We use them to watch the stock market or videos of dogs wearing liederhosen at the breakfast table. We instantly settle the argument that it was 1985, *not* 1987, when Sammy Hagar replaced David Lee Roth as Van Halen's lead singer.

Texting has taken the inconvenience out of simple communiqués, and there's no denying that the maps app is what veteran Savannah columnist Jane Fishman calls a "marriage saver." The problem is that we've gotten so needy that we can barely find our way out of a paper bag without plugging in an address.

These devices seem so shiny and innocuous at first, a perfect tool when we need a little extra speed in our everyday dealings. It doesn't take long for us to become intoxicated with the power, accomplishing in minutes what used to take hours. Before you know it, you're just another sallow-faced junkie at its mercy, fumbling with it in the bathroom and fretting over it like Gollum and his precious ring.

For real, precious, our obsessions with our phones can classify as a real addiction, similar to compulsive gambling and substance abuse, according to a study published in the *Journal of Behavioral Addictions*. The way I protectively clutch my phone definitely reminds me of how back in the day I used to worry over my cigarettes (housed in a similarly-shaped flat rectangular box, hmm), constantly patting myself to make sure they were still there. (Been quit from that habit for more than 10 years now, thank heavens.)

Even if you don't sleep with your phone under your pillow, the urgency to keep up with the barrage of texts and tweets can be mentally and emotionally overwhelming, sucking us into a time-evaporating vortex as we endlessly refresh multiple platforms. There's even a name for our hand-wringing anxiety about being separated from our devices: "Nomophobia" is the official psychological term for the fear of losing your phone.

But I'm hardly the person to provide you with a smug public service rant about such hazards. As I have illustrated above, having a smartphone certainly hasn't made me any less stupid.

After what the children now call Mommy's Big Hissyfit, I brought my battered phone to the techy people at iRepair on Bull Street to see if my phone could be resuscitated. They assured me it could, but I'd have to wait for a part to be shipped. Which meant I was looking at doing Thanksgiving weekend cold turkey, so to speak.

Witnessing the facial twitches, the nice pregnant lady at the desk apologetically offered me the use of a Blackberry so prehistoric it might have been exhumed by Fred Flintstone. (Come ON, when's last time you used a trackball?) Forced into technological exile, I went back to the Dark Ages, relegated to checking email on a computer and forgetting to update Facebook.

I have now been apart from my Precious for over a week. The first days of withdrawal got kind of intense when I tried to slide open the refrigerator with my index finger and asked a bar of soap for directions. After that, it became amazingly normal not to check my black box every 30 seconds. I especially have not missed the always-ominous possibility of it falling out of my back pocket and dropping into the toilet. (Which I, along with 19 percent of Americans, have done, according to another study.)

Here's the kicker: After months of feeling like I didn't have a minute to spare, I've suddenly had time to knit a pair of lopsided handwarmers and play board games with the family. Denied the digital download of the *Catching Fire* soundtrack, we rediscovered our vinyl appreciation, thanks to a stack of classics from Graveface Records. Still, I could've really used some instant Google action when my spouse challenged my knowledge of '80s glam bands.

The petroglyph Blackberry makes outgoing calls and receives texts, so I haven't missed any emergencies, but it's so hideous that I feel no need to whip it out in public. Instead, I've been doing a lot of people-watching—which is so much less interesting these days now that it's just a bunch of heads bowed over screens, faces aglow.

The call that my phone is fixed will come at any minute, and I wonder if it's possible to mindfully return to the world of status updates and selfies. It's been an eye-opening banishment from the realm. Like Gollum over his golden band, I remain torn by the obsession and the desire to be free of it.

Dec. 3, 2013

Death of the Absurdivan

Dearest community, we are gathered here today to mourn the passing of one of Savannah's most colorful figures.

The 2000 Mazda MPV known as the "Absurdivan" succumbed last week to complications from a warped engine block after months of hacking and overheating like an asthmatic, menopausal mule. Daily infusions with the garden hose could not prevent its mysteriously leaky radiator from leaving oozy puddles in the driveway, and its frequent hot flashes were often accompanied by a noxious odor akin to fried dog hair.

It had also been suffering from squishy brakes, a hissing fan belt and a terrifying pause while accelerating out of first gear before it quietly gave out at the corner of Price and Henry streets during rush hour.

The Absurdivan leaves behind a grieving driver as well as three other immediate family members who are deeply relieved that they will no longer be subjected to its mechanical whims or being snickered at in the carpool line. While it was an undeniably embarrassing vehicle to hand over to the parking valet at The Grey, it was also unfailingly hospitable and generated an endless supply of individually-packaged wintergreen Lifesavers from its side door pocket.

With its three hubcaps and terminal coating of pollen, the Absurdivan could never be called a beauty, but it made up for its lack of refinement with a most distinctive feature: A figurine-festooned dashboard that provided endless entertainment for its driver, passengers and anyone who bothered to stop texting at a stoplight.

From the first Little Pet Shop bobblehead to the South of the Border sombrero to the one-of-a-kind Troy Wandzel mini-sculpture, this loony exhibition represented a decade of family life events. Its demented plastic menagerie included Disney princesses, pirates, Smurfs, superheroes, toy soldiers, tiny dancers, champagne corks, naked Mardi Gras babies and a veritable safari of exotic animals, including a rhino, two giraffes, a gorilla, a Shetland pony and a sloth. Among its organic additions were hawk feathers, surf wax and a full set of swallowtail butterfly wings.

Ridiculousness of such magnitude does not happen by itself. Gratitude is owed to the birthday party goodie bags, Happy Meals and 183 tubes of Superglue that transformed it from an ordinary beige minivan into an enchanted multidimensional voodoomobile.

Indeed, there was a certain good magic exuding from all those juju eyeballs. Every *tsotchke* represented a prayer to keep its precious cargo safe as it navigated the treacherous paved world, each charm an appeal to the angels, the car karma gods and Lady Luck to keep the drunk drivers at bay and the senile in their own lanes. The superstitious adornment seems to have worked; for all of its crotchety feebleness, the Absurdivan never experienced so much as a fender bender.

Among its many adventures were a cross-country sojourn that wound through Yosemite National Park and Navajo Nation, across Texas, over the North Georgia hills and finally to Tybee Island, where, sadly, it never got to check riding in a parade off its bucket list. It once blew a radiator cap deep in the Appalachian Mountains, a crisis ameliorated by a roll of duct tape and a pair of tightly-folded boxer briefs. Mostly, it made its loyal rounds from home to school to work and back again, accruing knickknacks at every turn.

Though it began its tenure as a pragmatic decision paid for in cash, this accidental art project found purpose along the way. Its asinine cavalcade became a testament to the absurd avalanche of useless plastic crap we encounter unblinkingly every day, a way to remember that it will all eventually end up in landfill, not decomposing, ever. It also served as a good-natured rebellion against the status our society places on material possessions in general and cars in particular.

The Absurdivan never failed to provoke a reaction, and while most found it delightfully ludicrous, there were a surprising many disturbed and downright offended by its abject rejection of resale value. There were those who saw it rollin' and were hatin', them in their shiny, leased 500-series jobbies who have never known the joy of gluing one's fingers together while affixing Marge Simpson as the Bride of Frankenstein to the air conditioning vent. When they delivered their gas pump sermons on the topic of devaluation, the best response could only be, "Oh, yeah? What's your car payment? Bet it's not less than zero."

For the most part, the Absurdivan leaves behind a legacy of validating weirdos everywhere, and its loss will make road trips a lot less fun but definitely less alarming.

Those wishing to express their condolences attended a closed-hood memorial service at the First Friday Art March in the Old Starland Dairy on Desoto Row. In the spirit of its gaudy largesse, a raffle was held to help ArtRise Savannah continue its innovative community programs and Emmaus House and Old Savannah City Mission to feed and shelter the less fortunate. A variety of prizes were donated from sympathetic local businesses, including A Squad Bake Shop and SOS Tires & Auto. Each $5 ticket came with the opportunity to pluck the sun-bleached talisman of one's choice from the dashboard.

In closing, it must be said that the Absurdivan fulfilled a destiny far beyond its station as a shitty minivan. Yes, it got us where we needed to go, except for that time it fricasséed Seb Edwards' jumper cables.

But even then, it taught us that sometimes, all it takes to break down barriers between the diverse voyagers of this planet and bring them up to the same speed is a plastic Strawberry Shortcake, a couple of melted lizards, and plenty of Lifesavers.

June 3, 2015

A Radical Sabbatical

"Life moves pretty fast. If you don't stop and look around once in a while, you could miss it."

—from *Ferris Bueller's Day Off,* 1986

It's closing on 30 years since Ferris Bueller counseled us all to take a ditch day to keep our perspectives fresh.

But now that we're grown-ups with bills and snappy Twitter personas and these goddamn phone things attached to our faces, we can't seem to find the time. Even though we know this will eventually result in burnout, wrinkles, heart attacks, bad posture, unhappiness and the inevitable violent hurling of the phone thingie across the room.

We're consoled with the platitudes "Just breathe" and "Take time just for you" so many times they've become colossal clichés. In my head, I can hear the imaginary chorus of judgmental hipsters cynically muttering *yeah yeah yeah, I can quote 80s movies all day long, too, you dumb dork* as they scroll through their Instagram feeds clutching a Bulletproof coffee.

Even worse, the message of self-care has been co-opted by branding experts who use it to shill products from bubble bath (Calgon, take me away with your harmful sulfates and chemical irritants!) to checking accounts (I tell you from experience that in spite of the picture of the pretty lady meditating on a cliff on the website, banking with Suntrust is *not* the path to inner peace.)

Deep down, we know the truth: You cannot buy your way or roll your eyes to serenity. There isn't an app for it, either.

Sometimes, when things get really whacked and you find yourself red-faced and hyperventilating that someone left the box of cereal open again and it got stale, you need more than a few breaths. You need to do something radical. You have to steal your life back from the deadlines and the iPhone calendar and the to-do lists.

Earlier this summer, after months of general malaise and a recurring nightmare about fire ants making a nest under my desk, I decided that the most revolutionary action I could take for my mental, emotional and physical well-being was a sabbatical. College professors take sabbaticals all the time to further their hands-on knowledge in a particular area of research. As a person with no academic authority whatsoever, mine was to deepen my expertise in creative navel-gazing.

I humbly recognize that not everyone is in the economic position to take six weeks of unpaid leave to do a whole lot of nothing. I didn't believe I could do it either, until I committed to the idea. With a couple of well-timed freelance gigs and the support of my bosses, I took the longest ditch day I could.

Here is a brief account: The first week, we entertained guests from the West Coast that we hadn't seen in 12 years. We grilled hamburgers and mortified the kids with our dance moves. We learned that Facebook isn't a terrible way to stay in touch with distant friends, but surviving a flash flood together on Tybee is way more fun.

The second week I helped the children pack for summer camp. If you've ever had to stamp 50 pairs of underpants with indelible ink, you understand why it took an entire week. There were also quiet moments to make a mommy's knees buckle, like holding hands with my soon-to-be high schooler while we walked the dog. Even when our neighbors came outside and saw us, he didn't let go.

The third week, struck dumb by the silence of an empty house, I sat at my kitchen table, drank tea and watched birds. All. Freaking. Day. I watched a watermelon plant take over the backyard. Later in the week, two rats invaded the pantry, probably attracted to the open cereal boxes. An epic BB gun battle culminated in a hurricane swath of destruction and a bloody standoff in our daughter's closet. There was a solid two-day block of washing pink princess sheets and hunting down tiny bronze pellets before the dog could eat them.

The fourth week, I went to visit my parents. I haven't really had them all to myself since I was in diapers, and it was a real gift to spend time with the two funny, interesting people who raised me. Especially now that we can all drink wine.

The fifth week the air-conditioning broke. I escaped to the beach, where I drank too much beer and gave my dermatologist tremendous reason to scold me for my amazing tan. One morning, I paddleboarded all the way from Alley 3 to the end of Horsepen Creek just because I had nothing better to do. On the way back, I passed a pair of dolphins slopping up shrimp in the marsh banks. They ignored me like I was part of the scenery.

Towards the end of the sixth week, we rented a tiny cottage near some waterfalls outside Brevard, North Carolina. It rained a lot. I sat at the kitchen table, drank tea and watched some different birds.

By now, my mind and heart had settled back into a rhythm that more closely resembled the life I believe in, one of nourishment and gratitude, of faith and justice. From the polestar of my rediscovered self, I have found myself more able to respond with authentic to a world spinning off its center: Carnage in the Middle East. The spate of local shootings and our city leaders' audacious helplessness. Cops in Missouri lined up like they're going toe-to-toe with ISIS militants instead of American citizens exercising their right to congregate and grieve over the shooting of an unarmed young man. The suicide of one of our most beloved and beneficent bodhisattvas, Robin Williams.

So many tragedies to remind us of the sadness and injustice inherent in this confounding place we've found ourselves in together. More than ever, we must do whatever we can to cultivate our essential compassion for each other. And that means taking the time to tend to it for ourselves.

Six weeks might not be feasible, but I implore you to do whatever it takes to get your own life back. Even if it means sacrifice, it probably won't be a financial disaster (unless your AC breaks, but the repairman will tell you it would've happened anyway, and that's what credit cards are for.) Let us rise up against the dogmatism and cynicism, though Ferris also advised, "Ism's, in my opinion, are not good. A person should not believe in an 'ism,' he should believe in himself." (Or herself, as it were.)

As I return to my desk and its deadlines, perspectacles freshened, I plan to hang on to the long, slow moments of my sabbatical. I will try to remember that we're all just a bunch of idiots running around trying to make everything OK for ourselves and the people we love.

So be patient. Just breathe. Take your time. It'll all still be here when you get back. I'll remind you if you remind me.

Aug. 19, 2014

Enveloped by the Beloved Community

Everybody knows that in this world, you gotta have a thick skin to survive.

Some seem to be born with the ability to shake off adversity and insult, untroubled by the distractions of injustice and imminent environmental catastrophe. The rest of us fashion reptilian armor to protect ourselves from the slings and arrows of this outrageously unfair and hectic life. Hearts on sleeves are rarely rewarded and not recommended.

I don't know about yours, but my alligator hide must've been manufactured at the same Taiwanese factory that makes crappy dollar store umbrellas. The weather's may have finally turned fall gorgeous, but last week still brought in quite a storm: ISIS and Ebola and the Koch Brothers marauding our political system like a couple of sociopathic pirates in pinstripe suits. Pile that on with raising a teenager, a barrage of emails from unhappy readers and a weeping blister accrued by a shitty pair of shoes, and I'm feeling as shredded as a piece of laundry left on the line.

Fortunately, there was a salve last Tuesday at Muse Arts Warehouse, where activist authors Tom Kohler and Susan Earl had arranged to film the telling of their book, *Waddie Welcome and the Beloved Community.* The book follows the life of Savannah citizen Waddie Welcome, born with cerebral palsy and relegated to a faraway nursing home after his parents passed away in the 1970s. Mr. Welcome managed to charm practically everyone who crossed his electric gaze, drawing Kohler, Earl, "angel-on-earth" Addie Reeves and dozens of others into a circle of advocacy that eventually helped bring him home. It's both a biography and a fable, with a moral lesson far more joyful than any of Aesop's: "Keeping the 'social' in social change" is the rallying cheer that continues to buoy the story and its message: We all matter, and we can all help.

Waddie Welcome and the Beloved Community has also inspired a play, a spectacular quilt by "artivist" Beth Mount, an interactive walking tour and other forms of art. Tuesday's reading—filmed and edited by Jay Self and Andy Young and assisted by Jay's daughter, Emily—will be released by Inclusion Press and used as an educational resource for organizations like Citizens Advocacy that work to increase the dignity of those living with disabilities.

I have a copy of the book on my nightstand, and I wouldn't miss the opportunity to see it presented in person. And as it turns out, there couldn't have been a better place to show up with one's protective shell in tatters.

As the slowly-dying Absurdivan puttered up to Muse with all the *oompf* of a hippopotamus in the last stages of emphysema, I glimpsed a Who's Who of some of Savannah's biggest champions of social change: Standing at the stoop of the concrete staircase was Molly Lieberman, who spends her days funneling love and art into the children of this city through Loop it Up Savannah. Standing next to her was Clinton Edminster, the ever-smiling, octopus-armed arts booster. And then came kisses from my favorite preschool teacher in the world, Ms. Maggie Smith, who has preserved playful childhoods for over 30 years at Maggie's Morning School. Within minutes, my drooping spirits were bolstered from their friendly squeezes.

I traveled down this gauntlet of love straight into the arms of Barbara Daughtry, with whom I shared some laughs at the last Citizens Advocacy potluck. She may only be barely four feet tall, but Barbara has an embrace that can knock even the heaviest chip off a person's shoulder. I also got a hug out of former Citizens Advocacy chairman Robert Cohen, but only after he gave me the hard sell for his book of poetry, *Joys Fears and Tears*, a lovely read based on his experiences living in a wheelchair and earning his degree from Savannah State University.

I collected more handclasps and hugs from fellow writers Amy Paige Condon and Kris Monroe, and pressed cheeks with author and SCAD professor Susan Falls. I flung some good hard vibrations at JinHi Soucy Rand and her husband, Mark, always so busy behind the scenes in both the theater world and real life, tirelessly holding space for art and authenticity in this town.

I didn't want to scare assistant city attorney Lester Johnson, so I let him off with a firm handshake. But Tammy Kenckel, a service coordinator for Williams Court Apartments, and her husband, Tom, who's on the board of community radio station WRUU, didn't escape my squeezes.

By the time punk rock goddess Angel Bond and Missionary Blues' singer Mike English (the bluesiest bank president that ever lived) began to croon and strum Sam Cooke's "A Change Is Gonna Come," I was a bit punch-drunk on the love, in a totally non-Beyoncé kind of way.

For this was the kind of event for which The Civil Society Column was conceived: A gathering of some of Savannah's most courageous and outrageous souls, people unafraid to be helpful and hopeful, ready to act but not willing to move ahead until everyone else has caught up. Martin Luther King, Jr. called it the Beloved Community. I've come to think of it as a far better safeguard for our survival than spiky stegosaurus skin. A lot cozier, too.

"What we believe has so much to do with what happens in the world," counseled Tom Kohler from the podium, reminding how powerful we are when we are brave enough to be vulnerable with each other. He enjoined us to share what lessons we learned from Waddie Welcome's story on big posters in the Muse lobby.

I thought a minute, then wrote, "The antidote for despair is service."

After many warm good-byes and "see y'all soon"s, I went home to repair my armadillo fleece for another day. Amid snuggles from and gratitude for my beautiful family, I thought of something else:

That hugs from the people we live among are the best kind of medicine, especially when given with arms wearing their hearts all over their sleeves.

Oct. 7, 2014

An Epilogue, of Sorts

Back in September 2011, I had this idea for a society column that went against everything the genre stood for. Instead of focusing on debutantes and fancy fêtes, I thought it would be hilarious—maybe even helpful—to spotlight regular folks making Savannah better and the issues that affect us, as well as poke a stick at the ironies that make living here an endless, absurd adventure.

"An Anti-Social Debut" offered up the Civil Society Column as a place to "bridge differences, offer solutions and create community," which honestly sounds as naïve and pretentious as all get out but hey, I was young(er) and more idealistic back then.

Aw hell, I may be older now but I'm still the same starry-eyed tenderheart who believes in loving our neighbors as ourselves, fighting for liberty and justice for all and breaking out into song and dance when the chaos and crazy get to be too much.

And every time Savannah makes me so mad I want to throw fire ants in the air and move somewhere else, something—a slice of Southern kindness, a soul-searing art exhibit, the moon rising out of a golden marsh sunset—reminds me just how blessed we are to belong here.

As a West Coast weirdo who never tasted a boiled peanut until her 30s, I experienced a certain feeling of alienation when I first moved to

Savannah. Even as the bride of a native son I stood out like a red balloon stuck in a maganolia tree, which only made me try harder to find acceptance. (Wearing my husband's letter jacket to the homecoming football game of his alma mater may have been too enthusiastic.)

I know now that you can be born and raised here and still feel excluded, and it's been my mission to practice radical acceptance of all of those who don't fit into the square box of the status quo.

This space was always meant to be for and about us: The outsiders and the outliers, the curious and the queer, the service folk and the worker bees, the rebel beekeepers and the animal rescuers, the grieving mothers and wide-eyed kids, the forgotten and the voiceless.

It's been a platform for the justice keepers and the jubilee raisers, the wild places that need to be protected and the neighborhoods that aren't nearly as scary up close as they are on the evening news.

Every week, as I've invited myself into people's lives and asked them nosy questions, I've tried to keep in mind this quote from modern sage and my former California neighbor Ram Dass: "We're all just walking each other home."

It reminds me that regardless of our zip code, our politics, our skin color or our opinion of who serves the best fried chicken in town, we're all living together here in this glorious, ever-complicated little moss-draped city, in a still-democratic country on this sparkly blue planet.

It also helps me remember that at the deepest level, we all come from and are going back to the same place.

This isn't so much a good-bye as a "see ya 'round." Sure, I might toss around a few fire ants over Savannah's pernicious problems, but I have no plans to live anywhere else. Like the rest of you radical tenderhearts, I will continue to champion all who share the idea that our community's greatness is measured by how we treat each other, and that none of us can truly be free if a single one of us is chained down by institutional and systemic barriers to progress. It might be two steps forward, one step back forever, but my boots remain happily stuck in this charmin' lil' swamp.

And though we might conduct this velvet revolution with our faces in our phones, I will always maintain that it's far more effective to meet each other face-to-face: Every day, each of us has the power to build a most just and civil society by showing up. We don't even have to shout our opinion or carry a sign; our simple presence speaks volumes when we bring our bodies to public spaces, fill the chairs at City Council and County Commission meetings, support public art and local music, and spend our hard-earned dollars at independent bookstores, family-owned restaurants, and other small businesses. That goes double for those of you just visiting.

There are so many opportunities to break out of our silos, break bread with new friends and break down the barriers that keep us from feeling like we belong. I hope to see all y'all on the streets and out in the squares, all us weirdos shoulder to shoulder as we walk each other home.

February 7, 2018

Acknowledgments

I can barely make it through a week without depending on the kindness of strangers and friends alike, and this book would still be at the bottom of the birdcage of my mind if it weren't for so many good people. I humbly offer thanks in particular to the following folks:

To editor extraordinaire and teacher Amy Paige Condon, who helped me shepherd this from a cut-and-paste disaster into something more refined while handling my artistic hysteria with patience and grace.

To the multi-talented groove goddess Molly Hayden, who designed the cover and body of this book with one hand, because she was holding mine through the entire process.

To the staff of *Connect Savannah* for putting out a consistently valuable, informative, attractive and awesome publication every week of the year and for enduring my off-key singing during deadlines.

To photographer and left-hand man Jon Waits, a literal rock star always ready to follow me into the woods for a story.

To creative powerhouse and compassionate listener Rubi McGrory, for always appearing just when I need her.

To my Mama Bear Posse—Kim Spencer, Natasha Gaskill, Kristen Harward-Grant and St. Claire Mars—for all the walks and laughs and toasts, for the sympathetic ears and strong shoulders to cry on, for being the village that our family could not do without.

To my parents, Marcia and Skip Feinstein, for their unfailing encouragement, support and example that creativity and productivity only increases with age.

To my father-in-law, Dr. Harvey Lebos, for his generosity and good humor and for claiming me even though I'm sure I've embarrassed him on countless occasions.

To my kids, Abraham Lightning and Liberty Ruth, for modeling what it means to be a true Savannahian by always being yourself.

Finally, to Mark Lebos, without whom I would never have known this enchanted city nor what it means to truly belong to someone. I love you, babeleh.

ABOUT THE AUTHOR

Jessica Leigh Lebos has been writing about interesting people, vexing issues and anything involving free food for more than 20 years. She was voted Best Newspaper Columnist by the readers of *Connect Savannah* and received a First Prize for Humor from the National Society of Newspapers Columnists in 2017. Swept off her feet by a Savannah son sometime in the last century, she introduces herself at cocktail parties as "Southern by marriage." Reach her at yoyenta@gmail.com.